Portrait of Juan de Grimaldi by Federico de Madrazo, 1849
(courtesy of the Biblioteca Nacional, Madrid)

CAMBRIDGE IBERIAN AND
LATIN AMERICAN STUDIES

GENERAL EDITOR
P. E. RUSSELL F.B.A.
Emeritus Professor of Spanish Studies
University of Oxford

ASSOCIATE EDITORS
E. PUPO-WALKER
Director, Center for Latin American and Iberian Studies
Vanderbilt University
A. R. D. PAGDEN
Lecturer in History, University of Cambridge

Theatre and politics in nineteenth-century Spain

The Frenchman Juan de Grimaldi was instrumental in the development of the Spanish theatre in the 1820s and 1830s, at a time when censorship, repression and economic chaos had left it in a state of stagnation. As impresario and stage director, he trained actors in the new style of declamation, made physical changes in sets and lighting, translated recent French plays into Spanish, and encouraged the writing of original Spanish plays. His own magical comedy, *La pata de cabra* (1829), was outstandingly successful.

Grimaldi was also a wealthy businessman and newspaper editor, and the patron of many important Spanish Romantic writers. He was active in politics, vigorously defending not only his own intellectual and business interests, but also the moderate policies of the Queen Regent, María Cristina, and of the Prime Minister, Ramón de Narváez. Even after his return to Paris he continued to work secretly as an agent of the Spanish government.

This book, based on original archive materials, is the first in-depth study of Grimaldi's involvement in the literary and political progress of nineteenth-century Spain.

Theatre and politics in nineteenth-century Spain

Juan de Grimaldi as impresario and government agent

DAVID THATCHER GIES

UNIVERSITY OF VIRGINIA

The right of the
University of Cambridge
to print and sell
all manner of books
was granted by
Henry VIII in 1534.
The University has printed
and published continuously
since 1584.

CAMBRIDGE UNIVERSITY PRESS

CAMBRIDGE

NEW YORK   NEW ROCHELLE

MELBOURNE   SYDNEY

Published by the Press Syndicate of the University of Cambridge
The Pitt Building, Trumpington Street, Cambridge CB2 1RP
32 East 57th Street, New York, NY 10022, USA
10 Stamford Road, Oakleigh, Melbourne 3166, Australia

First published 1988

British Library cataloguing in publication data
Gies, David Thatcher
Theatre and politics in nineteenth-century
Spain: Juan de Grimaldi as impresario
and government agent.–(Cambridge Iberian
and Latin American studies).
1. Grimaldi, Juan de   2. Theatrical
producers and directors–Spain–Biography
I. Title
792'.0233'0924   PN2788.G7/

Library of Congress cataloguing in publication data
Gies, David Thatcher.
Theatre and politics in nineteenth-century Spain.
(Cambridge Iberian and Latin American studies)
Bibliography.
Includes index.
1. Grimaldi, Juan, d. 1872.   2. Theatrical producers
and directors–Spain–Biography.   3. Theater–Spain–
History–19th century.   4. Spain–Politics and
government–19th century.   I. Title.   II. Series
PN2788.G7G54   1988   792'.0233'0924 [B]   87-3007

ISBN 0 521 34293 7

Transferred to digital printing 2004

The publishers are grateful to the Program for
Cultural Cooperation Between Spain's Ministry of
Culture and United States' Universities for a
generous subvention towards the production
of this book.

SE

For Mary Jane, Mary Jo and Bitsy,
the women in my life

Contents

Preface

This work of literary historiography attempts to bring into focus the life and milieu of Juan de Grimaldi. It is an attempt to report on Grimaldi's activities, failures, and accomplishments rather than to speculate on his motives and intentions. The perspective is multiple: many of the documents quoted are originals written in his hand; others are responses to his requests and demands. More objective commentary (although in the world of nineteenth-century Spain, objectivity was a rare trait) is culled from the newspapers and contemporary reports of the period. Finally, modern scholarship is brought to bear when it helps to clarify or underscore a point.

All of the translations, unless otherwise indicated, are mine. I shall endeavor to include appropriate documentary citations in parentheses within the text.

For simplicity, the following abbreviations will be used throughout:

AHN   Archivo Histórico Nacional, Madrid
AHP   Archivo Histórico de Protocolos, Madrid
AV   Archivo de la Villa de Madrid
BN   Biblioteca Nacional, Madrid
DM   *Diario de Madrid*
MAE   Ministerio de Asuntos Exteriores, Madrid
RAH   Real Academia de la Historia, Madrid
RE   *Revista Española*

Acknowledgments

This study is the result of many years of research and study on Juan de Grimaldi and the world in which he lived. During that time I have been the recipient of the generous help of several institutions and numerous individuals, whose support I wish to recognize here.

Financial support has been provided by the John Simon Guggenheim Memorial Foundation, the National Endowment for the Humanities, the American Philosophical Society, the Comité Conjunto Hispano-Norteamericano para la Cooperación Cultural y Educativa and the Center for Advanced Studies of the University of Virginia, to each of whom I express my most sincere appreciation.

Many friends and colleagues have helped with the conception and creation of this book by providing details, answering queries, sending materials, correcting errors and reading drafts of sections in progress. My deepest gratitude goes to Russell P. Sebold, John C. Dowling, Javier Herrero, Donald L. Shaw, Tibor Wlassics, Frank M. Duffey, Robert Marrast, Carlos Seco Serrano, Ermanno Caldera, Gregorio Martín, Antonietta Calderone, Gabriela del Monaco, Victor Ouimette, Mary McKinley, Katy Vernon, Linda Maier, Lee Fontanella, Pedro Alvarez de Miranda, Sandra Strauber and Ron Quirk for that very generous and selfless aid. In addition, I wish to thank Professors P.E. Russell and Enrique Pupo-Walker for giving this work their support, and Kevin Taylor and Margaret Jull Costa of Cambridge University Press for their excellent editorial assistance.

Without access to the documents cited in these pages there would be no book on Grimaldi and the Spanish theatre. I am indebted to the kind assistance provided by the directors and workers at the following libraries and archives for their patient professionalism: In Madrid, the Biblioteca Nacional, Biblioteca Municipal, Archivo de la Villa, Real Academia de la Historia, Real Academia Española de la Lengua, Ateneo, Hemeroteca Municipal, Archivo del Ministerio de Asuntos

Exteriores, Archivo de Protocolos, and the Iglesia de San Sebastián; in Valencia, the Hemeroteca Municipal; in Paris, the Archives de France and the Bibliothèque Nationale; and in Washington, the Library of Congress.

A preliminary draft of chapter 3 "A smash hit: *La pata de cabra*," appeared as "'Inocente estupidez': *La pata de cabra* (1829), Grimaldi, and the Regeneration of the Spanish Stage," in *Hispanic Review*, 54 (1986), 375–96. Likewise, sections of chapter 4, "Masked Balls and Troubadours," appeared as "Juan de Grimaldi y la máscara romántica," in *Romanticismo 2: Atti del III Congresso sul Romanticismo Spagnolo* (Genova, 1984), 133–40. I am grateful to the editors for their permission to draw upon that material.

To all, my most sincere appreciation.

Introduction

The story of Juan de Grimaldi (1796–1872) is the story of much of the intellectual, cultural and political life of nineteenth-century Spain. His life parallels – and indeed is intimately tied to – many of the turbulent political upheavals and cultural advances of that century. During his lifetime he was revered and criticized, feared and consulted. After his death he was remembered as one of the most significant figures of Romantic Spain, and he has even appeared in fiction written by authors such as Benito Pérez Galdós,[1] Antonio Espina,[2] and Antonio Buero Vallejo.[3] Still, he remains for us today largely underestimated or misunderstood.

Grimaldi was a Frenchman who came to Spain with the invasion of the 100,000 Sons of St. Louis in 1823. Between that year and 1836, when he left the country permanently and under mysterious circumstances, Grimaldi exercised powerful control over theatrical life in Madrid. He acted as either impresario or stage director of the two major theatres in the capital, the Príncipe and the Cruz, and made important decisions concerning repertory, set design, the makeup of the acting companies and physical improvements to those theatres. He was so influential that he was remembered by Ramón de Mesonero Romanos, one of his friends from the *tertulia* "El Parnasillo," as being a veritable "theatrical dictator."[4] Another participant in the artistic life of the capital, José Zorrilla, also remembered Grimaldi as being an "autocrat of the theatre,"[5] and both individuals issued enthusiastic praise for his intelligence, cleverness, clear thinking and impact on the development of the theatre during the initial years of the Romantic period.

Yet, surprisingly, Grimaldi has remained unknown and unstudied. José Alberich has commented that

Those who write the history and criticism of Spanish literature are similar to those who assault an ancient fortress: someone fires a cannon shot and opens a

I

hole in the wall, and seconds later the crowd of invaders presses through it. Hispanists gather together in bands which work themselves up into a fury over Unamuno, or Lorca or Machado, while in the meantime it is impossible to find a halfway informative article on Manuel Cañete or don Juan Grimaldi.[6]

This is sadly true (the excellent article by Frank Duffey[7] and the unpublished thesis by Bernard Desfrétières[8] are among the only serious works on Grimaldi to date). Grimaldi is one of those authors more alluded to than studied or understood.

One of the innumerable things said about Juan de Grimaldi in the last century was that he "had style". That style, and his way of manipulating it into power and prestige, is the subject of this book. It would not be an exaggeration to say that Grimaldi was one of the most influential figures in the intellectual and political life of nineteenth-century Spain and that his influence – while for the most part exerted behind the scenes – was felt in very disparate circles. His impact on the intellectual world of Spain was profound. Grimaldi was not merely a successful theatrical impresario. He was, at different and overlapping times during his long life, a soldier, diplomat, politician, journalist, wealthy businessman, historian, dramatist, and civic leader. Some of this activity occurred in Paris, where he lived from 1836 to 1872, but it was nearly always directed toward the country that he came to love passionately and understand completely. He left a mark on what people saw and read, how they reasoned and the decisions that were made which affected their lives.

His intellectual achievements were even more startling, since he had no formal education; he left the classroom for the battlefield when he was merely twelve years old. How did he become that "intelligent and extremely clever" man praised by Zorrilla and befriended by Larra, Bretón de los Herreros, Ventura de la Vega, Mesonero, Concepción Rodríguez (whom he would marry), Queen Regent María Cristina and her lover, the Duque de Riánsares, Queen Isabel II, Ramón de Narváez, Emperor Napoleon III of France, and other figures of the Franco-Spanish cultural and political scene? What raised in him the ire which expressed itself in corrosive public attacks on Juan Alvarez Mendizábal, Baldomero Espartero and the great French historian, Pierre Guizot?

To reconstruct Grimaldi's life and times it has been necessary to sift through numerous documents and printed materials, many of which are incomplete or riddled with error. His times were those of

Romantic Spain and revolutionary Europe, and the reconstruction of those times is still far from complete. There are many questions which remain to be answered and mysteries to be solved, but the gaps are not so great as to impede our ability to appreciate the importance of Grimaldi as a literary and cultural personality. It is to be hoped that further details will be filled in by future scholars, but the outline of the life he lived and the world in which he moved provided here should give us, for the first time, a coherent picture of a man at once brilliant, opportunistic, ambitious, clever, charming, manipulative, erudite, glib, stubborn, and endlessly fascinating.

I

The Spanish stage, 1800–23

Máiquez and the theatre before 1820

Since the reign of King Felipe IV in the seventeenth century, those who controlled the theatres in Madrid possessed the right to conscript actors from theatrical companies in the provinces. The capital's theatres were run, depending on political and economic circumstance, alternately by private individuals, the municipal government, or the acting companies themselves. Even though to act in Madrid represented the highest achievement in that profession, the conscription (called an "embargo") was not universally applauded by those men and women forced to abandon friends and family in order to perform on the stages in the capital. In the actors' minds, "that privilege enjoyed by the theatres in Madrid was, and is, excessive."[1] In addition, the cost of living in Madrid was significantly higher than elsewhere and wages, surprisingly, were significantly lower, so that the move represented at times a real economic hardship for the actors, who already were locked into a low-paying profession.[2] In recompense for this disruption in their lives (and the threat of never working again if they refused), the actors were guaranteed – but not, as we shall see, always paid – retirement benefits.[3]

In the first two decades of the nineteenth century, actors struggled for respectability and for stability in a city beset by war, censorship, turmoil, and general indifference to their offerings.[4] With the maturation of the great actor, Isidoro Máiquez ("a true prodigy in his profession," according to Antonio Alcalá Galiano),[5] the acting companies had hoped that their work would be looked upon with some favor, and in fact, during the reign of Napoleon Bonaparte's brother, Joseph, the theatres acquired a semi-official status and received generous monthly subsidies.[6] The return of Fernando VII to the throne in 1814 changed all that, even to the point where "actors

4

and actresses were prohibited from using the title 'doña' or 'don', a sign of esteem when attached to a name, which clearly underscores the desire of the authorities to humiliate them."[7] The "embargo" continued in full force.[8] But Máiquez was successful in bringing much popular attention to the theatres and to a few actors who performed with a degree of skill generally absent from Spanish theatrical performances in the past. As Díaz de Escovar notes,

With [Leandro Fernández de] Moratín we find a unique case: while trying to return the theatre to classical naturalism, he became the liveliest incarnation of the French school of Boileau, and its tidiness, smoothness, decorum, and regularity brought with it as a natural consequence a style of acting that was sloppy, homespun, weepy, and which spread from the comedy to serious plays and from serious plays to tragedy, and from which only Rita Luna and Isidoro Máiquez managed to free themselves in time.[9]

Isidoro Máiquez (1768–1820) was one of the first Spanish actors to view his vocation as a true profession. Although he had been "schooled" in the typical Spanish style of acting (that is, the little technique he knew he learned by imitation rather than formal study), he desperately wanted to travel to Paris to train with the famous French actor François-Joseph Talma. Máiquez knew that he came from a tradition lacking in technical preparation and wanted to improve his craft. In addition, the collection of plays that the companies inherited and were accustomed to performing were what he called "dramones," which, according to Antonio Colao, required "all manner of looseness and all sorts of excessive gestures, hand movements, outcries, strained effects, and low-brow means. No subtlety, no balance, no contemplation, no sobriety, and how little naturalness!"[10] Máiquez was passionately committed to raising the standards of acting, and overcoming the mediocre – often execrable – level of acting common in his day. There were exceptions to this general rule, of course – his own wife, Antonia Prado, was frequently praised for her skill, and Rita Luna is invariably included along with Máiquez on the list of those few who set high standards for themselves. But more often than not, complaints were heard throughout the latter half of the eighteenth century and, notwithstanding the Neoclassical theorists' attempts to regulate acting style by decree, little progress was made.

The actors demanded little of themselves, as little as the audiences demanded of them.[11] Moratín was of the opinion that the theatre was at the "mercy of the public, in the hands of ignorant actors," since the public reserved its applause – and had done so since the time of Lope de Vega – for hyperbolic and artificial performances, wild gestures, sweeping emotion, and bombastic rhetoric. José Rodríguez claims that Máiquez knew and studied a collection of letters on acting style, entitled "Letters on Gesture, Pantomime, and Theatrical Posture," which appeared in the Madrid newspaper *Espíritu de los mejores diarios literarios que se publican en Europa* in 1789–90 (translated from the German original of Johann Jakob Eugel).[12]

In Paris, Talma was developing a style of acting that was more natural, more relaxed. He was accused of being cold and distant from his audience, but Máiquez respected him for his natural style, and was determined to imitate him. His decision to travel to Paris was almost unprecedented for an actor; few had ever ventured north to improve their skills, since the journey was difficult to arrange (permission had to be secured from the municipal government and from the acting company itself, and funds had to be raised – Máiquez was forced to cash in his pension and sell his wardrobe of costumes in order to underwrite his trip). The two years he spent in Paris (1799–1800) enabled him to combine his innate talent with studied technique, and upon his return to the Madrid stage he was more confident, secure, and in control of the deep emotions demanded by the role he chose as his first performance, Othello. It was an instant success. Revilla, remembering Máiquez's natural style, wrote

Máiquez did not gesticulate the way other actors I have known did; he walked around the stage just like any man does in his home; he did very little wringing of his hands; his tone and diction differed little from that which we use in everyday discourse, and his energy and fire were clearly evident, but without the stamping around that shakes the scenery, those powerful blows to the chest and thighs that are heard all the way to the rear of the theatre; and when he sobbed, he did not use the old-fashioned moaning style nor wave his white handkerchief up and down to dab his eyes (which was presumably to let us know that the actor was supposed to be crying).[13]

In Colao's words, "Máiquez was not only a reformer of the stage, but also a reformer of theatrical life in general. With him there began a totally new period in Spanish theatre."[14]

Máiquez's success was to bring about his ultimate downfall and official disfavor. By 1818 he was weak and ill, and often forced to take time off from his acting duties. Manuel de Arjona, the magistrate of Madrid, feared that Máiquez was faking his illnesses (and thereby collecting his salary without working) and forced him to return to the stage. Máiquez responded to the demand with an angry letter which irritated Arjona to such a degree that he forced the actor into retirement and eventual exile. The King, tired of Máiquez's constant demonstrations of independence and subtle incitations to his audiences (once, for example, during a performance of López de Ayala's *Numancia*, Máiquez received wild applause when he intoned the verses, "It is written in the Book of Fate/That the nation wishing to be free *is* free"), was glad to be rid of him and did nothing to intervene.[15] He was forced to resign in 1819 and he ended his life in semi-obscure exile in Granada, where he died in 1820.[16] But his movement toward the professionalization of the Spanish stage left, if not tangible results, at least a deep and honored memory which actors would hold dear and aspire to in the coming decades. The ghost of the great Máiquez hovered benevolently over the Spanish stage for most of the nineteenth century.

The apprenticeship of Concepción Rodríguez

In 1818, a young actress of modest and undeveloped talent from the provinces was brought to Madrid by the *autor* (director) of the Cruz Theatre, Bernardo Gil. She was sixteen years old and had been acting since 1815 in theatres in Seville, Granada, and Barcelona with her father, Bruno Rodríguez, and her mother, Rosa Abril y Velasco, who was herself the older sister of a well-known actress, Concepción Velasco.[17] Concepción could hardly lay claim to being a star performer from regional theatres, since her parts were restricted to those young *ingénues* seemingly present in every play written or performed during the period. Nor was she, if reports are to be believed, even very skilled in her profession, but she did possess an acute intelligence and a respectable education imparted to her by her parents: ". . . Miss Rodríguez owed to them an excellent education without which, it must be admitted, it is doubtful that she would have excelled in the art she has chosen."[18]

Bernardo Gil, perhaps alerted to her possibilities by Dolores Pinto, a well-known actress of her day who had worked with the young Rodríguez in Granada, "using the privilege held by the companies in Madrid, requested and received permission to conscript her."[19] Hence, on Easter Sunday, 1818, Concepción Rodríguez joined the Cruz company in the novice roles of *segunda dama*.

The Cruz company, like that of the other theatre, the Príncipe, was a company of rigid hierarchies and uncertain future. In 1818 the two theatres shared sets, opera and dance companies (they alternated monthly), props, and at times even actors. Manuela Carmona and Antera Baus were the leading ladies who dominated the other actors, while Bernardo Gil, as Director (he doubled as leading man), made decisions on repertory, role assignments, and performance schedules for the Cruz. Rules of conduct were frequently commented upon, if not very strictly enforced, and periodic statements issued by the Juez Protector de los Teatros del Reino (in 1819, José Manuel de Arjona) attempted to insure proper conduct both on the part of the spectators and on the part of the actors.[20] One such proclamation, published in 1819, outlined the responsibilities of the acting companies and the dance and music companies, as well as the financial arrangements to be followed. It even attempted to address such questions as whether words or sentences could be added to or eliminated from approved scripts, how the director should deal with an actor who feigns illness or refuses to accept an assigned part, when the companies can take vacation, what to do for fire safety, how the actors should divide and balance their parts (no one should be allowed to outshine the others), what time the actors must appear at the theatre, and so on (AHN: Consejos 11.408, n. 41).

Gil, his wife, Antera Baus, and Loreto García would remain part of Concepción Rodríguez's professional world for years to come. The chance to act at the Cruz, and to meet and watch Máiquez at the Príncipe, somehow compensated for the low pay – Rodríguez received 16 *reales* per performance; Baus and Carmona received 40, Gil received only 24 in 1818, but that salary was raised in 1819 to 40 (AHN: Consejos 11.408, n.1). Within a week of the formation of the company and the opening of the new theatrical season, Concepción was performing in a two-day run of *Lo que son los vecinos*. That year her performance schedule was relatively light. She appeared in the usual mix of translated plays imported from France or salvaged from the standard repertory of Golden Age "refundiciones" ("rewrites"). Those performances included: *Lo que son los vecinos* (March 29–30), *Reinar después de morir* (April 1–3), *El recto ministro o el duque de Craón* (April?), *El hombre gris* (April 17), *El desafío y el bautizo* (August 3), *El avariento burlado* (August 24–7), *El huérfano y el asesino o El valle de Torrento* (September 2–4), and, in October, *Una mañana de Enrique IV*, *El tesoro* ("a very boring play; interminable; full of repeated episodes"), and *Los huéspedes o el barco de vapor*.[21] In the following year she received a small raise (to 20 *reales*) and she was able to work once again with Dolores Pinto, who had just returned from Barcelona, but her performance schedule – and talents – remained similar to that of the year before.

These salaries were standard, but in general actors were poorly recompensed. Earl J. Hamilton warns of the dangers of comparative pricing (which can lead to distortions due to "difference in weights and measures, seasonal variations, quantity purchased," etc.)[22] but it might be instructive to provide some information on the relative worth of the *real* (one *real* = 34 *maravedíes*) during the first third of the nineteenth century. Reliable statistics are difficult to locate ("Economic historians have devoted very little attention, in Spain, to the period between the War of Independence and 1836",[23]) but some salaries and pricing information will enable us to understand more clearly the financial status of actors during this period. Hamilton records that in 1800 a loaf of bread cost 1.3 *reales*, twenty-five pounds of chickpeas 27.8 *reales*, eggs 4.05 *reales* per dozen, writing paper 46.3 *reales* per ream, olive oil 46.5 *reales* per *arroba* (approximately 12.5 litres), and white sugar 6 *reales* per pound. A journeyman cabinetmaker earned up to 20 *reales* per day, while an unskilled laborer earned barely over 5.[24] Twenty years later, as recorded by Angel Fernández de los Ríos, bread cost 1.5 *reales*, meat 1.5 *reales* per pound, chickpeas 34 *reales* for twenty-five pounds, and olive oil 80 *reales* per *arroba*; a carpenter earned 14 *reales* per day, and a laborer 7 or 8.[25] The economic crisis of the 1818–30 period did little to help the situation of the actors or their directors; we shall return to these statistics when we discuss theatre prices below.

Concepción Rodríguez enjoyed some small successes in her apprenticeship years:

She did not manage in her first year, nor in the following year of 1819, nor in 1820, to rise out of the category of second player which, as we all know, is an unrewarded leftover from the old plays which constitute the principal repertory of the Cruz Theatre, but she always distinguished herself with an undeniable originality: in *Sotano y el Torno*, in *Marta la piadosa* and several other plays she had the satisfaction of earning not insignificant applause playing beside Antera Baus, who was outstanding in these dramas and who did not normally share with anyone the well-deserved public favor which she possessed almost exclusively.[26]

Máiquez's forced resignation from his position as Director of the Príncipe and the revolution headed by Rafael de Riego, which swept a new constitutional government into power, changed the way theatres were run and opened up several years of troublesome conflict and uncertainty.

The theatre during the Constitutional Triennium, 1820–23

The change of government in the capital affected the theatrical season, which, for reasons of bureaucratic infighting and stalled petitions, came close to not beginning on time on April 1 (Easter Sunday), 1820. Bernardo Gil tried valiantly to convince the municipal authorities to permit the acting companies to function as impresarios to straighten out the threatened delays. At issue was who owned what and who was responsible for the payment of the special charges levied on the theatres. Two days before the season was to begin, Gil and Antonio González, Director of the Príncipe, issued yet another petition, begging the authorities to make up their minds and let the actors get to work. Part of the problem was the mere incompetence or nervousness of those individuals pressed into serving as interim officials (as was Pedro Sáinz de Beranda, the "Acting Constitutional Mayor of Madrid"), but the real blockade was that, with the reemergence of the constitution, it was felt that all previous rules and regulations became invalid and that it was impossible for the theatres to continue to operate "as they had last year." It was a matter of Royal seals, proper authorizations, and published decrees, and whether or not a Theatre Regulation, approved on December 11, 1812, would legally be in effect in 1820 (Riego had proclaimed the reinstitution of the Constitution of 1812). According to Gil,

The authorities of the *ancien régime* were used to dealing with actors in a demeaning and fierce manner, issuing decrees despotically and quoting the King when it served their purpose to deal with them whimsically and arbitrarily, depriving them of the property earned by their industry, and at times jailing or banishing them, as they saw fit. When the King signed the Constitution, the inequality among Spanish citizens disappeared, as did secret judgments and commissioned judges, bringing together all citizens under one law and one judicial power. In accord with the spirit of that sacred document, the Regency that legitimately governed during the King's captivity established a rule of law for the theatres in which were written various articles that outlined the limits of the Town Halls, and the powers enjoyed by them, by the town leaders and by the judges in matters of legal dispute.[27]

Gil was not convinced that the theatres could be run "as they had last year," and his four petitions to the authorities received unsatisfactory replies. He finally demanded, in the name of his acting company, that "said Theatre Regulation be approved and put into effect, so as to avoid that the authorities arbitrarily dispose of the property of the claimants, and so that the duties and obligations of both parties be explicit and limited, and in this way to insure that the light which has shined over all of Spain, will shine as well upon her acting companies."[28] Since it was too late to formulate new regulations and still open the theatres on time, the actors decided to open the new season under a plan formulated by Arjona (but "as an interim measure, and under protest"). Even after the King and the chief political officer of Madrid had approved the Reglamento, no action was taken and the actors remained in the same state of uncertainty as before. It was not until weeks later, on May 26, that the authorities even asked for an accounting of the charges being disputed.[29]

These charges were one of the most contentious points of theatrical ownership in the 1820s and 1830s and the cause of much acrimony and financial hardship. They were the "hot potatoes" of all parties involved, and each potential impresario, whether it was an individual, the acting companies, the municipality, or the Supreme Council, wanted to toss them off onto someone else. "During the first half of the nineteenth century complaints are continually repeated by actors, impresarios, literary critics and even the Town Hall against the charges that weighed so heavily upon the Cruz and Príncipe theatres."[30] The charges were an "inheritance from the past but an important obstacle in the development of theatrical life in the capital"[31] and were comprised of two types: actors' retirement payments (pensions) and "good works," that is, payments to charitable institutions which the theatres had supported since the end of the sixteenth century.[32] In addition, there had been added to the general costs of running the theatres certain other expenditures such as free seats for designated municipal authorities, rental payments for the theatres, dividend payments to individuals or institutions with historic rights to receive them and a fixed annual payment to help underwrite the actors' infirmary. All such payments came out of box office receipts, of course, which reduced the pool of funds available to pay the actors their salaries or to produce any sort of profit. The "good works" charges were protected by Royal Decrees; the salaries were not. Bernardo Gil was frustrated by 1820 and he complained bitterly of "the enormous charges that . . . weigh daily upon the theatres . . . and being requested to suit the purpose of the theatres themselves . . . and in view of the unfortunate situation of the actors, who suffer an enormous loss of income, as well as of work," since he felt it unfair that the actors themselves were being forced to carry the charges (Gil, *Manifiesto*, pp. 18–19). The actors viewed a regulation signed on June 28, 1820, as a document of enslavement ("being a Regulation of the government, which the actors were forced to subscribe to, or be blacklisted in the entire country"). Gil presented a detailed explanation of their position to the municipal authorities on July 14. Put simply, it was their belief that "to continue these charges this year would produce desolation in the theatre and the devastation of the actors' capital," and he asked the municipality to pay for the seats they use, take over the payments to the Colegio de Niñas de la Paz, the Hospital del Buen Suceso and the Hospital de Antón Martín, and reduce the rents charged for the theatres (Gil, *Manifiesto*, p. 21). He even implied that there might be a strike if the conditions were not honored. His demands were met with silence.

By August 14, 1820, Bernardo Gil and Antonio González, both Directors of their respective theatres and official spokesmen for their companies, issued yet another bold statement in which they rehearsed once again their reasons for complaint, the hardships they were suffering, and their debts ("they increase daily"), and proclaimed that "as a result there can be no more performances, and these will cease next Sunday, August 20, if before that date the municipality does not institute the Regulation of the Regency, which deals with the conditions under which the acting companies are to work" (Gil, *Manifiesto*, p. 24). This was not their last try. On August 19, Gil and González repeated yet again their complaints and warned that on August 21 all theatre performances would stop. They did. On August 30, the two directors took their case to the people in the form of a *Manifiesto que dan los autores de los teatros de la Cruz y Príncipe*.

By the time the new season got underway in the spring of 1821, the theatres were in the hands of a private impresario, Clemente de Rojas.[33] Concepción Rodríguez was selected to move to the Príncipe as "leading lady," where she received much popular acclaim and continued to develop skills which would later carry her to the triumphant heights of the Romantic stage. But her popular successes were not matched by those of the impresario, who by September, 1821, was so deeply in debt that he had to ask for a loan from the municipal government. His reasons? The costs of the "good works" and pensions he was forced to pay. He subsequently went bankrupt, and the theatres were turned over to José Sáenz de Juano on December 31, 1821, for a five year period (AV: Contaduría 4-56-1).

Sáenz fared no better. The instability of the revolutionary government, the continuation of the immense cost of mounting theatrical productions in Madrid, and, finally, in 1823, the war situation created by the invasion of Spain by the French troops of the 100,000 Sons of St. Louis, backed by the Holy Alliance, brought his business to a halt. In June, 1823, Sáenz, citing "the enormous losses which I am suffering," asked the city government for a bailout. "The intake of the theatres diminishes every day and they are reduced to almost nothing, my reserves are gone, I have no means left," he complained (AV: Secretaría 2-472-31). The loan was refused, and Sáenz was forced into bankruptcy. The theatres closed on June 9 and one week later they were put up for public auction (AV: Secretaría 2-472-31). The future of theatrical activity in Madrid remained uncertain.

Bankruptcy and the battle for control, 1823

On January 28, 1823, King Louis XVIII of France proclaimed, in the Louvre, that one hundred thousand French troops were prepared to march against Spain in order to restore Fernando VII to the throne ("one hundred thousand men, commanded by a Son of France are about to cross the Pyrenees . . ."). The army was under the command of Louis's nephew, Louis Antoine de Bourbon, known as the Duke of Angoulême.[34] Among those who served in that army was a twenty-seven year old career soldier named Jean-Marie Grimaldi.

Grimaldi, born in Avignon on April 2, 1796, of a humble family of Corsican descent, was not an extremely cunning "Italian" as Zorrilla and others have mistakenly claimed.[35] When he was not yet twelve years old he abandoned his formal schooling to enter the military, securing a position in the army of his fellow Corsican, serving in Avignon in the supply depot of the Army Service Corps (the Commissaire des Guerres, later known as Commissaire des Intendants). He worked there from the beginning of January, 1808, until October 4, 1810, and was such an able administrator – he was less than fourteen years old! – that he was sent in 1811 to Vaucluse as interim Director of the Service Corps, and shortly thereafter, because of his "zeal, intelligence, and activity," he was named head of the warehouse in Toulon charged with securing and distributing uniforms and other clothing for the troops. He remained in this position until October, 1814.

Grimaldi took advantage of a period of convalescence he had been granted during Napoleon's short period of exile in 1815 to work for the Emperor's return. His loyalties paid off: Napoleon returned to power in March, and by May Grimaldi was situated in Paris as a Lieutenant in the Parisian National Guard. It is not known what happened to Grimaldi when Louis XVIII was restored to the throne in June of that same year following the One Hundred Days, but some years later (in the petitions he wrote to take over the theatres in Madrid in 1823) he claimed that he was a "Retired Head of the Commissariat, licensed lawyer, member of various scientific and literary societies" (Letter dated July 10, 1823; AV: Secretaría 2-472-25). That he survived the radical upheavals of French politics is not difficult to believe, for his chameleon-like nature and ability to use his quick intelligence to ingratiate himself with those whom he served – or wished to serve – are characteristics which would surface again and again, and rescue him from delicate political and financial situations. He was an opportunist whose loyalties at times underwent surprising modifications, depending on the necessities of the moment. In 1815 he was an ardent, active supporter of Napoleon; by 1823 he was invading Spain to replace a constitutional government with an absolutist monarch. His "liberalism" was at times only skin-deep and later in his life it would be tempered with huge doses of middle-of-the-road moderation. As Desfrétières has stated, "Grimaldi, who had 'contributed to the triumph of liberal ideals,' went to combat liberalism in Spain."[36]

Angoulême's 100,000 Sons of St. Louis passed through Burgos (where they were greeted by José Zorrilla's father, at that time governor of the province) and arrived in Madrid in May, 1823. Commissioner Grimaldi took a room near the Puerta del Sol, at 9 Calle del Carmen, and settled into learning the language of his new host town. Perhaps it was boredom, perhaps it was a result of discussions he overheard or even entered into with the leaders of the French army, but whatever motivated his next decision, the result was startling: less than six weeks after arriving in the foreign capital, Juan *de* Grimaldi (as he now began to present himself) decided to become impresario of the Spanish stage. The decision was surprising for its intrepidity. He possessed no formal education, no experience in the theatre, no knowledge of the theatrical structure in Madrid. He did not even possess the language yet (although he appears to have learned it extremely quickly and well: as Patricio de la Escosura remembered, "Grimaldi's talent – for everything – was enormous, as is proven, among many other examples, by his having made himself such a master of our language in so few years that he ended up writing it with a truly enviable elegance and fluency.").[37] Grimaldi quickly saw that the theatres were in a state of ruin, that Sáenz was bankrupt and that the French troops had insufficient entertainment, and so on July 4 he boldly presented a letter to the municipal government proposing himself as impresario of one of the theatres, the Príncipe. He intended to put on French tragedies, comedies and vaudeville performances in the service of the French troops. The letter of petition proposed the staging of "an entirely new entertainment" for residents of Madrid who had never lived in France. He would establish "a French theatre," composed of actors "of fame and renown" who would work fifteen days each month. During the remaining fifteen days the theatres would host performances of Italian opera. He thought that such entertainments would bring "lustre" to the Spanish capital as well as calm to the occupation troops, who needed to "enjoy in the midst of their military labors in a foreign country a diversion reminiscent of the theatre of their home country." He was careful to insist that this idea was not his alone, but that it had the backing of the head of the occupation force, the Duke of Angoulême.

He addressed the issue of the charges and the actors' retirement benefits, and even as he insisted that he had absolutely no desire to "harm in the least" any of the actors, he offered to pay only half of their existing pension rights and only then if he was granted full use of the goods and props kept in the theatres (AV: Secretaría 2-472-25; the letter is reproduced by Desfrétières, pp. 142–3).

Grimaldi revealed in this letter that his first interest was in providing entertainment for his countrymen, and that the Spanish actors would, perforce, be excluded from his offerings at the Príncipe. It would have been thought that the City Council ("Ayuntamiento") would have seen Grimaldi's petition as a chance to resolve the sticky issue of the theatres, but as negotiations progressed over the next few months, it became clear that such was not the case.

The strongest opposition to Grimaldi's plan to take over the Príncipe came, not surprisingly, from the actors themselves. In fact, they must have got wind of his plans early because on July 2, two days before Grimaldi wrote to the City Council, the actors themselves presented a statement to the authorities. It contained a notice of their offer to join with the company of Italian actors currently in the capital to present interim functions in both theatres until the issue of ownership could be resolved ("the Spanish actors offered fraternally to join forces with them in order to share a common fate and to divide whatever earnings might result" [AV: Secretaría 2-472-25].), but this offer was rejected by the Italian company. As Gregorio Martín has pointed out, "The Spanish actors must have thought that Grimaldi had been guilty of convincing the Italian actors to abandon the project of working together with them."[38] They did claim surprise at the decision ("the Spaniards wondered about that decision" [AV: Secretaría 2-472-25].), since they prided themselves on their generosity in allowing foreign actors to act on Spanish stages, a custom previously prohibited by Carlos IV. But a few days later, the actors' attorney, Agustín Toraño y Roldán, "having received notice that an impresario had come forth, requesting that he be granted the Príncipe Theatre, in order to establish a company of French actors, which, alternating with the Italian opera singers," demanded that any new impresario be held responsible for the *full* payment of the actors' pensions. Toraño made two key points: one, that the pensions should not be linked in any way to the use of goods belonging to the actors and two, that the payment of pensions was protected by Royal mandate and had never been abrogated before. He pointed out that the present closure of the theatres and the bankruptcy of Sáenz had brought more than seventy families to "a state of mendacity." Their concern for the protection of the payment of retirement pensions was intense and he insisted that "In view of what has been expressed, the petitioner can only indicate that if the theatre is given to the new impresario, he must be made to understand that he must satisfy the daily payments of the retired actors, and fully, especially during the time when only one theatre is open (whether there is a daily performance or not), as has been the practice in the past. The Spanish actors will also conform to this stipulation if they manage to take charge of the theatres" (AV: Secretaría 2-472-25).

Several days following Grimaldi's letter, on July 9, 1823, the actors sent another letter, signed this time not just by their lawyer but by all of them, in which they denounced "the application of the impresario who wishes to take over the Príncipe Theatre for the French and Italian companies to the exclusion of the Spanish actors" as "*an attack upon Spanish theatre which will bring about its ruin"* (emphasis mine). They reiterated their position on the payment of retirement benefits. The list of signatures included those of Concepción Rodríguez, Antera Baus and Antonio Guzmán, who had joined the company recently and who was destined to rise to fame acting in the most popular comic role created in the first half of the century, in a play written, ironically, by the "foreigner" he was now so vociferously opposing.[39] Grimaldi feigned surprise at the actors' resistance. His rather arrogant reply stated:

I did not consider the possibility that the Spanish actors could oppose this plan, since I was prepared to contribute one half of the retirement payments, as long as they were prepared to turn over to the impresario the decorations and goods which belong to them. The Cruz theatre remains free for the use of the Spanish actors, who certainly cannot assure better results with two theatres, given the decadence in which, unfortunately, acting and the dramatic arts find themselves currently in Madrid.

This attitude hardly endeared him to the acting companies, who, as he had heard, "are begging the officials to reject the proposal." The tone of his letter was aggressive, but understandable, for he felt it hypocritical and unjust that the actors, who could not sustain the theatres by themselves, sought to prohibit him from doing so. His strongest protest, however, was marshaled against the actors' contention that his plan would ruin Spanish theatre.

They say that the establishment of this theatre would ruin Spanish national theatre. What does the one have to do with the other? The theatre being proposed can only be an object of luxury for those Spaniards who like music or who know French or really just a special diversion for the allied troops. But Spanish theatre will always appeal to the majority of the people and principally to the lower classes ["el Pueblo"] who would not understand anything about French acting. Even more can be said: a foreign theatre can only stimulate the envy of the Spanish actors, and bring them out of the stupor in which they are now immersed, to the great detriment of their art, which has remained languid for the past few years.

Besides, he wrote, "my establishment cannot last very long and it should naturally be limited to the time the French army remains in Madrid. It is nothing more than a provisional test of a new entertainment that the current circumstances demand."

Grimaldi thought, however, that he might be able to neutralize the actors' resistance to his plan by somehow bringing them into it. He discussed with them the possibility of joining forces and, in effect, their opposition disappeared the next day. Grimaldi, together with the actors' lawyers Juan Carretero, Rafael Pérez and Agustín Toraño, proposed to the City Council a short five-clause contract in which they agreed to work together to open the theatres, pending approval by the City Council (AV: Secretaría 2-472-25; Desfrétières, pp. 145–6). Grimaldi's longer, formal contract was presented on July 12.[40] This longer contract contained thirteen stipulations, but it was phrased in language less contentious than before. Grimaldi's principal conces- sion was his agreement to take over not just the Príncipe but the Cruz as well, noting that since "nobody wants to take over said theatre and it would be unseemly that two foreign theatres exist in Madrid while the Spanish theatre remains closed, I have decided to run the risk of huge losses by taking over both theatres" (AV: Secretaría 2-472-25; Desfrétières, pp. 147–49). His statement about running the risk of substantial losses was not entirely exaggerated since he was well aware of Sáenz's fate ("one impresario ended up ruined because of the lack of paying public and ever since this business ceased, nobody has come forth to take over the theatres"), but his proposed contract certainly attempted to minimize those risks. He went so far as to claim that he was doing the City Council a favor by offering to take over the theatres and that the City Council should meet his demands out of gratitude.

Those demands were not insignificant: he requested both theatres rent free, with the use of the income-producing cafés attached to them; he insisted that he should not be responsible for the social welfare fees; he demanded free use of all the goods, costumes, and machinery, in both theatres; he refused to be responsible for any repairs which dealt with general maintenance of the theatres (these were the City Council's responsibility); he protected himself against any liens or debts accrued by the previous impresario; he insisted on the right to hire or fire the actors, musicians, stage hands and other workers he chose to employ; he demanded the right to bring foreign actors to Madrid (this had been a particularly troublesome point for the Spanish actors); he requested that all other theatrical performances in Madrid be banned (in order to avoid competition) or if banning was not in order, he demanded a payment for performance rights (this was standard policy and "it is practiced in all the theatres of Europe");[41] and he included a clause which stipulated that the contract would become null and void if the theatres were closed by fire, death of the king or queen, or other catastrophe.

The Theatre Commission met to study Grimaldi's request and responded to his offer on July 17. Not surprisingly, a number of his clauses were turned down. The particularly difficult points were the concession of the theatres and the cafés free of charge, and Grimaldi's attempt to absolve himself from the "good works" fees. The City Council was apparently willing to go along with the first demand in part ("Madrid's generosity in this matter is only an experiment," and the City Council did not control the use of the cafés) but it was unable to release Grimaldi from his responsibilities to the hospitals and other annuities. Grimaldi responded the following morning quickly and forcefully ("it is absolutely impossible for me to take charge of the theatres under the conditions proposed by the Commission"), but the City Council remained equally intransigent and even turned back to the actors to pursue additional possibilities. It set up a special meeting for the next day and invited the actors to attend. Several meetings were needed to iron out the details of the arrangement and before any concrete decisions were made, Grimaldi, apparently seeing the direction in which things were moving, finally gave in and offered to accept the City Council's terms. On July 21, he confessed that both his honor ("I cannot abandon a matter which has progressed this far so publicly") and pressure from the Duke of Angoulême and other high officials of the resident troops ("they all await the French theatre that I have offered them") obliged him to "make sacrifices" and to take over the theatres "under the conditions approved on the 17 of this month."[42]

Even with Grimaldi's concession, by July 23 the City Council still had not decided whether to give the theatres to him or to the actors. The decision was finally made on August 5 in Grimaldi's favor, with one seemingly insignificant addendum: Grimaldi was to provide a security payment of 100,000 *reales* in cash or twice that amount in property as a security measure for the Town Hall's investment (AV: Secretaría 2-472-25). This security would cover not only the charitable payments but also the actors' pension costs (Grimaldi's previous offer of 30,000 *reales* was discounted by the city, and protested by the actors themselves as grossly insufficient). The city was clear as to the seriousness of the proposal: on August 14 it declared that if Grimaldi refused the established conditions or could not come up with the guarantees it would recommend that "the theatres be turned over to the Spanish actors." Grimaldi's actions were being watched closely by everyone concerned and his intentions were suspect, particularly in regard to the payment of pensions, which the actors (with reason) feared would be ignored or reduced by the prospective impresario.

Their lawyer, Toraño, issued a firm statement on August 18 asking the City Council to include in Grimaldi's contract a clause concerning pensions, so as to avoid the harsh fate which befell the pensioners, widows and orphans under the stewardship of Sáenz de Juano.

Grimaldi offered 65,000 *reales* – 50,000 up front and the remaining 15,000 in two months (AV: Secretaría 2-472-25) – but the City Council refused to bargain. He then asked for an extension of six days, and once again heard the threat that if he did not come up with the money, the theatres would be turned over to the actors. He apparently succeeded in convincing an acquaintance to back his project, for at last, on August 25, Grimaldi offered as collateral a house in Madrid belonging to a woman named María Juliana del Barrio. The house had been appraised, according to his letter, at 200,000 *reales*. It is not clear who this woman was nor why she would be interested in mortgaging her property for Grimaldi, but her offer appeared to be his immediate salvation.

The battle over rights and ownership was seemingly won; Grimaldi prepared himself to take over the theatres. But the City Council and the actors had been so shaken by the economic chaos of the past that nothing was to be left unsecured this time around. Another delay ensued as assessors were sent out to prove the worth of the house and the legal status of its ownership. By the end of August it was determined that the house was indeed worth more than 200,000 *reales*, but that it had a number of outstanding debts against it which reduced its cash value to under 190,000. More meetings were held to determine whether such a guarantee was sufficient and acceptable to the city. And there was still an issue of a cash down payment of 60,000, which Grimaldi was having trouble raising. By September 17, the pressure on him was enormous; he signed a statement promising to have the money by the next day or "I agree to allow the theatres to be given to the actors."[43]

The actual contract for his takeover of the theatres had been drawn up on September 14, but it was not certain that it would be put into effect. It contained twenty-seven clauses, most of them favorable to Grimaldi, but still meeting the major demands of the actors (pensions) and the City Council (charitable payments) (AV: Secretaría 2-472-25; Desfrétières, pp. 150–4). He would stage French and Spanish plays, and Italian operas, and would receive both theatres and their adjoining cafés free of charge, although he had to honor the payments made to those individuals or institutions which traditionally received benefits from the products of the theatres and cafés (these charges totaled more than 19,000 *reales* per year). But he would receive any profits generated by the cafés after these payments were met.[44] Grimaldi was likewise responsible for payments to the Colegio de Niñas de la Paz and to the lamplighter, nightwatchman and doorkeeper who guarded the theatres (an additional 30,000 *reales*).[45] While nobody was completely satisfied with the terms of the contract, all parties concerned – the actors, the City Council, the French troops, and Grimaldi – agreed upon the importance of opening the theatres and salvaging what could be salvaged of that year's theatrical season.

By September 16, when the contract had been approved and the inventories of both theatres certified, the issue was resolved. The theatres, closed since June 9 (with a two-day hiatus in August to celebrate the queen's Saint's Day)[46] were set to reopen on September 21. Juan de Grimaldi became impresario of the Príncipe and the Cruz theatres.

2

Grimaldi at the beginning of the "Ominous Decade"

Manuel Bretón de los Herreros recalled the years 1820–3 as years of "decadence" for Spanish theatre and viewed Grimaldi as a true savior of the theatre. "Under the direction of Mr. Grimaldi," he wrote, "the work of Máiquez was completed, abuses and habits that were still obstacles were eradicated, and stage art reached its highest point."[1] This fundamental renovation took years to accomplish, but in his first year as impresario, Grimaldi made a number of significant changes which he would continue to build upon throughout the next decade and beyond.

Grimaldi Impresario: 1823–4

What did Grimaldi inherit along with his new title, "impresario"? Why did he take this bold step into an area in which he had no experience? Why did he consider the theatre an endeavor in which he should invest his administrative skills and money? Where did he get the money to invest? Besides a risky financial investment, contentious and undertrained actors and a limited (and censored) repertory of plays to perform, he received two buildings which were decrepit and uncomfortable and which contained a grab bag of painted curtains, sets and props. "The poor state of the costumes, decorations and stage equipment at that time ... would hardly be believable to anyone who has not witnessed it," commented a contemporary theatregoer, Dionisio Chaulié.[2] The detailed inventories "of all the goods and materials existing in both theatres owned by Madrid" (AV: Secretaría 2-472-45)[3] reveal that the Príncipe contained an odd collection of lanterns, candlesticks, barrels for oil and tallow, chandeliers, flies (for the scenery), large painted backdrops (representing a jail, a poor man's house, a garden, a seashore, a forest, a street), set decorations (a door, garden gates, a throne, a precipice, a fountain, two caves, benches, tables, chairs, stools, and even thirty clothes hangers) and other assorted goods which Grimaldi promised to return intact at the end of the season in 1824. The Cruz contained a similar collection of items (but more of them, including a triumphal carriage, a jail cot, a carriage with two swans on it, two dogs and a goat made of wood, and a large rug "ripped to shreds"). Most of the items were made of wood, cloth, or tinplate.[4] The low quality of these goods did not go unnoticed and the scant quantity of them produced similarly low expectations on the part of the audience ("large forest, small forest, garden, stately salon, narrow room, poor house, jail, and a street scene for *sainetes*: here is the catalogue of sets that everyone was familiar with, that everyone saw at the theatres. In some plays the scenery was varied a little by adding some indispensable household item or by putting doors on a backdrop, and nothing more was demanded," remembered Chaulié).[5]

The two theatres themselves were dusty, dark and uncomfortable. The modern Príncipe, built in 1745 and reopened in 1807 following the disastrous fire of 1802, contained space for twelve hundred spectators.[6] The Cruz, built in 1737, could accommodate slightly more than thirteen hundred people. Two testimonies from the period provide somewhat differing views of the theatres. For Fernando Fernández de Córdoba, they were unbearable: he witnessed paltry oil lanterns which left the whole place in shadows and gave off an "intolerable odor"; ridiculously small boxes, "poorly painted, poorly decorated, and abysmally furnished," which were so dirty that women feared to wear even a "moderately fine" dress to the theatre because of the dust and oil; backless seats which were so uncomfortable that people had to bring their own seat cushions from home; rickety orchestra seats covered with torn, filthy goatskins; "pestilential" smells emanating from the galleries; a dense and continuous haze ("smoke") inside; asphyxiating heat in summer and bone-chilling cold in winter; nasty, "gross" ushers; and finally, a rude and noisy audience.[7] But a French traveler, Adolphe Blanqui, visiting Madrid in the mid-1820s, painted a more benevolent picture of the physical aspects of the theatres (and made some sociological observations as well):

The interior (of the Príncipe) is laid out intelligently, and the public has numerous advantages there that are not found in any of the theatres of Paris. The pit is divided in three sections: the first, which they call the principal seating, is similar to what we call the stalls, which are, in Madrid, real arm chairs perfectly adorned and very comfortable; the second resembles what we call the orchestra: the spectators are seated there with their backs supported against a ramp, but they are not numbered; this is the second section. Finally the third division corresponds to the pit in our theatres. There are three rows of uniform box seats in two galleries. . . . The boxes present a sad spectacle. All the women are dressed in black, and they wear on their heads a type of veil of the same color known as a *mantilla*, which falls gracelessly over their shoulders and which hides their hair, their neck, their bosom and their shoulders; they look like a gathering of mummies. The rapid and tiresome fluttering of their fans hardly breaks up this singular monotony. However, it would be wrong to reproach the Spaniards for their choice of gloomy dress in the present circumstances; in the midst of the enormous sorrows that weigh upon the country, gaiety would be unseemly among the ladies of the Peninsula.[8]

His was a minority voice, however. The majority of those who commented on the Spanish theatres in the 1820s and 1830s found them disagreeable in the extreme ("both are ugly and small inside, oppressive and vulgar; the Cruz much more than the Príncipe" is the way Ferrer described them in 1835),[9] and even a compatriot of Blanqui's found "the theatres in Madrid fairly sad."[10]

Under such circumstances, what could be expected of an untrained ex-soldier – even one with vast administrative experience – who by sheer stubbornness found himself in charge of the Madrid stage? As Chaulié wrote, "the Príncipe Theatre was lucky enough to be taken over by D. Juan Grimaldi, a model of impresarios and stage directors, who at the cost of great effort and intelligence reformed many of the defects I have mentioned."[11] Grimaldi began his new task in late September, 1823.

The political climate was changing and the King initiated a period of political and cultural repression which would later come to be called the "Ominous Decade." On October 1, Fernando VII annuled all legislation passed during the Constitutional Triennium. This repression, and the censorship which accompanied it, manifested itself visibly in the types of theatrical productions approved and performed in Madrid's two theatres.[12] Grimaldi was not unmindful of the political climate, and later he remembered these years in general as "the melancholy year of 1823 and those which followed it" and October 1 in particular as a day which "ruined thousands of families, that eliminated all jobs, that outlawed the country's most worthy sons."[13] He would have a modest degree of success in expanding the repertory in his years of influence during the "Ominous Decade," but it would not be until after the death of the King that any significant change of style would be in evidence. Fighting censorship was a task that even the bravest souls rarely undertook. Even Larra – and not until after 1828 – was circumspect in his criticism of the regime. What Grimaldi could do, however – and did do – was to infuse the companies with a new and previously unimagined spirit of professionalism, improve the physical accoutrements of the stage, enrich the repertory with plays imported from abroad (mostly from France, naturally) and attract a wider audience to the theatre. As we shall see, these advances were slow and arduous, but by the time the political atmosphere accepted what even then were vaguely called "Romantic" plays (after 1834), there was an audience interested in attending them, a group of actors trained to act in them and theatres prepared to give them quality productions.

Grimaldi opened his first season with the standard fare: at the Príncipe he offered a symphonic excerpt from Rossini's *Tancredi*; a two-act comedy called *El sordo en la posada*, translated from the French; an operatic duo from Rossini's *Zoraida*; a short dance number; a *sainete* by González del Castillo called *El recibo del paje*; and yet another excerpt from a Rossini opera, *La cenerentola*.[14] These pieces had been performed previously (mostly in 1822).[15] At the Cruz, the so-called "national" theatre, the audience witnessed a performance of a rewrite ("refunación") by Dionisio Solís of Tirso's *Don Gil de las calzas verdes*, a dance number, a symphonic piece from *Los dos ciegos*, and a *sainete* called *El muerto vivo*. In spite of Grimaldi's claim that he wished to provide entertainment for the French troops, none of the performances was in that language, a surprising and puzzling fact, given his still-strong allegiance to the Duke of Angoulême. (Did he perceive the possibilities of making a profit from the Spanish audience, thereby abandoning his interest in the French troops?) Concepción Rodríguez acted in *Don Gil* along with Gertrudis Torres, Ramona León, and others who would be steady, if undistinguished performers during the 1820s.[16] The following evening she was acting at the Príncipe in *El viejo y la niña*, another of the Moratín plays in which she had achieved some degree of notoriety.

From the announcements of the first months' performances in the Príncipe and Cruz we can discern some of Grimaldi's goals and the direction his theatres would take over the next few years. His first goal was clearly to please the public and to present plays, operas, and spectacles which would attract an audience. When it became clear that neither he nor the Italian opera company was sufficiently well-organized to begin a full series of performances by the end of September, he promised Spanish operas, sung by members of the regular acting companies who possessed – or claimed to possess – voices sufficient to carry them.[17] He likewise promised magic spectacles, plays which had always enjoyed popularity among Madrid theatregoers ("the company is preparing to put on very soon at the Cruz Theatre a grand performance of a magical play ("función de magia") entitled *A falta de hechiceros lo quieren ser los gallegos*, embellished with transformations, flights, trap doors, new sets and all sorts of theatrical apparatus"),[18] and which would culminate in 1829 with the debut of his wildly popular *La pata de cabra*. And above all, he promised to present an array of melodramas, which had become increasingly popular with Madrid audiences.

He did his duty to the King and crown by holding special functions on auspicious occasions, such as the celebration for the King's release held on October 5. The Royal Boxes were left open (normally a curtain closed them off when the royal couple was not in attendance), a portrait of the King was perched on his chair in the box, the exteriors of the theatres were illuminated with hundreds of candles (at substantial expense) and a play with political implications, Lope de Vega's *El mejor alcalde, el rey* (in a rewritten version by Solís), was performed. That evening also witnessed an allegorical tableau "showing France removing Spain's chains and placing our august sovereign, Fernando VII, on his throne." Another politically inspired evening took place on October 14 (the King's birthday). *Una función cerca de Cádiz* had its debut that evening, and once again the King's portrait was perched in his box and the theatres were illuminated. The newspaper reported that a French soldier was given a part in the play: "a fan (a French soldier) will perform a part written in French."[19] A similar political evening was held privately in honor of the Duke of Angoulême on November 3; the following day the pieces were put on for the general public, and yet another official function, "which alludes to the present circumstances" and performed before the King and Queen on November 26, was installed at the Príncipe on December 1. This piece, *La noticia feliz*, was written by José María Carnerero and scored musically by Ramón Carnicer.[20] It lasted for a few days on the stage, but closed for this reason (as printed in the *Diario de Madrid*): "Because the performances of Italian opera are about to begin and because the actors deserve a rest, the performances of the play entitled *La noticia feliz*, which alludes to the present circumstances, will be suspended, and will resume when the acting companies are reconstituted." Performances of this play did not resume.

Multiple performances were the common fare of Spanish theatre at the time. Performances were lengthy (usually three or four hours), and the audience sat through several musical interludes, a one-act farce (*sainete*) or other one-act piece, a two- or three-act comedy or tragedy and two or three dance numbers. The actors, musicians, singers and dancers were each separate, but related, companies within the larger company. They were contracted to work in a set number of performances.

Grimaldi tried many things to lure people into the theatre. He attempted to capitalize on Rossini's popularity by presenting a play entitled *El hombre gris, o sea el ceniciento*. In addition to the "comedias de magia," he presented several French melodramas, whose complicated stage apparatus appealed to the public's (and Grimaldi's own) enjoyment of spectacle and which would help to foster it. (One notice, for the play, *El víctor o el hijo del subterráneo*, promised "a general battle and several military encounters," and newspaper notices usually commented if a play was a showy spectacle ["de gran espectáculo"]). He allowed the actresses to do special Christmas Eve, female-only shows in both theatres – in the Cruz, the traditional *El alcalde de sí mismo* and in the Príncipe, *También por flores hay duelos*[21] – and also during that first holiday season he put on a play which, although already an annual staple in the repertory in its original form, would inspire Grimaldi the following year to create his own rendition of it and provide Concepción Rodríguez with one of her most enduring hits. The 1824 version was Estrada's translation of J.N. Bouilly's *L'Abbé de l'Epée*, but it only remained on the boards for two performances. Grimaldi achieved more success with *La rosa blanca y la rosa encarnada*, a new two-act opera by G.S. Mayer and first played on January 1, 1824. That year it was seen ten times at the Príncipe.

Grimaldi had somewhat less success with the plays he introduced to Madrid's audiences during that 1823-4 season. Most of them had just a few performances, although one or two managed to remain in the repertory for most of the decade. The nine plays he introduced in the first season were: *El tutor celoso y la lugareña astuta* (a reworking of a Tirso play, first played on September 26 and managing ten performances during the decade);[22] *El celoso por fuerza* (October 14; one performance);[23] *El víctor o el hijo del subterráneo* (December 19; six performances); *Triunfar sólo por la Fé* (January 5; three performances); *El asentista* (January 20; two performances. This play was announced as a "comedia nueva," but often that term merely designated new translations, not original plays); *El hijo asesino del padre por socorrer a la madre, Carlota y Federico* (a translation of a German original; February 7; eleven performances); *El durmiente despierto* (February 14; three performances. This play was advertised as a "new original comedy" in the *Diario de Madrid*); *El fisonomista engañado* (February 24; two performances); and *El divino Sansón* (evidently by Pérez de Montalbán; February 27, 1824; eight performances).

Every now and then special events were announced. These could be a special performance for an actor's benefit (such as Loreto García's benefit show of the opera *Las juventudes de Enrique V*, on February 24, 1824) or the debut of new actors (José García Luna and Carlos Latorre both made their debuts in early 1824). Perhaps the oddest special event during that first season was the benefit performance for the actors' trade union – the Cofradía de la Virgen de la Novena[24] – and for their infirmary. The play to be presented at the Cruz on March 1, 1824, was *La vieja y los calaveras* and the novelty was that ("with the authorities' permission") "men will come out dressed as women, and the women as men." A similar function, based on the comedy *La novia impaciente* (translation of Etienne's *La jeune femme colère*, 1814), was held that day at the Príncipe.[25]

During his first season, then – September 21, 1823, to Mardi Gras Tuesday, March 2, 1824 – Grimaldi presented a mixture of French plays by Beaumarchais, Arnault, Destouches, Etienne, Regnard, Molière,[26] Scribe, Duval, and Désaugiers (in translations by Bernardo Gil, Gorostiza, Comella, Ramón de la Cruz, Carnerero), *sainetes*, operas or excerpts from operas (mostly by Rossini), rewrites of plays by Golden Age authors such as Calderón, Fernando de Zárate, Tirso, and Lope, and odd novelties such as the "magical *sainete*" ("sainete de magia"), *Diablos son las mujeres o el barbero mágico*, performed in mid-October. Some additional performances were given at theatres not controlled by Grimaldi (for example, the five-act tragedy by Trigueros, *Sancho Ortiz de las Roelas*, given in a theatre on Cava Baja on October 13), but he presumably exercised his contractual rights by agreeing to them and by collecting a fee. Grimaldi also presented some "new" authors and plays, but few of any consequence except José María Carnerero, who would work for Grimaldi's theatres as playwright and translator before turning to journalism – the field in which he would have his greatest impact on the intellectual life of Fernandine Spain.

An analysis of that first season reveals that Grimaldi and his companies staged 102 different one- to five-act plays (not including *sainetes* or dramatic panegyrics [*loas*]) in 163 days. No play received more than nine performances that year and only eight received more than six performances. The most popular were: *El perro de Montargis* (translation of a French melodrama by Pixérécourt);[27] *Los jueces francos* (translation of a French version of a German melodrama by Viet-Weiber); *Del rey abajo ninguno* (Golden Age *comedia* by Rojas Zorrilla); *El leñador escocés* (translation of a French melodrama by Mélesville); *El hechizado por fuerza* (post-Golden Age *comedia* by Antonio Zamora); *La casualidad a medianoche* (one-act comedy; author unknown); *A falta de hechiceros lo quieren ser los gallegos* (magical play [*comedia de magia*] by González Martínez); and *El mejor alcalde, el rey* (Solís's reworking of Lope's Golden Age drama). Operas were the most popular: of the five operas presented that year, two ran for ten days each (Rossini's *La cenerentola* and Mayer's *La rosa blanca y la rosa encarnada*) and a third was staged nine times (Mercadante's *Elisa y Claudio*). There were thirty-five performances of the opera. But most regular plays lasted for only one performance or two: of the total number of performances, fully fifty-nine per cent were of plays which disappeared after two performances. The small but assiduous theatre going public demanded a constant influx of new material and it was Grimaldi's intention to meet that demand. He would not let the popularity of the melodramas and the *comedias de magia* go unnoticed.

If Grimaldi failed to reinvigorate the repertory during his first year as impresario, it was due to two clear, and related, reasons. One was the strict and suffocating censoring apparatus headed by the zealous Father Fernando Carrillo who controlled which plays were permitted. The other was the lack of fresh new plays. Chaulié talked of "the implacable theatrical censorship" which "destroyed or condemned to silence those works of genius which fell under its authority," and noted that "dramatists were in short supply."[28] Grimaldi would later turn his attention to the problem of new plays and playwrights, but in his first year two different areas attracted him – the physical improvement of the two theatres and the location and development of good actors and opera singers.

Grimaldi gave considerable time and attention to his attempt to improve the condition of the two dirty, miserable theatres he controlled. He first closed the Cruz for four days at the end of October in order to paint new sets and to make some small general repairs inside.[29] The Príncipe was shut down for more than three weeks (November 4–27) and then reopened "completely repainted,"[30] and following that, his attentions were once again turned to the Cruz, which was closed "in order to carry out a restoration similar to the one done at the Príncipe."[31] In addition, new sets were constantly being painted, an activity which reached its apogee later in the decade with the arrival of the talented French painter, Jean Blanchard.

With regard to the actors and opera singers, Grimaldi's first move was to dispatch his treasurer, Cristóbal Fernández de la Cuesta (who, before the decade was out, would himself be named impresario), to Italy to hire new performers for the opera. He knew opera was gaining popularity in Madrid and his contract with the City Council stipulated that part of the "public entertainment" would be performances of Italian operas. He needed to expand his pool of singers. Opera ultimately became so popular in the capital that it threatened to suffocate the regular theatre, but Grimaldi's immediate goal was to import some new talent (AHP: Protocolo 22945, folios 403–4. October 11, 1823). He had a similar interest in improving the skills of the dramatic actors (the company charged with putting on comedies and tragedies was called the "compañía de verso" to distinguish it from the opera company or the dance company). Concepción Rodríguez was improving in her roles as first lady, Antonio Guzmán likewise continued to develop his craft, and two new names were added to the company that year: José García Luna and Carlos Latorre. These four actors formed the core of an important resident repertory acting company that would grow and develop in stature and would, with the addition of Matilde Díez and Julián Romea in the 1830s, bring before the public the radical new plays of the Romantic period.

José García Luna (1798–1865) made his debut on January 11, 1824, in a role made famous by Máiquez – García del Castañar, in Solís's version of Del rey abajo ninguno – and returned to the stage on February 7 in Eduardo Gorostiza's Indulgencia para todos. He remained with the company throughout his career until his severely declining eyesight forced him to seek retirement in 1846.[32] He served in several capacities beyond that of actor (ticket dispatcher, impresario),[33] but it was in his roles in Bretón de los Herreros' plays and as Rivas' Don Alvaro that he reserved a place for himself in the annals of Spanish theatrical history.[34] His mother, Andrea Luna, was a recently-retired member of the company.

Carlos Latorre (1799–1851) also joined the Príncipe company early in 1824. John Dowling has noted that "The beginning of his career in 1824 coincided with the renovation of the theatre in Madrid under the stimulus of Grimaldi."[35] His first performance was in the title role in *Othello* (in a Spanish translation of Ducis's French version of the play) on February 21, a role he would repeat with great success throughout the decade. Latorre specialized in tragic roles and a "natural" style of acting. "He brought naturalness to the stage, a naturalness that had not arrived previously in spite of the impressive tragic performances given by Máiquez. Latorre, more intelligent, practiced a natural style of acting, but his case was isolated."[36] He formed his reputation acting in such plays as *Oscar, hijo de Osián* (in which he was an instant hit – by June, 1824, he was receiving the incredible sum of 750 *reales* per performance),[37] Quintana's *Pelayo*, Alfieri's *Los hijos de Edipo*, *El Cid*, and Martínez de la Rosa's *Edipo*. His greatest triumphs would come, like those of his fellow actors Concepción Rodríguez and García Luna, in Romantic plays: he starred in *La conjuración de Venecia*, *El trovador*, and *Don Juan Tenorio*, among others. Latorre had spent years in France – his family lived in exile there from 1813 to 1820[38] – and his attraction to Grimaldi was immediate. As Zorrilla remembered: "Latorre was the only tragic actor to inherit the traditions of Máiquez and to be trained in Talma's good school of French acting. His father had been an employee of the Treasury, an official in the provinces, in times past; and Carlos, a good horseman, skilled in the use of arms and of elegant and excellent appearance, had been a page to King Joseph [Bonaparte], and he acquired in France an education and social graces which made him a model stage performer. Grimaldi, the most intelligent director that our theatres have ever had, had shaped his classical habits and his Greco-French acting style to the demands of the modern theatre."[39]

Rodríguez and Latorre acted together in scores of plays between 1824 and 1836. One French commentator wrote that they "carried on in the footsteps of Máiquez, giving tragedy a new glamour, increasing the public's interest in seeing performances of many plays from our dramatic repertory."[40] Latorre became so well known and so appreciated as an actor that when Fernando VII's fourth wife, Queen María Cristina, convinced her husband to establish a Royal Conservatory of Music and Acting ("Real Conservatorio de Música y Arte Declamatorio") in 1831, Latorre was named Professor of Acting[41] and in 1835 he was invited to join the newly-inaugurated intellectual society, the Ateneo, along with the most distinguished literary and political leaders of the day.[42] Carlos Latorre was the first Spanish actor to receive official permission to use the distinguished appellation "don" before his name,[43] and by the end of his life his fame was such that his salary had soared to approximately 90,000 *reales* per year.[44]

Grimaldi's first year was not problem-free. Besides the strains created by the demands of the performance and production schedules (102 different plays in 163 days), the high costs of running the theatres and the payments to the charitable organizations were still problems which were not completely resolved. Said institutions were not always regularly paid, and petitions and demands were constantly exchanged between the impresario – who claimed inability to pay or need for more time – and the institutions, which demanded that they receive their rightfully contracted and agreed-upon sums (AV: Contaduría 4-56-1). The impresario was also responsible for the myriad bills presented by those who provided articles to the theatres (glassware, candles, utensils) and by those who historically received payments for previous investments ("réditos de censo") (AV: Contaduría 4-56-1). Even the alcaldes who were left unpaid by Sáenz demanded payment from Grimaldi (although by contract he was not responsible for Sáenz's debts). One issue left unresolved that year, and which would come back to haunt Grimaldi a decade later, was a bill presented to him by the man in charge of the theatres' storehouses, Eustasio Nieto y Castaños, in the amount of 12,252 *reales* for charges accrued for the rental of storage space for the theatres' effects (AV: Contaduría 4-56-1 and Secretaría 2-472-57).[45] The debts were never satisfied (Grimaldi claimed that he was owed similar amounts from the City Council for income lost on the free seats given out to the French generals). In fact, when Nieto came finally to collect the money in September of that year *Grimaldi hid from him* ("but seeing that when they searched his house he hid and could not be found; I tried to do my job and when I caught up with him he began to offer excuses for not paying, instead saying that he was owed money for the seat that the French general had enjoyed free of charge . . ." (AV: Secretaría 2-472-57). The two parties finally decided that the debt was only 5,987 *reales*, but even so Grimaldi refused to pay and Nieto was forced to sue him. When Grimaldi bid again for the takeover of the theatres eight years later the authorities began to question why these debts were left unresolved and those questions became obstacles between him and the municipal authorities.

He was upset with the demands for free seats that he was receiving from influential members of the French occupation troops. The Commander-in-Chief, Comte de Bourmont, wanted "to have a seat reserved for him every day in one of the two theatres free of charge." Grimaldi, citing his contract with the City Council, refused to honor this demand, but Bourmont's chief of staff sent an armed guard to each of the theatres to prohibit anyone other than the Count (or the Royal Family) from occupying the boxes. Grimaldi asked the authorities to expel Bourmont or make him pay for the seats (AV: Secretaría 2-472-39; Desfrétières, pp. 155–6). The debt still had not been settled by February 24, 1824 (AV: Secretaría 2-472-57; Desfrétières, p. 157) and by July of that year the King himself decided that the French generals could have their free seats (with the theatres absorbing the costs, which ran as high as 14,000 *reales* per theatre per year) (AV: Secretaría 2-472-39). Grimaldi also faced the problem of limited repertory possibilities, censorship, and personnel difficulties (such as illness, which at one point forced suspension of the performances of opera).[46]

Grimaldi's problems multiplied when it came time for him to renegotiate his contract as impresario for the next season, 1824–5.

Grimaldi behind the scenes

Ironically, Juan de Grimaldi, remembered as one of the most influential impresarios ever to work in the Spanish theatre, was "impresario" no more than one single season, 1823–4. Never again would he be successful in achieving a takeover of the theatres. His influence – and it was profound, as we shall see – would henceforth be carried out behind the scenes as director, manager of his own traveling company, friend and supporter of the actors, playwrights, and critics, and resident *éminence grise* (even at an early age) of the companies.[47]

Grimaldi had run the theatres from September 21, 1823, to March 2, 1824, when they closed for the traditional Easter break. They were set to open again on Easter Sunday, April 18. Just eight days after the close of his first season, Grimaldi once again turned to the Municipality with a proposal to continue the work he had started. He had been planning to continue for some time: the letter accompanying the contract proposal indicated that the document he was turning in on

March 11 contained the same stipulations that he directed to the authorities months earlier, on January 10 (AHN: Consejos, 11.411, n. 35; Desfrétières, pp. 158–79) and it contained clear evidence of the plans he was already formulating for the improvement of theatrical representations in the capital. He bothered to cite his previous communication of January 30 because he was battling an unexpected foe in his attempt to take control once again of the theatres – the acting companies themselves ("I understand that the actors are requesting the theatres for themselves"). He offered to show proof that he had already been in contact with a scenery painter and a stage machinist ("maquinista") in Paris who could carry out the improvements he promised in his attached contract; that he had laid the groundwork for improving the lighting scheme of the theatres; that he had contracted the renowned musician and composer Ramón Carnicer[48] as well as several famous singers (including one Bonoldi, "one of the three best tenors in Europe") for the opera; and that he had recruited six trained dancers from Paris, Milan and Bordeaux to work in Madrid.

Grimaldi sneered at the thought that the acting companies should be given possession of the theatres. He claimed that their numbers were severely reduced (of the seventy-four members comprising the companies in 1817, only twenty-three remained, the others having died, retired or fled – and those who were left were hardly, in his opinion, "the cream of the companies"). He possessed a copy of Gil's *Manifiesto* of 1820 and cleverly quoted it against his rivals by insisting that to return to the pre-1820 system (i.e., with the actors in charge) would be to return to the lack of individual freedom which they had so vociferously protested previously. "Was it not they themselves who asked for help from the very managements against whom they are now screaming?" Their plan, he claimed, was doomed to failure: "Have they perchance come across better resources in the interim? On the contrary: at that time the acting companies were whole; now only a skeleton of them remains to do a job that they were unable to do when they were robust and full of vigor. What a foolish calculation on the part of their misguided pride! They demand your protection only to return to a situation in which they will encounter certain ruin." In conjunction with the authorities, he saw himself as a benevolent dictator, a "father-figure" who could save the actors from their doom:

Just as a watchful and wise Father often protects his inexperienced children when they believe he is operating against their interests, you will certainly have the generosity to reject the actors' demands. Democracy is as lamentable in the dramatic societies as it is in political societies; as much the former as the latter need an enlightened, strong, and absolute power to guide them; with it, order, advantages and security; without it, confusion, bitterness, ruin.[49]

His actual proposal was a lengthy, detailed discussion not only of his specific plans to keep the theatres for the next few years, but of his ideas about what theatre in general should be and how it should be developed in Spain. It was a blueprint for what he would attempt to achieve and it laid the groundwork for much of his later success. The "Conditions and Propositions" contained thirty-four clauses and seventeen long explanatory notes, the first of which demanded the theatres for a three year period instead of the normal one. This demand, he argued, was necessitated by the "terribly costly improvements" that the theatres needed. A short-term investment would impede proper development, since the impresario "would not dare to make such huge expenditures" which could only be realised with time.

He proposed to combine the two acting companies into one, doubling the parts (two leading ladies, two leading men, etc.). In the course of this clause, he launched a tirade against the poor acting the Spanish public had heretofore been subjected to:

I propose to establish a single Spanish acting company, but doubling the principal parts, for as long as the actors remain without the competent direction *which can bring them out of the lofty indolence in which they lie*, and which can restore some semblance of decorum and variety to their performances, two companies can in no way be sustained given the dissatisfaction with which audiences now attend theatrical performances. Another reason is that, in order to maintain two companies, the impresario would be forced to keep some truly bad actors, who were hired years ago when there was a lack of qualified actors, and who during the entire time have given *proof positive of their absolute worthlessness*, who are *unworthy of the profession* and who *degrade with their very presence* the royal theatres of this capital. (Emphasis added).

In addition, he was convinced that the threat of being fired from the company would force bad actors to be more mindful of the skilled actors who might be out in the provinces and willing to come to Madrid to replace them. In this same clause he detailed his view that the Príncipe would be the theatre which housed opera and dance functions, and that the Cruz would be the "national" theatre. He showed his scorn for the two reasons which, in his mind, were the cause of the Cruz's decline: first, the "dullness and negligence" of the actors and second, the "barbarous and depraved" taste of previous theatrical producers who "prostituted" the stage with dog shows, acrobats, and "demagogic and repugnant" farces which the licentiousness of times past permitted to the great detriment of "literature, dramatic art, and good customs." In order to insure that such things did not happen again, Grimaldi insisted on the right to select *all* members of the acting company (although he did concede that the selection could be subject to the Mayor's approval).

Grimaldi was one of the most cosmopolitan and internationalist figures ever to work for the Spanish stage, and his awareness of the status of dramatic and operatic arts in the rest of Europe exerted a forceful influence in Madrid. His most passionate goal (and it was reflected in this contract) was to bring the Madrid theatre up to the level of theatre in the rest of the continent. To that end, he insisted that for the opera company fully two-thirds of the performers must be of international stature, that is, they must have performed in the premiere houses of Naples, Milan, Paris, or London. As for the dance company, he stipulated that it be complete, and French, "in order to begin to give the theatres in Madrid the *tone* of other capitals of Europe" (emphasis added). Even Lisbon, capital city "of one of the most limited kingdoms," possessed its own professional dance company. For Grimaldi, dance was "a spectacle of luxury which has in many ways made itself indispensable to the splendor of any Court."

One of Grimaldi's most startling and most important clauses contained the promise to create an acting school, maintained at his expense and open three days a week to help young actors prepare themselves for the rigors of stage performance. And it would be free. Grimaldi envisioned a school with two professors, students both from the resident companies and from the outside and a Director whose goal was to teach "good taste." To stimulate this activity he even promised to fund prizes ("as long as they do not exceed 100 *duros*") which the Mayor would distribute to the winners. In Grimaldi's view, an actor needed not just innate talent, but a solid education – both a general literary education and training in specific dramatic art – something sadly lacking in Spain. It was no wonder, he commented, that their "miserable education" left them so "backward." How was it then, he asked, that an individual like Máiquez could rise up out of mediocrity to the heights of his profession? Because he was lucky enough to be able to travel to Paris: "there he saw true theatre, the Royal schools of acting and there he learned that the art he loved possessed fixed rules and principles."⁵⁰ But Grimaldi lamented that Máiquez was unique, that he had failed to train actors in his new style, that he "carried to his tomb the secret of his training." For Grimaldi, no advance, no restoration of the Spanish stage was possible without a School of Acting, a place where actors could learn

the difference between speaking verse and prose, where they could be taught to combine the harmonious cadence of verse with the expression of naturalness and the tone of truth; where they might see the difference between the manners of a king, of a grandee and of a watercarrier, between the look of an ambitious young man and that of a jealous lover, that of a daring criminal immune to feelings of remorse and that of a repentant sinner, from whom all passions are extracted, necessary things but which are foreign to the majority of Spanish actors. In that way actors – true actors, not mere reciters of verses, whose sole merit consists of their memories (which are often untrustworthy and weak) – can learn and grow.

In this contract Grimaldi also formulated important plans for the physical improvement of the two theatres. He promised to change the lighting to make it safer, cleaner and brighter. He promised to repaint the curtain of the proscenium arches, to rebuild the scenery – back curtains, wing scenery – to make it quickly mobile (as it was in European theatres), to put up a back curtain which could be pulled up (at that time the backdrops were rolled up, which naturally destroyed the paint and the cloth quickly), to institute changes in the guide wires and flies in order to make them both aesthetically better (concealed in order to maintain the scenic illusion) and safer for the actors, and to build six new sets every year for the Príncipe and three for the Cruz.

As far as his relationship with the actors was concerned, Grimaldi demanded total control over them. He claimed hiring and firing rights and, while he promised to respect the payment of retirement benefits (based on a percentage of the daily gate receipts), he refused to deal with the actors as a corporation or to negotiate with their lawyers. If the actors banded together into a union "as has happened previously," Grimaldi held that the Mayor should intervene in order to "avoid similar excesses." His attitude could not have been more clearly expressed:

Several times it has happened, and principally on the eve of the present theatrical year, that the actors have refused to contract individually with the managements of the theatres, while the managements were in disagreement with the companies' lawyers over certain points containing the most disorganized principles; and from which are derived all of the absurdities which stupefy and bring about the decadence of the theatres. The managements have capitulated out of necessity because the actors at that time were powerful and the result was as could be expected, that is, the ratification of contracts which subjected the managements to all manner of strictures while leaving the actors alone. If such a situation recurs and a similar coalition comes into existence again, it would render impossible any reform of the abuses which attempt to perpetuate the laziness, bad faith, and ridiculous vanity of some actors, whose despotic and malignant influence has been the primary cause of the ruin of the theatres.

Such attitudes were hardly calculated to endear him to the acting companies, but he insisted over and over that his main interest was not financial but rather his "irresistible passion for the fine arts" and his "love of literature and the advancement of the arts."

Still, major parts of the contract concerned rental of the theatres, ticket costs (each ticket had a two-tiered price: one basic cost – the same for everyone – to get into the theatre, and a supplement based on the type of seat desired), storage space, charitable payments, and retirement benefits, and emphasized Grimaldi's interest in minimizing his financial responsibilities. He discussed in detail the ruinous charges faced by any impresario and attempted to demonstrate that many of those charges were unreasonable or unnecessary. Much of what he wrote made sense, since in those days the impresario was obligated to pay separate rentals not only on the theatres themselves, but also on the adjoining ticket booths, cafés and storage spaces, subjecting him to capricious increases levied by the individuals in charge of those spaces. As far as the charitable payments were concerned, he made another effort to convince the municipality that such payments should be the government's responsibility, not the theatre's. His argument was that in the past, when the King conceded these support payments he did so knowing that there was some profit left over after regular expenses had been met, but "those times of prosperity for the theatres have disappeared." Now, he repeated, such charges were suffocating the theatres (and he offered to open his books for inspection to prove that he was losing money). If the theatre remained obligated to these payments, "its ruin is unavoidable."

The issue of retirement benefits was another matter that Grimaldi addressed here. He claimed to approve of the *idea* of actors' pensions, but he lamented the "abuses" which had conspired to bring ruin to the impresarios. In the days when payments *into* the retirement account were sufficient to cover payments *from* it there had been no problems. But now, due either to poor administration of the account or negligence of the actors themselves, the account did not contain sufficient funds to cover those payments, so that pensioners, widows and orphans were paid out of current gate receipts. These costs reached, according to Grimaldi, 300,000 *reales* per year. What right, he asked, did these widows and orphans have in claiming money from the impresario? The money had not been used up by the theatre owners and he saw no reason why he, as impresario, should be penalized for that fact. He proposed that the actors begin once again to contribute to the maintenance of the account. "Nobody is unaware of the fact that this is the fatal origin of the ruination of every theatre owner."

Grimaldi addressed other issues in this long prospectus (repair and maintenance of the actors' chapel in the Iglesia de San Sebastián, relationship with secondary theatres, etc.) and his final clause was a passionate defense of his qualifications. He was somewhat disingenuous in his claim that he was "unaware of who his competitors were" (as we have seen, his previous letter clearly stated that "I understand that the actors are requesting the theatres for themselves"), and he dismissed the actors as inept and incapable of running the theatres without Italian opera (their experience in 1820 proved that to be the case). But he was apparently nervous about his possibilities for success since he attempted to disarm his detractors by rehearsing his qualities and flattering the authorities. He also found himself in the uncomfort able position of having failed to bid on time for contract renewal (according to his first contract he was to advise the authorities one month prior to the end of the season if he intended to ask for renewal) and he excused himself claiming that "said condition, although it is in the contract, is not as clearly stated as the impresario, *who had little familiarity with the Spanish language at that time*, thought." (Emphasis added.) He defended himself against charges that as a foreigner he was incapable of running Madrid's theatres – a serious issue which the actors kept coming back to in their own bid to take over the theatres – by reminding the authorities that he had fought for the restoration of King Fernando VII. "Grimaldi is a Frenchman, but a Frenchman who loves his King, and as such is no stranger in Spain."

In sum, the main thrust of his plan was threefold: 1) to improve the physical properties of the theatres, 2) to train the actors and 3) to create an appreciative audience. The contract proposal of March 1824, was written to convince the city government that he was the best man for the job – "a strong hand, intelligent, and with resources."[51]

Unfortunately for Grimaldi, the city fathers were not convinced. The actors had indeed petitioned for takeover and they clearly wanted no part of a "foreign impresario or foreign actors" ("to the exclusion of a foreign impresario or foreign actors" [February 28, 1824. AHN: Consejos 11.411, n. 35]). Their application was based less on a strong desire to control the theatrical arts in Madrid than to insure, once again, the sacredness of the pensions which they had "earned by the sweat of their brows." They warned the municipality against being taken in by "the propositions of an impresario, which although they are adorned with pompous sentences and words, can be annuled and even destroyed, as some poor pensioners and actors are now experiencing."[52] Two other private individuals, Manuel Marqués and José Saavedra, had also petitioned the authorities for the theatres. Marqués, according to documents kept with Grimaldi's contracts, turned in "conditions identical to those of Grimaldi, whose confidence and protection he has apparently abused, since there is no difference between the two proposals other than a light addition here and there." Saavedra proposed operas, dances and verse performances, but his application was so sloppily presented that it was never taken seriously by the authorities (AHN: Consejos 11.411, n. 35). The relative merits of the proposals were debated in City Council meetings over the next few days. The Council harshly condemned Grimaldi's document, finding many of his clauses "repugnant" and "fueled by a blind greed which would sacrifice the interests of the actors and those of the public if they were adopted" (letter dated March 22, 1824. AHN: Consejos 11.411, n. 35). The Mayor found the actors' application, while fraught with problems, to be "less bad, less unstable and less prejudicial to the public," and therefore more acceptable. They had a personal and vested interest in the success of the undertaking, he thought, and would consequently work harder for its ultimate success. On April 2, the King issued a decree returning the theatres to their pre-1820 state (i.e., when the actors ran them) and on April 18 the theatres passed over to an actor and sometime opera singer named Eugenio Cristiani at the Príncipe, and to Antonio Campos at the Cruz.[53] As it turned out , they were no more successful than Grimaldi at reducing costs[54] and by August they were complaining as much about the same charges that had "suffocated" Grimaldi as about the other performances being permitted in Madrid which were jeopardizing their economic stability and their ability to keep both theatres functioning ("we will arrive at a situation where it will be impossible to keep even one theatre open" [AHN: Consejos 11.411, n. 35]).

But Grimaldi was no longer legally entitled to concern himself with the finances of the theatres and so he turned his attention to putting into practice some of the ideas he had laid out in this contract proposal – creating pieces for the repertory, making suggestions about physical improvements and working with the actors. To this he added one additional goal, not mentioned anywhere in his written statements: courting and marrying the leading lady of the Príncipe company, Concepción Rodríguez.

The rise of Concepción Rodríguez

When the 1824–5 theatre season opened, Concepción Rodríguez, Antonio Guzmán, José García Luna, and Carlos Latorre[55] occupied key places in the acting company of the Príncipe. Concepción's aunt, Concepción Velasco, served at both theatres, but her father, Bruno Rodríguez, was not listed on the actors' rolls that year.[56] From this point until her retirement from the stage in 1836, Concepción took an increasing series of acting challenges, performing in hundreds of dramas, and improving her skills with the help of the foreign "dictator" who was soon to become her husband.

The marqués de Molins recounted a tale of how Grimaldi and Rodríguez met, a story which has been repeated numerous times. In his version, their meeting was the stuff of fairy tales: Grimaldi was living in an apartment at 11 Calle del Príncipe when one day the floor collapsed, sending him tumbling down amidst the rubble into the bedroom of the lady occupying the floor below. The lady was of course Concepción Rodríguez. According to this account the young actress nursed him back to health, they fell in love, and soon thereafter were married.[57] It is an attractive story, one worthy of being put on the stage (*El galán caído del cielo y la bella joven inocente?*) – but the facts of this alleged mishap have been embroidered and distorted. There is reason to believe that some sort of accident did occur, but it is clear that Concepción, as a leading actress in the Príncipe company, and Grimaldi, the upstart impresario, would have known one another since the summer of 1823, when the serious negotiations (or conflicts) between the acting companies and the new impresario began. She had signed the petition protesting his attempted takeover of the theatres and his actions were certainly the main topic of conversation among the actors during those troubled months. Be that as it may, they did fall in love and were married on January 11, 1825, in the old San Sebastián Church.[58] He was twenty-nine; she was twenty-three.

Grimaldi was to exercise considerable skill and invest considerable energy in helping Concepción to grow as an actress. He undertook a campaign to train her in the "new" style of acting as he knew it. She was a willing apprentice. She increased the number of times she appeared on stage in the 1824–5 season (although she still did not appear as many times as the other "leading lady," Agustina Torres) and acted alongside Guzmán and García Luna on numerous occasions.[59] José María Carnerero was more active this season and his labors as translator, "arranger" and author in the Príncipe company brought him in close contact with Grimaldi, with whom he would work for another decade. Their collaboration culminated with their work on the important newspaper, *La Revista Española*, in the early 1830s.

Grimaldi recognized that his fiancée had talent and that she enjoyed a rapidly-growing popularity. She competently performed in the translations, revisions, melodramas, and comedies that dominated the repertory in the early and mid-1820s. The newspapers praised her and the audiences applauded her. "The most serious newspapers used up all the encomiastic language on her. Some proclaimed her the 'pearl' of our stage, others the 'diamond': we have these notices before us. But better than the newspapers' praise and the nightly applause, what demonstrated the high regard in which she was held was the steady audience that came to even the least attractive plays when her name appeared on the theatres' posters."[60] But for Grimaldi, such praise was not enough. He believed that her popularity was based less on her skill as an actress than on her freshness (and the lack of competition), and that "our facile southern enthusiasm often clouds our judgment."[61] In short, there was a disparity between her "intrinsic merit" and "the fame that at that time she enjoyed." Her voice was flat, her actions unnatural, and her expressions at times exaggerated:

They praised her voice, but she did not know how to modulate it sufficiently, she still had not corrected in it several harsh tones; she lacked projection, "bite"; she did not mold it to the complete expression of the variety of passions that a leading lady needs to express and she only used it to express tenderness (but which she did with irresistible allure). Her sensitivity was astonishing and she plied it with great effect; it was exquisite and accessible, but she exaggerated it at times and she did not know how to use it with the prudent economy that art teaches and experience reveals; and like all new actresses, if she had to play a young girl who, anywhere in the play, was called upon to sigh and cry, she came out from the first scene waving a handkerchief and said even her first greeting to the maid in weepy tones; in this way she diluted the effect of the tears which the poet had carefully prepared, and created a contradiction since only then would someone ask, "Are you crying?"[62]

This whining and exaggerated tearfulness was not uncommon on the Spanish stage. Actors had for decades been castigated by critics for the stupidity of their acting, which often consisted of jumping around, winking and grimacing at the audience, waving their arms and hands wildly and even carrying handkerchiefs soaked in onion juice to produce tears. Concepción was not untouched by many of these faults, although she did avoid the dual traps of delivering her lines in the typical sing-song manner and displaying certain mannerisms which the public showed preference for, and repeating them for effect. Still, at this stage of her career her style lacked modulation and, according to her husband, "whoever had seen her in one role had seen her in all her roles."[63]

She demonstrated a keen intelligence, but the closed repertory – and her refusal to break out of the comfortable circle of typecast roles she played – prevented her from developing swiftly enough into the star status that Grimaldi envisioned for her. He set out to change all that by identifying her weaknesses and working with her to overcome them. He saw that she "often confused certain expressions of emotion which were similar but not equal, for example, melancholy, sadness, affliction, grief," that she transformed "ingenuousness" into "folly," and that when playing a young girl she frequently became a silly child instead. "In short, she fell into many of the traps which, if they are inherent in inexperienced actresses and therefore should not have been censured too hard, should nonetheless have toned down the praise she received." And she was modest enough – and interested in her development as a professional actress – to listen to the advice offered by her husband and by others.[64]

Grimaldi believed that the actor held a key place in the important process of relaying literature to the populace. As spokesman for the author, each actor had a real "role" to play in bridging the gap between the poet and his audience. He believed that the actor needed to be mindful of the demands of his profession.

The artist is an interpreter of the grammatical and literary meaning of the ideas of the poet; the artist should search in the continuous study of the human heart for the means to give different shapes to similar thoughts spread among different characters, in accordance with the physical and moral circumstances with which the writer has infused them; he should vary and shape his movements, modulate, alternate his voice in harmony with the wide spectrum of human emotions; he cannot aspire to lasting fame if his soul is not prepared to receive different impressions, if his natural talent, no matter how great it may be, has not received from a solid education the orderly development which can only fertilize it and make it grow.[65]

Many of the ideas expressed here and put into practice by Grimaldi echo those of the great Talma, who published a treatise on acting in which he outlined what he considered to be the essential character-istics of a good actor: diction, gesture, study, and practice. The treatise influenced Máiquez, of course, and, although we have no proof that Grimaldi read the work, it is possible that he knew of it (he was French, after all, and lived in Paris) and that he even saw Talma perform on stage.

For his wife, though, above all, Grimaldi thought that she must act; so, beginning with the 1825 season her performance schedule increased dramatically. Between April 3 and September 20 she appeared in forty-six performances of seventeen different plays. At the end of September her performances halted, however, for she was pregnant at the time with their first child, a daughter born on December 19, 1825.[66] Performances this season included her debut in one play that her new husband translated from the French with her specifically in mind and which would become one of her most enduring successes – *El abate l'Epée y el asesino o La huérfana de Bruselas*. By the time she returned to work in August, 1826, she was ready to take on an even more demanding load, and between that time and the end of December of the same year, she acted in ninety performances of twenty-nine different plays. Some of these plays she had appeared in before; some were new, including a second work translated by her husband, *Lord Davenant o las consecuencias de un momento de error*, and one translated by Bretón de los Herreros which would become another of her most famous roles, *Dido, fundadora de Cartago*.

Improving acting was an exceedingly difficult task, and progress was slow. Things periodically got so out of line that the King himself was forced to step in and issue injunctions against the worst abuses of the audience and of the actors. On September 1, 1826, he issued a decree which underscored once again the rules of conduct that should be observed in the theatres, "in order to avoid the disorder that the disregard of the police rules can cause." The decree banned the spectators from, among other things: jumping up and down, shouting, or pounding on their seats (the punishment for such behaviour was two months at hard labor, "with one shackle on the leg for the first offense, and four for the second"); blocking the view of other members

of the audience; calling out to friends or to the actors during the
performance; smoking or carrying lighted torches inside the theatre;
throwing money, paper, or candy at the actors, and so on (AV:
Secretaría 2-178-18; see Appendix 2). Similar rules were outlined to
control the behavior of actors, who were given to repeating favorite
passages, waving and calling out to their friends in the audience and
taking bows at every opportunity (unscripted bows could also result in
time on the chain gang). The King's decree likewise banned loitering
within thirty yards of the theatre – to avoid the unseemliness of "a
certain class of people who frequently can be seen standing in the
doorways of the theatres and in front of the Cruz Theatre" (thirty days
at hard labor if caught) – and scalping or touting tickets.

Even such decrees, however, did little to change a situation which
had existed for decades.[67] Concepción and the principal actors with
whom she worked did improve, but many of the minor players were
hopeless. Within months of the King's decree, Antonio José Galindo,
the temporary Corregidor of Madrid, wrote to the head of the
company at the Príncipe and demanded that he control the behavior
of his actors. He emphasized in particular those who came late to
practice or skipped altogether and those who let unauthorized
personnel backstage (Letter dated January 22, 1827; AV: Secretaría
3-477-20). Galindo was not above putting spies in the theatres to
insure that his wishes were followed. At one point, being particularly
incensed by the unscripted sentences and gestures that the actors
frequently included in their on-stage speeches, he issued a severe
warning:

Having observed the scandalous abuses perpetrated by some members of the
verse and song companies, who add expressions to the pieces they are
performing and take liberties with improper and gratuitous actions, in total
disregard for the writers whose compositions they disfigure and ruin, I beg
you to insist that all members of these companies desist from uttering on stage
any word that is not found in the text of the piece as approved by the censor
and to refrain from making gestures which are not in keeping with the parts
they are playing; this is a matter of public morality and decency. The slightest
transgression of these rules should result in the payment of a fine of 20 *ducados*
for the first infraction, and double that amount for the second, infractions of
which I shall inform the political censor, since I am charged with watching
and denouncing any excesses which might occur.

(Letter dated February 8, 1827; AV: Secretaría 3-477-20)

But such threats had little impact on the actors' behavior. The
October 23, 1829, issue of Carnerero's *El Correo Literario y Mercantil*
published a scathing attack on the abuses still being perpetrated by

the actors. Among the many defects the author of the article found were the failure to have the role properly memorized (which resulted in "confusing the phrases, mutilating the sense, disfiguring the verses, and destroying the illusion"); chorus members who gazed out at the audience, giggled and whispered among themselves, grinned inappropriately or failed to pay attention to the play in which they were performing; the wearing of inappropriate costumes; stepping out of character (being overly familiar with the person playing the part of a king or laughing at the jokes told by the comic *gracioso*, for example); adding and subtracting lines from the script; and forgetting the attempt at illusion which the play was trying to create.

These very abuses were the object of Larra's brilliant satire, "Yo quiero ser cómico," which appeared in *La Revista Española* on March 1, 1833. He, too, criticized the general ignorance of the actors, especially those who thought that study and professionalism were not part and parcel of their trade. He mocked the young supplicant, the man who wanted to be an actor because "it's a job in which there's nothing to do," and ridiculed his ignorance of history, humanities, diction, grammar, acting style, costume design and literature. Larra's trenchant satire addressed the worst abuses of the day, abuses which Grimaldi was deeply concerned with and passionately interested in correcting.[68]

Grimaldi's call for a School of Acting eventually led to the creation of the Real Conservatorio de Música y Declamación, founded in 1831 by Queen María Cristina, and staffed with some of the best actors and musicians of the capital. Joaquín Caprara and Carlos Latorre were named among the first professors of declamation, and Julián Romea, soon to become the leading actor of the Romantic stage, was counted among the Conservatory's first students. (Forty-six students applied for admission; thirty-six were accepted.) Previous attempts to create a resident school for actors had failed (most notably, the one established at the Teatro de los Sitios Reales in 1768),[69] but it was expected that the new Conservatory would be a proper training ground for actors. Hopes were expressed in this new school, "whose results would be far reaching for many families and for the glory of Spanish theatre."[70] It certainly was welcomed as a necessary addition to theatrical life in Madrid: "Until now the art of theatrical declamation has been conducted among us without any previous study ... It is certainly not one of the least causes that have contributed to the discredit of the acting profession, in which only he who had some natural talent or a rare drive to apply himself and study has progressed."[71] But it met those hopes only in part. According to Bretón, "we now have a very useful institution which has produced many positive results,"[72] but it was underfunded and it operated in a sort of vacuum, not tying in its curriculum or internships with the activities (or needs) at the Príncipe and the Cruz. Consequently it failed to become a real force in the theatrical life of the capital and as a result the impresarios and the actors remained, as usual, dependent on their own devices.

Carnerero, in his famous *Cartas Españolas*, likewise took note of the sorry behavior all too much in evidence in the capital's theatres. To the above-mentioned complaints, he added his protests against false and hysterical death scenes, like the ones in which the actor sipped his poison as though it were a cup of hot chocolate and delicately mopped his brow with a lace handkerchief before arranging himself carefully on the floor of the stage for his expiration. He also complained about the disruptions caused by cats and dogs in the theatre, which invariably scurried around or mewed or barked inappropriately during interesting passages, "whatever their interest in the plays might be."[73]

Bretón, like Grimaldi, Carnerero and Larra, voiced frequent concern for the state of acting in Madrid. He published several pieces in *El Correo Literario y Mercantil* which discussed acting techniques, styles, and gestures.[74] In addition, he wrote a long and thoughtful article on the art of acting entitled "Declamación. Progresos y estado actual de este arte en los teatros de España," in which he credited Grimaldi with important improvements and commented on his work with Concepción Rodríguez:

The Príncipe Theatre enjoyed the good fortune at that time of being taken over by Mr. Juan de Grimaldi . . . who, smitten with the young and already acclaimed actress Concepción Rodríguez, married her and, increasing his enormous love for the theatre, which theoretically and practically he knew better than most people , he first dedicated his energies exclusively to the artistic education of his wife and to cultivating the innate talent that she had displayed from the beginning of her career. . . Under the direction of Mr. Grimaldi, Máiquez's work was completed, abuses were banished, and habits which were still hindering the art of acting were eliminated. The art of acting reached its highest point.[75]

Bretón did, however, consistently praise the skills of Concepción (he was careful to record that "her flexible and unique talent contributed to bringing my humble name out of obscurity"). Following their second season in Seville (see below), Bretón reviewed her performance in the tragedy *Gabriela de Vergi*, and noted that the Madrid audience was delighted to have her back: "The announcement of this play brought in a considerable number of people due to the genre to which it belongs, and also due to the presence of an actress whose absence has been felt for a year. The attendance was substantial; and Mrs. Rodríguez, far from diminishing the fame she had acquired as a consummate actress, exceeded in more than one place the high expectations of the audience. . . The audience saw her triumph over numerous difficulties, recognizing and rewarding her talent with applause and frequent streams of praise."[76] More triumphs would soon be hers.[77]

Grimaldi and friends

Grimaldi had always been concerned with the repertory. As has been seen, the theatrical repertory was not being enriched with new plays fast enough to meet the demands of a daily (and on holidays, twice-daily) performance schedule. During the 1824–5 season, Grimaldi had been instrumental in encouraging two new talents to become involved in the life of the capital's stages, and these two authors – Manuel Bretón de los Herreros and Ventura de la Vega – were destined to become the two most important playwrights of the decade preceding the staging of the first Romantic plays in Spain.

Bretón, the same age as Grimaldi, ironically had fought against the French invasion in which his new friend participated in 1823. Without employment or resources he came to Madrid and, as Patricio de la Escosura later wrote, "we don't know how, but he had the good fortune to meet Grimaldi, who has been called the Maecenas of the illustrious author."[78] When Bretón made his debut in October, 1824, with his first comedy, *A la vejez viruelas*, he initiated both a solid friendship with Grimaldi and Concepción, and a prolific career as the leading exponent and heir of the comedy form perfected by Leandro Fernández de Moratín.[79] At Grimaldi's insistence, Bretón translated scores of plays from the French, arranged Spanish Golden Age pieces for the contemporary stage and wrote original comedies.[80]

None of these activities paid very well. For example, he received 1,000 *reales* for *A la vejez viruelas* and another 800 for his translation of *Lujo e indigencia* during his first season (AV: Secretaría 3-478-9).[81] He received only three hundred for his successful *A Madrid me vuelvo* (1828). A piece sold to an editor, for which the author lost all future rights, brought in a mere 500 *reales*, the cost of a carriage trip from Madrid to Valencia.[82] Years later (in April, 1831), he received a little less than 3,000 *reales* for "several dramatic pieces that he has sold to the theatres" (AV: Contaduría 3-182-2). Translations paid only marginally less than original pieces, but the efforts (and the risks) involved were significantly less. In addition, it was safer to translate, since censorship was normally directed at the authors of the original plays, not at the translators.[83] Larra lamented a few years later that there was "very little difference between the price paid for an original work and that paid for a translation,"[84] but he nonetheless praised Bretón's skills: "This is the proper occasion to do justice to someone who deserves it: one of those who has best translated vaudeville, one of those who has been able to make the new genre Spanish is don Manuel Bretón de los Herreros. Certainly, if all the vaudevilles adopted here had been translated like *La familia del boticario*, *No más muchachos*, and others by the same translator, true models of this kind of work, then only praise would come forth from our pen." Larra later commented that

to deny this author praise for his infinite hard work would be a grave injustice: since 1825 [*sic*] when, if I remember correctly, he presented his first productions, until today, not only has he been a tireless partisan of the dramatic muse, but he has been the only one to persevere, the only one who has kept the sacred fire constantly alight; the only one who has paid little or no homage to the political spirit which agitates us; he recognized his true mission and, never abandoning the place that his vocation and our gratitude made for him, he has been a pillar of our national theatre. Unfortunately for us, that theatre has degenerated horribly from its ancient glory; but at least we owe Mr. Bretón the recognition that he has worked in his way with all his efforts so that this light will not be extinguished.[85]

Bretón's popularity and productivity remained constant during his years of association with Grimaldi, even in his role as translator. As N.B. Adams has shown, Bretón's popularity and productivity were unsurpassed during the Romantic period.[86]

Concepción Rodríguez performed in the majority of Bretón's plays and translations, and enjoyed particular successes in his translations of Pompignan's *Dido, fundadora de Cartago* and Scribe's *Valeria o la cieguita de Olbruck* ("she excited the public and filled the theatre's coffers").[87] Bretón dedicated the printed version of *Dido* to "Miss Concepción Rodríguez, first lady of the Príncipe Theatre. The public, so moved by the worthy performer of *Dido*, *Andrómaca*, and *La huérfana de Bruselas*, will no doubt view with pleasure at the front of this play the name of an actress who brings such honor to the Spanish stage and whose friendship makes her loving servant Manuel Bretón de los Herreros proud."[88] Grimaldi, who was for Molins "a hugely successful diviner, capable of discovering hidden sources of genius,"[89] and Bretón, "Grimaldi's best aide,"[90] became intimate friends for both personal and professional reasons. Bretón's arrival was fortuitous, and Grimaldi, "quickly and with sure instinct,"[91] perceived the opportunity to develop this fresh new talent. According to Molins, Grimaldi discovered the best source of aid to help him carry out his two overwhelming desires, desires which filled his heart and his mind: to give eternal glory to the virtuous and beautiful actress to whom he had linked his fortune, and to restore Spanish theatre, which at that time, given over to plays such as *Asesinos generosos*, *Hombres de la selva negra* and *Vampiros*, lay truly enchained as in the *Cárceles de Lamberg* or in *Herrerías de Maremma*. For the first goal he needed . . . he needed, well, Bretón.[92]

As Duffey has recognized, "Grimaldi's aid, advice, and friendship were of great value to Bretón during the years when the young dramatist was most in need of help and counsel."[93]

But Grimaldi needed more than a handful of actors and one playwright if he was to achieve the goal he set for himself – nothing less that to "restore Spanish theatre." On that same evening in October 1824 when Bretón opened *A la vejez viruelas*, another young playwright, Ventura de la Vega (1807–65), made his appearance with a one-act comedy entitled *Virtud y reconocimiento*. Ventura and Bretón became close friends and key members of the group being slowly assembled by Grimaldi.[94] (The three of them – Grimaldi, Bretón, and Ventura – remained intimate enough friends to collaborate on an original drama eleven years later, in 1835.) It was Grimaldi who "launched Ventura on the path of the theatre."[95] Ventura's first play never made it past four performances, but he was nonetheless congratulated by his old professor, the important teacher and critic Alberto Lista, who had cultivated the boy's passion for literature and who now encouraged him to continue writing.[96] During this first stage of his career, while he was associated with Grimaldi, he produced – as did Bretón – translations and original comedies.[97] Larra, while typically lamenting the fact of translation, nevertheless issued praise for Vega's skills in that area: "The only translations which compare with those produced by Mr. Bretón are some done by another well-known young poet: our readers will have guessed that we are speaking about Mr. Vega . . . in some of his works the translations are done so well that they can justly be called almost original pieces."[98] Ventura's career faced a temporary setback in 1825 when he was caught conspiring with a group of boys dedicated to the overthrow of the repressive government then in power. The group, which called itself "Los Numantinos," included one of the most radical youths of Romantic Spain, José de Espronceda,[99] and after their discovery Ventura was sentenced to spend the summer of 1825 under the careful watch of some Trinitarian fathers in Madrid.[100]

A third author/translator to link his fortunes early with those of this dynamic group of intellectuals and actors was José María Carnerero. Carnerero was to emerge, along with Grimaldi, as one of the arbiters of literary taste in the Fernandine and Romantic periods. Marrast has correctly claimed that the two "reigned over the theatre and newspaper worlds."[101] Carnerero had been in Paris during the early years of the century and had befriended Máiquez there. Later, he became quite famous (and powerful) as editor of the most original and influential newspapers of the late 1820s and early 1830s, the *Correo Literario y Mercantil* (begun in July, 1828; Bretón was also one of the editors), the *Cartas Españolas* (founded in March, 1831), and the *Revista Española* (a continuation of the *Cartas*, edited by, among others, Antonio Alcalá Galiano and Grimaldi)[102] and encouraged the brightest young writers to contribute to his newspapers. His activities in the early and mid-twenties, however, were mostly limited to his, as Le Gentil put it, "rather coarse translations of Picard, Duval and Bonjour."[103] He had been working for the theatres before the arrival of Grimaldi, having staged plays and "magical operas" during the Constitutional Triennium (*La antesala*, *Las citas*, and *La novicia* in 1820; *La huerfanita o lo que son los parientes*, 1821; and *La campanilla*, 1822). Later, he wrote translations, adaptations, "imitations," and "arrangements" of works by Scribe, d'Aubigny, Planard, and De Courcy, plus a few original pieces and allegorical *loas* (*La tertulia realista*, 1824, starring Concepción Rodríguez, *El afán de figurar*, and *El regreso del monarca*, 1828). These translations and one-act plays did not garner him much of a reputation as a creative playwright, but in his newspapers he voiced strong and informed opinions on literary matters and his opinions were heeded. Molins called Carnerero a "dean of journalists and a man who, although with no great standing among literary types, had more than passing influence in the salons and no little influence in literary criticism and the theatre."[104]

The last playwright to join forces early with Grimaldi was Antonio Gil y Zárate (1793–1861), who came from a family of actors – his parents were actors and his stepmother was the famous Antera Baus. His first work performed in Madrid (on August 10, 1825) was a three-act comedy entitled *El entrometido o las máscaras*. It was followed by a limited number of translations of works by Scribe, Arnault, and Ancelot (he had lived in France for a number of years).[105] Just one other original comedy (*Cuidado con los novios*, 1826) followed in these years. One of his plays, a tragedy entitled *Don Rodrigo*, failed to receive the approval of that "obese friar" – the censor Fernando Carrillo – for a reason which underscores the arbitrary nature of censorship during those years: "Although there have been, in fact, many kings like don Rodrigo, it is not seemly to present them in theatres so frequented by young girls."[106] Gil's real popularity came after the death of Fernando VII when he entered into the spirit of the new Romanticism and produced the beautiful and scandalous *Carlos II el Hechizado* (1837). His popularity was hard-won: Gil recounted that to earn a mere 400 *reales* a playwright dedicated six months to writing the play, another three waiting for the actors to decide whether to play in it or not, another three waiting for a committee to read it and recommend changes, an additional month to incorporate corrections, two more months waiting for the second reading, and a final five months anticipating the premiere. "And after all that you are a dramatist," he wrote.[107] Although he was remembered by Mesonero as being, along with Bretón, one of the "only poets who at that time came onto the scene with original productions,"[108] it is not surprising that his translations outnumbered his original compositions, even during his most productive period.[109]

The circle of friends that Grimaldi was collecting around himself became a cohesive unit with the gradual formation of the most influential literary tertulia to flourish in the capital in the first half of the nineteenth century. He and his friends began to meet for discussions over coffee at the café located next to the Príncipe Theatre. The café belonged to the theatre, as we have seen, and had so belonged since Máiquez took the initiative to establish it in 1816.[110] Grimaldi had "owned" the café during his year as impresario of the Príncipe. An impetus (and the name by which it has become famous – "El Parnasillo") may have been given to the meetings when Alberto Lista's students, searching after 1826 for a new place to conduct their discussions, "discovered" the Príncipe Café and joined those already meeting there.

Public cafés in the early 1800s were places in which, according to Moratín, one should have a quick drink and leave. For the most part, they were unkempt, small, dark and disagreeable.[111] The Príncipe Café was no exception. Fernández de Córdoba pointed out "the logjam of tables, the huge throng that habitually invaded its extremely narrow space, its poor and miserable decor, the noise that was produced by such a mob,"[112] and Molins remembered it as "a black and gloomy café."[113] Even Ramón de Mesonero Romanos, one of its staunchest supporters, remembered it as "jumbled, somber and solitary."

This small room, of hardly any depth, narrow and uneven ... was at the time, as a café, completely barren of any signs of luxury, and even of comfort. A dozen pine tables painted the color of chocolate, with a few Vitoria-style seats, comprised the principal furnishings; the rest was made up of a large open lamp hanging from the ceiling, and on the walls about a half dozen what were at that time called *quinquets* [oil lamps], named after their inventor. The place was enclosed by simple glass doors, with tinplate air vents on top of them. At the back of the room, and occupying a hole in the staircase, was an old cupboard, and near it were two tables with their corresponding Vitoria chairs.[114]

The poets, dramatists, artists, and impresarios seemed to pay little attention to "the ugliness and filth of the glassware or porcelain" or the "gloomy light of the lamps," and felt at home in this theatrical spot. Besides, there were few other places to meet, and in the late 1820s and early 1830s there existed none of the official intellectual circles which would come into being after the liberalization of the cultural atmosphere in the mid-1830s (the Ateneo, the Liceo Artístico y Científico. In a gathering such as a *tertulia* ideas could be discussed which had no outlet in print. The "Parnasillo" became "the literary and intellectual center of Madrid."[115] Fernández de Córdoba (a soldier) remembered the "endless and for me boring literary discussions"[116] which took place there. The discussions flourished and the café became the focal point of the literary rejuvenation taking place in Madrid, and the center of the growing debate on Romanticism.[117] Mesonero Romanos remembered the discussions at the *tertulia* and its members as being eccentric, lively, youthful, ingenious, and spirited. He included among their numbers Grimaldi, Carnerero, (who lived above the Café), Bretón,[118] Vega, Gil y Zárate, the *costumbrista* Serafín Estébanez Calderón and himself, but it was Grimaldi who presided over the discussions: "There, at the head of the table that we might call *presidential*, the theatrical dictator, Grimaldi, talked at length and discussed dramatic art and poetry with great intelligence."[119]

The activities at the "small, nasty and dark Príncipe Café" – as

Larra called it[120] – changed Spanish intellectual history, for it was there that many of the most important discussions concerning literature, art, and artistic theory took place. A modern critic has claimed that "The meeting at the Príncipe Café, called quite justifiably 'El Parnasillo,' had a decisive influence, not only on the propagation of Romanticism, but also on the preparation of the literary, artistic, cultural, political and of course journalistic fashions of the important times that were near at hand."[121] As the literary climate heated up, the founding members were joined by others who were to leave their marks on the course of Spanish literature: Larra, Espronceda, Patricio de la Escosura, the poet Juan Bautista Alonso, the bookseller Manuel Delgado, Antonio García Gutiérrez, Juan de la Pezuela (the future Conde de Cheste), Miguel de los Santos Alvarez, Eugenio de Ochoa, Gregorio Romero Larrañaga, the Marqués de Molins, José Zorrilla and Juan Eugenio Hartzenbusch.[122] One of the most significant friendships was that formed during this time between Grimaldi and the young Mariano José de Larra.

If Grimaldi was the brilliant "dictator" of the Spanish stage and the "president" (he was placed at the "presidential table") of the *tertulia*, Larra was the ingenious observer of the complex society in which he lived. Their friendship was close and important. Grimaldi encouraged Larra to write plays, got him jobs as a translator, secured him a position on the staff of the *Revista Española* and suggested to him his most famous pseudonym, "Fígaro." It was Grimaldi who helped him stage his first work, *No más mostrador*, in 1831 and who took care to see that his Romantic play, *Macías*, was given a quality production. Larra published reviews of many of the productions put on by Grimaldi and his actors (especially Concepción) and fought tenaciously, like Grimaldi, for the improvement of the dramatic arts. We shall return to their friendship later.

Grimaldi: Translator/Dramatist

Grimaldi not only encouraged his young friends to write original plays for the stage and to translate French dramas but he also engaged in these activities himself. Mesonero's admiration for Grimaldi was enormous, and he recalled this man who,

blessed with a superior talent and a supreme clear-sightedness, had penetrated our language, our society and our customs so thoroughly that, following his irresistible calling for the theatre and his profound literary

knowledge, he not only managed to become an oracle for poets and actors ,
not only rose up to dominate the stage, but, rushing into the battle himself, he
also wrote versions of French dramas with a truly astonishing originality.[123]

Grimaldi produced two translations, one "adaptation" and one
original play, none of which, as Duffey correctly points out, would
reserve for Grimaldi "a prominent place in the hall of fame,"[124] but
the adaptation, entitled *Todo lo vence amor o la pata de cabra*, was destined
to become the most popular play performed in Spain in the first half of
the nineteenth century and one of the most stunning successes ever
seen on the Spanish stage.

   His initial attempt to expand the repertory was a star vehicle for his
wife, first performed in Madrid six months after they were married. *El
abate l'Epée y el asesino o La huérfana de Bruselas*, staged on July 6, 1825,
was a translation of Ducange's *Thérèse ou L'orpheline de Genève* of
1820.[125] A different play with a similar title – J.N. Bouilly's *El Abate
l'Epée y su discípulo el sordomudo de nacimiento, conde de Harancour*,
translated in 1801 – had been playing in Madrid for twenty years, and
overlapped at times with performances of Grimaldi's, although
Bouilly's never achieved the popularity of the Ducange/Grimaldi
version.[126] Grimaldi put on Bouilly's play – starring Concepción –
three times during his year as impresario and in 1832 Bretón criticized
the silly liberties the impresario Agustín Azcona permitted in a
performance of it.[127] Grimaldi's originality with *La huérfana* was
somewhat less "wonderful" than Mesonero remembered, since as
Desfrétières points out, "Grimaldi made only one important change
in order to adapt the piece to Spanish customs: that was to replace the
character of the Protestant pastor Egerthon with that of a Catholic
priest, the abbé L'Epée."[128] The play's melodramatic characters,
colorful scenes, complicated action and air of mystery attracted a
large following and provided Concepción Rodríguez with a role with
which she would be identified throughout her career.

   From its appearance in 1825 until 1848 it was performed in Madrid
(and elsewhere)[129] a minimum of 126 times.[130] At its opening, the play
ran for eight straight performances and after that it frequently
attracted a sizable crowd. One announcement in the *Diario de Avisos*
(November 30, 1826) read: "This afternoon at 4:00 at the Príncipe a
special function: *La huérfana de Bruselas, o el abate L'Epée y el asesino*, a
spectacular play in three acts, adorned with all of the theatrical
apparatus that its plot demands: its author is D.J. de G. The company
deserves general praise for putting on stage the play that has most

pleased theatregoers in this capital for many years, as can be inferred from the extraordinary attendance that its repeated performances always generated." Several years later (September 9, 1829) the same newspaper commented, "This play, which has always earned the general approval of the public because of its interesting plot and its well sustained characters, makes us hope that this latest version will not change that opinion that it so justifiably has acquired." Gradually, interest in it waned and even though it remained in repertory, the intake declined correspondingly: for example, when it played at the Príncipe on May 17, 1832, it pulled in a mere 3,340 *reales*, followed by less than half that amount (1,605 *reales*) the next night. When it reappeared on July 9, the box office receipts were a paltry 1,589 *reales* and after bringing in only barely more than 1,000 *reales* on July 10, it was dropped from the repertory until November 9, when it enjoyed a three-day run but earned a total of only 8,650 *reales* (AV: Contaduría: 4-18-1). These figures are comparable to most of the box office receipts for plays during these years, which generally fluctuated from a low of 500–600 *reales* when translations and revisions ("refundiciones") were being staged, to a high of 9,000 or so when operas were on the program. Still, it was one of the most frequently performed plays of the 1831 and 1832 seasons.[131] The one startling deviation from this pattern – Grimaldi's *La pata de cabra* – will be discussed below.

La huérfana de Bruselas is an interesting mixture of passion, mystery, pathos, spectacle and sentiment – that is, a combination of those melodramatic elements which, slightly modified, reappeared frequently in Spanish Romantic dramas. If melodramatic spectacle strikes us today as exaggerated (Desfrétières criticizes the play's "grandiloquent and today almost grotesque pathos")[132] it was hardly viewed so disdainfully by the audiences in the Madrid of the 1820s and 1830s, who eagerly embraced the theatre's ability to make them laugh and cry, transport them to strange and wonderful places, and involve them in stories of love, intrigue, danger, and suspense. Grimaldi maintained the setting in France (not "Hispanicizing" his locales, as he would do with *La pata de cabra*) and developed the tale of the young orphan, Enriqueta, who hopes to marry Carlos, the son of the rich Marquesa de Belvil. In Act 1, Enriqueta reveals her terrible secret to her guardian, the Abate L'Epée: she is in reality Cristina, the infamous escapee from Brussels, sentenced to death for the alleged theft of the estate of the Marquesa de Ling, who raised Cristina as a child and left all her possessions to her when she died. The Marquesa's family accuses her of fraud and has sworn vengeance. A friend of the family – Valter – who promised to help Cristina, instead betrayed her and forced her to flee. Valter has since arrived in France in search of Cristina. When they meet, he blackmails her into marrying him since only he can clear her name – he reveals that she really is the legitimate daughter of the Marquesa de Ling and therefore the true heir. She loves Carlos and she swears that she will never marry Valter, but Valter discloses her true identity to Carlos's family. They react with shock and disgust. The Abate promises to protect her, which he does by sending her away to his sister's house in Act 2. On the way, however, Cristina stops for a rest at the home of some of the Marquesa de Belvil's laborers on another part of the estate. Valter follows her, demands that she marry him and pulls a dagger to threaten her ("Yes. . . marriage . . . marriage or implacable vengeance!"). In a subsequent scene, Valter emerges from the house and claims to have stabbed Cristina. A lightning bolt ignites the house where the Marquesa de Belvil is resting and in the ensuing confusion Cristina wanders out of the burning building, disheveled and grasping a bloody dagger in her hand. Before she faints she says that the Marquesa has been murdered. In Act 3, which takes place in front of the burned-out farmhouse, the police discover that Cristina is the convicted orphan from Brussels and suspect her of the Marquesa's murder. Valter, who has been captured by some local peasants, is brought in and subjected to questioning by the Abate. The Abate cleverly weaves a trap around Valter and exposes his lies, but Valter feels safe since the only witness to his murder of the Marquesa was Cristina, whom he thinks is dead. In an ending of high emotion, calculated for shock effect, Cristina confronts Valter. He confesses, Cristina's rights are restored and the path is cleared for her to marry Carlos.

The play reveals two of Grimaldi's major achievements during his years dedicated to the Spanish stage: it provided him with a chance to display some of the improvements in the stage machinery that he had been working on and it reflected the intensification of dramatic emotion which would become one of the hallmarks of Romanticism in Spain. It was a relatively complicated drama to stage, particularly at the end of Act 2, which required a full-scale fire and a continuously threatening storm, replete with crashing thunder and bolts of lightning. The final revelation in Act 3 also necessitated some tricky stage business. He knew full well that theatrical success was tied to spectacle and he was not afraid to insist on this as much as he insisted on skilled acting. It would not be until 1829 (*La pata de cabra*) that his imagination would be matched by his technical abilities, but with *La huérfana de Bruselas* he began to demonstrate some of those skills.

The elements which provide this drama with an aura of Romanticism are precisely those elements which play on the heightened emotions engendered by death, tyranny, and frustrated love. The lovers' happiness is impeded by a tyrannical individual; there is much talk of death, vengeance, graves, and masks; there are mistaken and confused identities; there are suggestions of ghosts (Cristina appears dressed "in a white dress, her hair loose upon her shoulders, and with one hand pointing at Valter" in the penultimate scene); and so on. Scene 4 of Act 2 provides the clearest example of the images of frustration and horror so commonly witnessed by the later audiences of *La conjuración de Venecia, Macías, Don Alvaro o la fuerza del sino, El trovador*, and other Romantic plays.[133]

> *Crist.* Ah! It's you? (the lamp falls from her hands and goes out.) Good God! What do you want from me? Haven't you done me enough harm already? Will you pursue me to my grave?
>
> *Valt.* Yes: I will pursue you forever. You will see me everywhere, always, as a shadow, following your footsteps. You will not have a single day of respite; and just when a ray of hope shines to encourage you, you will hear me whisper the name, "Cristina."
>
> *Crist.* Oh! (horrified.). . . I am a victim abandoned to misfortune. But if I must choose between the calamity that persecutes me and the horror of becoming your wife, do not doubt, my cruel tormentor: misery, condemnation and the gallows will seem less horrible than belonging to a monster like you.
>
> *Valt.* You shameless. . .
>
> *Crist.* I have nothing left to fear. Hand me over to my executioners: bury my innocence in tortures reserved for my crimes; but you will never, never gather the fruits of your odious sins. . . You have sold my tears to my enemies and now you want me to turn myself over to my own tormentor? Never! Never! Before that, death![134]

Concepción Rodríguez was very effective in the role of Cristina and it was her interpretation which immediately set the standard against which other actresses in the part were judged. Within months of its debut, Concepción was pregnant with the couple's first child and took a pregnancy leave. A newcomer, a young girl named Emilia Villar, took over Concepción's place in the lead role in October, 1825, but could not sustain it and the play disappeared from the repertory until Concepción returned to the stage. When she took the play on a tour of the provinces in 1831, audiences marveled at her portrayal of the unfortunate orphan. In Valencia she received praise for making audiences forget it was a play they were witnessing, especially in the scene detailed above:

It is easier to remember than to record how the audience felt at the end of the fourth scene of the second act, when poor Cristina sees the dagger of the vile Valter raised above her head. The fright that took over her whole being, the horror depicted on her face, the nervousness and trembling of her body, her penetrating and highpitched scream, the noble way she fell faint to the floor: this entire lovely effect carried the scenic illusion to its highest peak and the spectators forgot for a moment about the actress and saw only Cristina. They felt for her and sobbed with her, and could hardly stop the tears that streamed from their eyes, and only recovered when it was time to applaud the artist's exellence.[135]

Gradually the public's affection for seeing Concepción in the roles of innocent young *ingénues* (she was now twenty-nine years old) began to fade and transfer to her greatest rival, the gifted Matilde Díez (1818–83). It was ironically in this role, the role of the orphan of Brussels, that the latter made her most memorable initial impression. At the age of nine, Matilde played Cristina in the theatre of Cádiz. When her family moved to Seville she was discovered by José García Luna, who had been working in that provincial capital for a couple of years. Grimaldi most likely witnessed her performances in Seville in 1830 and three years later he brought her to Madrid.[136] "At that time, more or less, another star of the Spanish stage began to shine: Matilde Díez, who at the age of fifteen had already captured audiences in *La huérfana de Bruselas*: when Matilde came to the capital, those two great stars [Concepción and Matilde] complemented one another."[137]

Grimaldi's next attempt at translation did not achieve the popular success of *La huérfana de Bruselas*. The play, *Lord Davenant o Las consecuencias de un momento de error*, appeared in Madrid on May 30, 1826, a mere seven months after it premiered in Paris. Grimaldi's version is very close to the French original by J.B. Charles Vial, Justin Gensoul and J.B. Marie de Milcent,[138] and it was announced in the *Diario de Madrid* as "translated from the French and arranged for the Spanish stage by the author of *La huérfana de Bruselas*." It received little attention and was played just six times that year, twice in 1828, three times in 1829, once in 1834 and not at all in the 1840s.[139] It fared better in Seville, where it played six times between May, 1829 and May, 1830 (in part, it is to be supposed, owing to the presence of Grimaldi and his company in that city for part of the time).[140] Concepción Rodríguez played the part of the young American girl, Cecilia, who comes to London in search of Sanders, who had married and abandoned her years before. She falls in love with Sir Carlos, the son of Lord Davenant. Davenant, married to Milady, turns out to be that very same Sanders, who remarried only after hearing that Cecilia had been killed long ago. Naturally, Davenant opposes the marriage of Carlos and Cecilia. Complications ensue, and even though Davenant finally explains it all and manages to restore his honor and family stability, his melancholy nature leads him to commit suicide.[141]

Once again it is evident that Grimaldi was attracted to the melodramatic spectacle of crossed lovers, complicated plots, intense and conflicting emotions, pathos and tension, although he was unable to create a version of this play which would excite Spanish audiences. This he would do with his next play, *La pata de cabra*.

Grimaldi's fourth and final attempt to write for the theatre came during the next stage of his career in Spain, the stage which spanned the years between the death of Fernando VII (September, 1833) and Grimaldi's move back to France (August, 1836). The play was a collaborative effort between Grimaldi, Ventura de la Vega, and Bretón de los Herreros, and it was an occasional piece (an "insignificant *pieza de circunstancias*," in Duffey's words)[142] which underscored their fierce support of the Queen Regent's moderate policies and their opposition to the Carlist insurrection causing disturbances in the north of Spain. After Juan Alvarez Mendizábal came to power on September 14, 1835, he ordered the conscription of 100,000 men to quell the civil war. Money had to be raised, and writers and intellectuals offered their talents to the cause (most did so willingly, although there are reports that poets were instructed to write patriotic compositions for performance in the theatres).[143] In October, Vega and Bretón collaborated on a play called *El plan de un drama*, while other authors such as Gil y Zárate, Molins and Espronceda read their poems from the footlights of the theatre.[144]

1835 y 1836 o lo que es y lo que será, a "political-prophetic sketch in two acts, on the civil war afflicting Spain,"[145] was written with the precise political aim of raising funds for the troops in the north. The entire evening of the debut, December 5, was a stirring political happening. As recorded in the *Revista Española*, it was "an extraordinary function whose intake the management is setting aside to help underwrite the war in Navarre. It will begin with the singing of the 'Hymn to Riego', followed by a one-act comedy entitled *Partir a tiempo*. Then another hymn will be sung and the evening will end with *1835 y 1836 o lo que es y lo que será*, a political-prophetic sketch, written by three wits, in two acts, on the war afflicting Spain; finally, there will be popular dances performed to the music of a patriotic symphony, composed by maestro don Ramón Carnicer, from themes taken from various national hymns and songs."[146] It played a total of twelve times through February, 1836.[147] At its first performances it enjoyed some popular success, due mostly to its patriotic theme ("it is not surprising that whenever a patriotic play is announced, all the seats are taken early. The people of Madrid have once again proven their impartiality and patriotism").[148] The evening brought together many of the individuals who had been with Grimaldi for years – Vega, Bretón, Carnicer, Espronceda, Latorre, Guzmán, and an actor recruited by Grimaldi in the early 1830s (Julián Romea) – and, much to the delight of the participants, the Queen Regent herself, who arrived with her two daughters, the six-year-old Queen Isabel II and the four-year-old Luisa Fernanda.

A review published in the *Revista Española* on December 7 provides the only synopsis of the plot available (the play has never been published and no manuscript has been found): in a tavern in the province of Vizcaya the innkeeper and his friends don Policarpo, a fish merchant, and an unnamed hypocritical friar play cards as they muse over the fortunes of war. They support the insurrectionist pretender to the throne, don Carlos, and have stored supplies to feed and arm his troops (the provisions include sixteen barrels of gunpowder). The innkeeper's daughter is in love with a soldier – not one of the Carlists, but a soldier in the Queen's army – and when her father catches them together one night a terrible argument ensues. The daughter, betrothed to don Policarpo by her father, swears never to marry an enemy of her country. Act 1 ends with a battle between the National Guards and the Carlist troops. Act 2, which takes place in the future (1836), presents a new Utopia in Spain: no oppressive friars, freedom of the press, various social services – in short, "a regenerated Spain." Only the daughter is unhappy since she misses her beloved soldier. Finally he arrives and they marry.

The reviewer claimed that the evening was a stirring success: "It was eleven thirty and all the streets surrounding the theatre were full of people who came out, happy and beaming with sweet emotion. Spectacles of this type are not like those where a stiff and uncommunicative formality presides: they are truly *national* happenings, in which Royal splendor intertwines in a dignified manner with the frankness and gratitude of the people." But he criticized the play's final scenes, in which "everything moves along slowly and coldly," and thought that some of the dialogues were better suited to "a political academy" than to the theatre. In the light of these observations, Grimaldi, Bretón, and Vega rewrote the second act for the next performances. That act, which had seemed somewhat too long the first time around owing to the "profusion of dialogues," was shortened and the results produced "a complete triumph." The play raised nearly 10,000 *reales* for the war cause in its first night on the boards.[149] *El Artista* praised the play, too, singling out its authors in this way: "We will only say that normally only one man of talent is needed to write a circumstantial piece; for this one there have been three, which means that it is triply good."[150] Grimaldi returned to the issue of Mendizábal and his policies in a series of newspaper articles published in the *Revista Española*, where he underscored the importance of the participation of the capital's intellectual community in the fight against the reactionary Carlist supporters.[151]

3

On the eve of Romanticism

A smash hit: "La pata de cabra" (1829)

If the two translations and one political play which we have seen thus far provided scant proof of Grimaldi's abilities as a playwright, the same cannot be said about his 1829 adaptation of César Ribié's and A.L.D. Martainville's *Le pied de mouton*, a three-act comedy first played in Paris in 1806.[1] It became the most popular play in Spain in the first half of the nineteenth century and surpassed in number of performances and box office receipts every other play produced until mid-century, including such major works as *Don Alvaro*, *El trovador* (the most successful Romantic play, which had twenty-five performances)[2] and even *Don Juan Tenorio*.[3] The people's insatiable hunger for this magical, silly farce brought enormous fame and substantial wealth to Grimaldi, and a newfound life to the Spanish theatre which was tottering, now more than ever, on the brink of financial ruin.

Grimaldi was director (not impresario) of the Príncipe when *Todo lo vence amor o la pata de cabra* (known popularly as *La pata de cabra*) was first performed on February 18, 1829.[4] From the outset, the newspapers recorded that this play had something special to offer Madrid audiences. Its sets, stage machinery and dance interludes would provide an agreeable evening "of grand spectacle". The first announcement promised:

At the Príncipe Theatre at six thirty: *Todo lo vence amor o la pata de cabra*, a mythological-burlesque and magical melo-mimo-drama, of grand spectacle, new, in three acts; written, directed and staged by don Juan de Grimaldi. The sets are the work of don Juan Blanchard, who has been a painter in the royal theatres in Paris, and is now working in this capital city. The machinery has been done by don Ruperto Sánchez, and the dances directed by Mr. Juan Bautista Cozzer.[5]

It was not an instant hit. In fact, another magical comedy, *Al asombro de Jerez, Juana la Rabicortona* enjoyed more performances than *La pata* over the next ten days, the last ten days of the season. But when the following season opened, on April 19, *La pata* gained in popularity and achieved a following unparalleled in the history of the Spanish stage. From the first day of this new season until May 8, *La pata* ran every day (except for May 2, when both theatres were closed for the traditional patriotic holiday) – nineteen straight performances. The norm was a run of three or four days; ten performances constituted a veritable triumph and many never made it past one day, as we have seen. *La pata*'s nineteen performances were not a record (*El sí de las niñas* ran for twenty-six performances in 1806), but soon it would outstrip every previous record set for stage performances. It ceased its initial run for three reasons: first, the actors were exhausted and needed a rest. Second, the crowds which were descending on Madrid needed to be controlled: "the need to arrange the return home of those who have come from outside the capital . . . forces the management to suspend performances of *La pata de cabra* for a time, making it impossible to satisfy the curiosity of all the people who wish to see it."[6] The third reason was the illness and eventual death of Queen Amalia (May 17), which forced the theatres to close completely until August 18.[7]

Once the theatres reopened and the summer holidays ended (late September), *La pata* reappeared on the boards and ran an incredible forty-eight additional performances through Ash Wednesday, February 25, 1830. *El Correo's* guess that, had the theatres not been forced to close in mid-1829, "it seemed as though it might have run an entire month" was not far from the truth.[8] It ran almost daily throughout October and every other day in November and December. The announcement in early November of the King's betrothal to the beautiful María Cristina de Borbón, stimulated the theatres to offer a special function in their honor. The play they selected? The very same *Pata* which had been playing steadily at the Príncipe. As the *Diario de Madrid* recorded:

Note: Since the management wishes to give the public the best entertainment possible in the three days of celebration set aside to honor the King's marriage contract, and to contribute in its way to the festivities, it has decided that on the 5th, 6th and 7th, days set aside when the theatres will be specially illuminated, there will be a play in the afternoon at the Príncipe . . . that play will be the magical comedy *La pata de cabra*, so that the part of the public which has not been able to see it yet, either due to lack of time or because they have not been able to get tickets, can satisfy their curiosity during these three days.[9]

When on November 11 the impresario decided to offer a different play, an announcement appeared in the newspapers assuring the public that this was the last performance of *La pata*, but just "for now."[10] The play was back on stage by December 23. In all, by mid-century, *La pata de cabra* had played more than 277 times,[11] and it remained in repertory until the end of the century.[12]

People flocked from everywhere to see the play. Astonishingly, they even made trips into Madrid from the provinces for this purpose. In 1829, Fernando's political repression was still severe and it was not easy to cross provincial borders, which were treated at times as national boundaries. In fact, the government issued passports to those individuals wishing to cross a provincial border, and the passport cards were stamped with the nature of their business. One French traveler described the process: "Farmers, market gardeners, travelers on foot and on horseback, cannot enter the city [Madrid] without obtaining permission, a passport or a letter of safe passage. The majority of them are subjected to a veritable interrogation, even when they are on standard business. Who are you? Where are you from? What are you doing in Madrid? Where will you stay? When are you leaving?"[13] Adolphe de Custine complained about this bureaucratic practice, calling it "a pretext for interminable fussing":

For a three day trip that we wanted to make, we had to have our passports checked over in several offices; this cost us half a day. In Spain, time is meaningless. We were unable to obtain visas for the whole trip. They would only give us permission to go as far as the first stop, so that each evening we were forced to send our passports to the chief of police in that place via one of the hotel's staff. When we returned to Madrid we were subjected to the same delay as when we first arrived from France . . . You cannot reserve your place in a carriage without a passport, but they will not give you your passport until the very day of your departure.[14]

These rules did not only apply to foreigners. As Ferrer recounted for the year 1831, when a traveler entered the capital through the "horrid . . . and very ugly" Atocha checkpoint the police collected all passports and returned to them paper visas which needed to be certified by the warden who watched over the neighborhood in which the traveler planned to stay.[15] This practice was not abandoned until two years after the King's death.

José Zorrilla's father, who had welcomed the French troops as they marched through Burgos in 1823, was by 1829 Superintendent of Police in the capital and in charge of security arrangements at all checkpoints. His responsibilities included signing the passports and indicating the reasons for the visitors' stay in Madrid. Many of those visitors came specifically to see *La pata de cabra*. In his son's words, "It was absolutely prohibited for any Spaniard from the provinces to come to Madrid without a justifiable reason, and the Superintendent signed 72,000 passports for this powerful and unimpeachable reason: 'Coming to Madrid to see *La pata de cabra*.'"[16] Zorrilla does not specify the year or years, but it seems clear that his figure is not an exaggeration. As reported in the *Correo Literario* (October 5, 1829), by October of the year of its debut it was already "famous," and whenever performances were announced the box office was "besieged" by people in search of a ticket. In fact, some people preferred buying a ticket to the play to paying their daily bills. The very nature of the audience began to change:

The famous *Pata de cabra* continues to alternate with the opera [in this case, Carnicer's *Elena y Malvina*], and to maintain the edge in this dangerous rivalry. Why should this surprise anyone, when *people even come from surrounding towns to see it? Let's not even speak of Madrid, where every neighborhood has been on the move and there is not even a washerwoman who has not wanted to laugh at don Simplicio Majaderano's bravery.* So the women's section ["cazuela"] is populated with a new class of spectators; and the stalls, which are normally the most select section of the theatre, are full of jackets and caps [clothes worn by working-class men]. Such a thing has not been seen for a very long time; certainly it's not *Pata de cabra* that will belie Tacitus's axiom, when he said that what the people needed was little more than bread and entertainment (*panem et circenses*). The minister d'Argenson, applying the expression to the French, said that they only needed *entertainment, although they had no bread.* That idea is also applicable to many Spaniards these days, who before giving up seeing Vulcan's forges [part of Act 3 of *La pata*], would give up paying the baker.[17]

Exact attendance and box office figures are difficult to obtain for the years encompassing the 1829–50 period. Three such sets of figures, however, available for October 1831, April through November 1832, and December 1832 through March 1833, are instructive and perhaps representative. In October 1831, a total of 5,037 people saw *La pata de cabra* at the Príncipe and the average day's intake was 6,421 *reales*. Theatre ticket prices varied greatly, from a low of 4 *reales* in the cheapest seats in the women's section to a high of 64 *reales* for a central box. There were numerous choices between those two figures: second-floor boxes cost 48 *reales*, front mezzanine 10 *reales*, gallery 6 and 8 *reales*.[18] Mesonero gives figures for the bullfights (a box in the shade cost as much as 120 *reales*) as well as comparative prices for other goods and services for the years 1831–3. For example, books cost anywhere from 6 *reales* in paperback editions to 25 or 30 bound in cloth; a room in a hotel, 20 *reales* plus 6–10 for a decent meal (4–8 in a guest house); a subscription to the thrice weekly newspaper *La Gaceta de Madrid*, 196 *reales* per year (220 in the provinces); a bath at one of the public bath houses, 2 *reales*; a post office box for mail, 120 *reales* per year; a cemetery niche at the largest cemetery (Fuencarral), 464 *reales* for a four-year stay (after that one needed to pay again or the bones were removed to an ossuary).[19]

The Príncipe held a total of 1,236 and a complete sellout brought in 9,669 *reales*.[20] This compared to an average of 4,400 *reales* for the Golden Age *comedias* and French translations being offered on the other days. Only the three-day run of Molière's *El avaro* (over eleven hundred people on average per night, and over 9,000 *reales*) and the performances of operas brought in more people and more money.[21] And it must be remembered that *La pata* was in its third year in repertory. The play was not shown from April 1832 until mid-November of that year and the plays that were performed brought in little money for the companies. (Bretón's *A Madrid me vuelvo* earned a mere 1,320 *reales* on June 30.) The following table provides some partial comparative receipts (AV: Contaduría 4-18-1):

Date	Play	Receipts in reales
April 27, 1832	*Paulina*	3,944
April 28, 1832	*Paulina*	1,504
April 29, 1832	*Paulina*	3,489
May 3, 1832	*El casamiento por convicción*	2,057
May 4, 1932	*El casamiento por convicción*	961
May 5, 1832	*El sitio del campanario*	1,300
May 6, 1832	*El sitio del campanario*	1,519
May 9, 1832	*Los herederos*	2,230
May 10, 1832	*Los herederos*	1,502
May 13, 1832	*Amar sin querer decirlo*	4,947
May 14, 1832	*Amar sin querer decirlo*	2,111
May 17, 1832	*La huérfana de Bruselas*	3,340
May 18, 1832	*La huérfana de Bruselas*	1,605
May 19, 1832	*Amar sin querer decirlo*	545

These figures for plays (operas showed consistently higher returns, but ticket prices were about one-third higher) remained constant until November when *La pata* reappeared. Where previously the second day's receipts normally experienced a dramatic drop (see April 28, May 4, May 10, May 18 above), with *La pata* no such drop was noticeable and the receipts remained high throughout the run.

November 13, 1832	*La villana de la sagra*	1,542
November 14, 1832	*La villana de la sagra*	1,055
November 15, 1832	*Felipe* (afternoon)	3,690
November 15, 1832	*La pata de cabra*	7,906
November 16, 1832	*La pata de cabra*	8,231
November 17, 1832	*La pata de cabra*	8,020
November 18, 1832	*El medico del difunto* (afternoon)	5,159
November 18, 1832	*La pata de cabra*	8,500
November 19, 1832	*Cristina de Suecia*	7,716
November 20, 1832	*Cristina de Suecia*	3,395
November 21, 1832	*La pata de cabra*	7,658
November 22, 1832	*La pata de cabra*	8,099
November 23, 1832	*La pata de cabra*	7,604
November 24, 1832	*La pata de cabra*	7,078
November 25, 1832	*Cristina de Suecia* (afternoon)	5,661
November 25, 1832	*La pata de cabra*	8,388
November 26, 1832	*La pata de cabra*	7,223
November 27, 1832	*El bandido incógnito*	2,636
November 28, 1832	*El bandido incógnito*	2,305
November 29, 1832	*La pata de cabra*	7,363
November 30, 1832	*El Cid* (afternoon)	1,501
November 30, 1832	*La pata de cabra*	6,170

As is evident from the above sample, during the months when *La pata* was taken off the stage, the audience virtually disappeared. The same was true for the December 1832 through March 1833 period, with the exception that *La pata* even triumphed over the exceedingly popular operas, bringing in an average of 7,300 *reales* per performance (9,595 on December 2) as compared with the opera's average of 5,600 (AV: Contaduría 4-108-9 and Contaduría 3-575-1).[22] It is small wonder, then, that as early as October 1829, the newspapers were predicting that *La pata de cabra* would be a new "golden calf" for the impresario.[23]

There is no need to accept what Duffey calls "Zorrilla's penchant for exaggeration,"[24] for if these figures accurately reflect the audience's interest in *La pata de cabra*, Zorrilla's guess that his father had signed 72,000 passports for their bearers to see this play was hardly exaggerated. Based on box office receipts and performance schedules, it can be conservatively calculated that between 1829 and 1850 more than 220,000 people saw *La pata de cabra* in Madrid, a city whose population scarcely surpassed 250,000 inhabitants.[25] Documents preserved in the Archivo de la Villa prove that just in the five years between 1829 and 1833, *La pata de cabra* earned nearly one million *reales* (AV: Secretaría 6-311-3).[26]

"Magic plays" ("comedias de magia") had been enormously popular throughout the eighteenth century in Spain, although the taste for them developed in the seventeenth century. Calderón and Lope wrote magic plays, and the Italian Cosme Lotte discovered ways to surprise the audiences with clever sets, quick scene changes, and new effects when staging them.[27] Gradually, however, the content of the plays became less important than the dazzling effects performed on stage, and the audiences came to the theatres to be entertained with flashy tricks rather than with well-written, well-developed new plays.[28] One of the first successful authors of magic plays in the eighteenth century was Juan Salvo y Vela, whose cycle *El mágico de Salerno* attracted much attention in the first half of the century.[29] Later in the eighteenth century it was José de Cañizares who dominated the genre:

Cañizares had another speciality as purveyor of popular plays in his century, which was the magic plays, with their complicated stage machinery and decorations, and the constantly interesting plots which made them charm the people [*el vulgo*] . . . . The four parts of *El asombro de la Francia, Marta la Romarantina*, and the three parts of *El anillo de Giges*, the two parts of *Don Juan de Espina*, and others, have been popular spectacles for many generations, money-makers for the actors, and a lifesaver for theatre companies.[30]

These magic plays belonged to what Ignacio de Luzán called "comedias de teatro," that is, plays which had recourse to trickery and frequent set changes. Because they often dealt with sinister figures (mostly the devil), the Neoclassicists abhorred them and demanded their banishment as being "contrary to religion, reason, custom, and decency."[31] They were in fact banned in 1788, but they did not disappear from the capital's stages, and the public interest in them remained high. Grimaldi tapped into that interest with his *La pata de cabra*.

At this point a summary of the plot of *La pata* is unavoidable. The play opens as the hero, don Juan, prepares to kill himself since he cannot marry his beloved Leonor, a rich Aragonese maiden who is kept locked up by her severe tutor, don Lope. In this first scene, the pistols with which he intends to carry out his suicide fly magically out of his hands and discharge in the air. Cupid then steps out of a tree trunk and presents don Juan with a talisman – the goat's foot – and promises him happiness with Leonor. Juan goes to Zaragoza to confront the suitor chosen for Leonor by don Lope, the comically-named don Simplicio Bobadilla de Majaderano y Cabeza de Buey. Simplicio is shown to be a coward and a buffoon, and when Juan goes to serenade Leonor the earth opens up and out march four musicians who transform themselves shortly thereafter into the four duennas whom Lope uses to guard Leonor. Simplicio, who has witnessed the transformation, cannot get anyone to believe that the duennas are really musicians (or "devils"), but he does finally convince Lope that don Juan is hiding in the area. A trick mirror in Leonor's bedroom produces a hiding place for Juan, and the duennas undergo yet another transformation, this time into nymphs. Simplicio again witnesses the entire spectacle but by the time he calls don Lope into the room things have returned to their previous state. Lope's anger increases with Simplicio's frustration until Juan reveals himself and is captured by don Lope. The lovers are taken away and locked in a tower, but at the end of Act 1 Cupid flies by their prison in an elegant carriage and rescues them.

Act 2 is taken up with Simplicio's frustrated efforts to capture the two lovers, and it is replete with complicated stage tricks and scene changes. When they are caught, Leonor is once again locked away, guarded this time by don Simplicio who, naturally fails miserably in his attempt to keep her guarded. In a startling piece of staging the cap he is wearing inflates to the size of a hot-air balloon and carries him up into the sky and away. The act ends with another rescue of Leonor and Juan by Cupid in his elegant carriage.

When don Simplicio finally returns to earth in Act 3 he recounts the incredible journey he experienced – a flight to the moon! As he is about to return home the earth opens up and swallows him, planting him below ground in the forges of Vulcan. Vulcan then decides to help don Simplicio in his battle against don Juan and Cupid. As can be expected, a number of transformations and tricks occur in the conflict between the antagonists, aided by their respective gods. But true love predominates and Lope finally approves the don Juan–Leonor marriage. Even Simplicio, defeated, has no choice but to accede.

"Todo lo vence amor" – "Love conquers all" (with a little magical help).

Grimaldi's propensity for spectacle and the motifs of the comic tradition were put on display in this work, but it was a difficult task to bring it to the stage. The play contained thirty-five pieces of stage "magic," some of which required extremely complicated and clever sets. There were transformations, flights, quick escapes, dazzling changes of color schemes and identities, fires, comic reversals, floating props, levitations, disappearances, and some real magic (candles which continuously relight, a long sword extracted from a short scabbard, and so on).[32]

Many of these tricks, which served various purposes in the play – suspense, surprise, humor – could be carried out simply (Juan disappears from behind the mirror/throne of flowers, the magician appears from the prompter's shell, flames roar out of the trap door in the stage floor).[33] Others, however, required new and ingenious solutions if they were to be presented with any degree of credibility. Certainly, the transformation of the shell into a "magnificent old Greek vessel" and manned by a crew of cupids was a difficult stunt, and the further transformation of the ship into a frightening sea monster required a high degree of technical skill from the stagehands and actors, as well as a backstage full of sets and props. Likewise, the inflation to balloon size of Simplicio's cap and his subsequent levitation demanded quick work from all parties if the play was to have any surprise or amusement value. By all accounts, the workers handled the numerous stunts cleverly. And Juan Blanchard's sets were the marvel of Madrid, generating admiration and curiosity in the populace.[34] The action of the play demanded eleven different sets and twelve scene changes[35] – some standard (a forest, a woodland, Leonor's room) and some displaying more originality (peaks of the snow-capped Pyrenees, Vulcan's forge, Cupid's heavenly palace).[36]

The multiple changes of sets and the complicated machinery needed to carry out the tricks were hard on the curtains and painted scenery, which deteriorated quickly with constant use. In 1831, performances of the play were temporarily suspended so new sets could be painted. New jokes and tricks were added as well; the performances were constantly evolving, reacting to the audiences' responses. Bretón published two reviews of the play in the *Correo Literario* (September 2, 1831 and November 19, 1832), both of which provide detailed summaries of what contemporary audiences were seeing and admiring.[37] Blanchard and the man in charge of the stage hands, Mateo Sierra, were singled out for the "perfection" of their work. Bretón mentioned that some of the dialogues were somewhat "tedious," but necessary in order to give the stagehands time to change the sets and prepare for the next series of magical effects, some of which were, he admitted, "very complicated." The sets were not always handled with care nor were the tricks performed with professional skill, however. In 1840 (well after Grimaldi had left Spain), performances of this "inexhaustible" play, while still much more popular and more attended than new plays, had become careless. "*La pata de cabra* could not have been executed with more sloppiness or laziness on the part of those in charge of the sets, that is, the forests got mixed up with the interior rooms, the flights were not done properly, nor were the tricks performed well . . ."[38] *La pata*'s sets were not the only ones to be mishandled, to be sure. Complaints were often heard about stagehands putting up the wrong set or the director's recycling sets so much that the audience became bored with them. Scenery even fell down with some frequency, injuring the players and startling the spectators.[39]

While *La pata de cabra* brought in a lot of money, it was also terribly expensive to produce. The extra costs of mounting regular plays normally reached only 8 or 10 *reales* per performance, but *La pata*'s special requirements (extra props and food for the picnic scene, the special sets) raised the average additional performance cost to thirty-six *reales* each (AV: Contaduría 3-182-2). In addition, for a three-day run in mid-October, 1831, numerous extra musicians had to be hired (at a cost of 270 *reales*, plus an additional 96 *reales* for eight performances by a guitar player). Forty-eight extra stage hands were put on duty when *La pata* was on the boards (ten men on the right side of the stage, nine on the left, fifteen in the back and another fourteen manning the curtain – at a total cost of 468 *reales*). Additional actors had to be hired to play the parts of the Cyclopses (twenty-two of them), furies, servants and peasants (435 *reales*) and even the rental of the bellows to inflate don Simplicio's cap cost an exorbitant 90 *reales* more. And last, but hardly least, the men who provided the fireworks for the stage charged another 216 *reales*. Costs for the November 1832 performances were even higher, since new props had been made (tinplate items were in great abundance) and extras were paid a little more. Some extras were hired in lesser numbers – there were eighteen

Cyclopses instead of the twenty-two of the previous year, for example – while stage hands were demanded in greater numbers (seventy-five men handling the flies, sets and curtains instead of the forty-eight in 1831) (AV: Contaduría 3-575-1). Other *comedias de magia* were not nearly so expensive (*El mágico de Astracán*, for example, cost a mere 9 *reales* extra per performance) and only the high spectacle of the operas rivaled *La pata* for expense – but even they averaged no more than 30 *reales* per performance on the whole. Not every performance of *La pata* itself contained the requisite number of performers and supporting stage hands: one of the manuscripts, evidently used for performance practice, lists three duenna/musicians instead of four, the number which appears in the printed versions.[40]

Don Simplicio is one of the great comic figures of the Spanish stage. Few other characters come close to his blustery humor, his physical slapstick, or his good-natured buffoonery. He is a caricature of the false nobleman, a suave and valiant swordsman turned inside out, and his constant hunger reminds us of the typical characters from Spanish Golden Age literature, the *pícaro* and the *gracioso*. His very name is an inspired piece of comic wordplay and allusion: in Spanish, "Simplicio" suggests simple, foolish (it also, of course, recalls stock characters from Italian drama); "Bobadilla" is a diminutive form of a word meaning dolt, dunce; a "Majadero" is a sottish bore; "Cabeza de Buey" plays on the old and noble surname "Cabeza de Vaca" but changes "cow" to "ox," and it is all incongruously preceded by the noble "don." The whole name thus sounds hilarious to Spanish audiences. (Grimaldi might have been inspired by a similarly silly name attached by José María Carnerero to the main character of his 1824 play, *El pobre pretendiente*: don Verecundo Corbera y Luenga-Vista.) To play this rich role, Grimaldi found an actor able to convey Simplicio's whole range of humor – from silly pratfalls to puns and self-mockery. Antonio Guzmán (who had played Carnerero's don Verecundo for Grimaldi in 1824) became don Simplicio and was associated with the role for years, even during his triumphs in the new Romantic dramas. He was so funny in the part that he was credited with making the normally dour Queen Amalia laugh in public for the first time in the court's recent memory. ("Fernando VII wanted to see what was causing such a fuss, and the entire court attended the play with him. And what a shock! The famous character actor managed to make Queen Amalia laugh hilariously, to the great surprise of the King's retinue, who had never seen the poor woman display any outward signs of mirth.")[41] Contemporary reports confirm that the play also buoyed the spirits of the King: "July 13, 1830. The King has decided to go out without his guards, after having gone to a performance of *La pata de cabra*. Good!"[42] When *Entreacto*, a new theatrical journal begun in 1839 and edited by Gil y Zárate, García Gutiérrez, and Molins, printed its first lithograph, it was a portrait of Guzmán dressed in his don Simplicio costume.[43]

The character of Simplicio became proverbial. Larra, for example, employed references to him in his attacks against the Carlists. *"Just as there are times that are on the wane*, says Moratín; so *there must be men on the wane*, I said to myself on the day of the proclamation, noticing a strange figure who, standing on a corner of this great capital, rolled his eyes around everywhere, like someone who was looking for something without finding it. Could this be some Carlist, I said to myself, looking for his political party? It wasn't a daring thought, because the man kept searching, as meticulously as don Simplicio Bobadilla searches for ghosts between the cracks in the antique armchair in *La pata de cabra*."[44] The role made other actors famous as well. The great Mariano Fernández first became notorious for accidentally stabbing himself in the groin during a performance of the play (they carried him off, but the play continued!),[45] then infamous as he ad-libbed some unseemly political remarks.[46] Finally he became famous as he repeated the role throughout his long career. His last public performance, a mere four days before his death in 1890, was as don Simplicio.[47] Even the music became famous in Madrid and was regularly played – especially the piece known popularly as "the Forge piece" from the scene in the Forges of Vulcan – during musical interludes at private *tertulias*.[48]

Not everyone reacted so positively to the play's charms. A hilariously satirical letter appeared in the *Correo Literario* in November, 1829, purportedly written by a poet, "D. Bobadillo Zarrambla y Monteginesuturruburraga," who, meditating on the popularity of animal parts in the contemporary theatre, proposed to write a play with a rhinoceros hoof as the protagonist. His title satirized the folly of Grimaldi's creation: instead of *The Goat's Foot*, his would be called *The Rhinoceros' Hoof*, subtitled "a heroic, mimic, romantic, high-sounding, and pantomimic-mythological play, adorned with transparencies, reverberations, trapdoors, flights, convulsions, burials, floods, fires, and a multitude of transformations and similar additions; written in a semicultured-metaphorical style to serve as an example for the living and as a warning for future generations: in 17 acts, accompanied by dances by monkeys, orangutans, and camels, and songs by roosters and snakes." He detailed the multiple transformations which his leading man would undergo and the spectacular stage effects to be included. The performance would conclude with an apocalyptic ending so "real" that the entire building would shake and the audience would quiver and fall about in their seats and stalls. In the *cazuela* the ladies will fall all on top of one another and at the point when the screams become the loudest, the theatre . . . what a marvel! . . . will change suddenly into the Elysian Fields . . ." If *La pata*'s three acts enabled it to remain on stage for some forty days, *The Rhinoceros'* seventeen acts – claimed its author – would promise it a run of seventeen months.[49] Another detractor, Antonio Ferrer, found *La pata* to be, of all the *comedias de magia* he had seen, "the most graceless and lacking in moral purpose."[50] Modern critics like Narciso Alonso Cortés have thought it "one of the silliest plays imaginable,"[51] while D.L. Shaw has characterized it as similar to the "absurd atrocities" satirized by Moratín in *La comedia nueva*.[52]

What was it about this, in the view of Grimaldi's contemporaries, "very witty, original and popular" play which could "awaken the appetite of the Spanish people and bring them to the theatre for months at a time,"[53] this, in the view of a more recent commentator, "concoction of absurdities [which] simply rocked Madrid, and much of the rest of Spain, too, with joy and laughter"?[54] As Bretón pointed out, the play contained, quite simply, everything: "In a word, this is a play for everyone; it is a grabbag of odds and ends; a dramatic encyclopedia, where anyone who puts his coins down at the box office gets his money's worth."[55] Zorrilla credited Grimaldi with having discovered the pulse of Spain: "Grimaldi had comprehended perfectly our country at that time, and he gave it a piece of puffery well in keeping with the ignorance in which it lay, as the base of a hygienic treatment which he proposed to administer in order to nourish and regenerate it. *La pata de cabra*, untouchable by ecclesiastical censorship, comprehensible by the lower classes, popular even with our country's critics . . ."[56] This "piece of puffery" was imitated, satirized, continued and even converted into a *zarzuela*.[57] It was exported as well, enjoying long runs in Mexico.[58]

La pata's stiffest contemporary competition came from another magical play which opened on January 14, 1830, at the Cruz, entitled *El diablo verde*. Advance notices suggested that it would "usurp [*La pata de cabra*'s] place and rival it" – and it did enjoy a respectable run – but nothing could pry *La pata* off the boards and out of the minds of the audience.[59] Notwithstanding the fact that Blanchard painted eight new sets for this play, the *Correo* wondered how such a spectacle could be staged at the Cruz Theatre, "whose scenery has become famous for its sloppiness." Apparently, Blanchard did not paint all of the new sets for *El diablo verde*. According to Larra, the sets for the 1836 performance of the opera *Othello* were sets recycled from *El diablo verde* and painted by one Gandaglia "and besides that they aren't in the best taste."[60] Another potential rival, a French melodrama "of great spectacle" translated by Bretón called *Jocó o el orangután* and containing as a main character a monkey (played with exhausting and impressive realism by a French ballet dancer, Mateo Alard), likewise failed to match *La pata*'s popularity.[61] *La pata*'s strength lay in that it had (in abundance) what had always drawn audiences to the theatre but what was in scant evidence in Spain during this time: showy spectacle, local color, stage tricks, topical humor, puns and jokes, knockabout comedy, wonderful acting, a fast-moving plot, and suspense. It drew people into the theatre in record numbers, even, as we have seen, people who had never before set foot inside a theatre ("It really was magic, since in turn residents of surrounding villages began to come to the theatre to see what was causing such a fuss: not to mention Madrid, where people who had never gone to the theatre overcame their inertia and came to see the deeds of Mr. Majaderano Cabeza de Buey, and to learn things in Vulcan's forges").[62]

La pata, with all its spectacle and foolishness, carried the audiences of Madrid one step further toward the Romantic plays they would be witnessing in a few short years. That it had some connection to the contemporary understanding of what Romanticism was can be seen in the satirical letter cited above, whose author claimed that, among his other virtues, he had dedicated himself to the "Romantic genre." (Remember, too, that one of the adjectives in Grimaldi's pompous subtitle was "romantic.") *La pata*, as a new *comedia de magia* written within a long, but (by the beginning of the nineteenth century) declining tradition, "was destined to give this type of work its last flourish during the short Romantic period."[63] It reflected a growing fascination with the dichotomies of modern life, the dualities of Spanish existence under Fernando VII which would take deep root and flourish following his death.[64] Clearly, *La pata* was not a Romantic drama, but as Caldera has pointed out in a recent study of the differences between Grimaldi's work and Martainville and Ribié's *Le pied de mouton*, it contained numerous Romantic elements such as the typical Romantic settings (forest, moonlit caves) and the ambience (storms, thunder and lightning, mystery and witchcraft).[65] The plot itself – the happiness of two young lovers frustrated by a tyrannical relative – would become, with added ideological colorings, the basic Romantic plot. Grimaldi was not unmindful of the ideological underpinnings of his play, although he claimed that his sole purpose was to "give the theatre's management some way to attract people, and nobody can deny that this play has succeeded in doing that."[66] It did contain subtle political and social commentary: all the figures of authority and power are ridiculed and defeated (the nobleman, the tutor, the lawyer) and there is a constant satire of the excesses of vain and shallow chivalric behavior. In Caldera's view, "what must, above all, have sealed the extraordinary success of the play was the ridicule and comic defeat of all those characters who could easily have passed for symbols of power, or what at the time would have made equal sense, of the *ancien régime*."[67] Caldera adds perceptively that in Act I, Scene 4, "for the scene to be more complete, and the allusion more explicit, Grimaldi surrounds Simplicio with a lawyer and some constables who were not in the model [the French version]. There is no doubt that the ridiculous roles they play, their semijuridical language, and above all the traps into which they fall and the disappointments they suffer would have delighted the audience in Madrid, which took revenge (through scenic illusions) on the inflexible political persecutions they suffered in reality." Zorrilla, too, noted that with *La pata*, Grimaldi "distracted the populace of Madrid from politics for a number of months."[68] Grimaldi likewise satirized the intellectual élite. In the opening soliloquy, Juan made fun of his own failure in numerous professional positions because of his efficiency and scruples – he failed as a lawyer because his honesty prohibited him from taking on an overabundance of clients; he failed as a doctor because he cured his patients; he found only hard knocks and no promotions in the army; he wrote music, but since he wasn't Italian . . ., and so on. Grimaldi could not resist noting the book publishers' penchant for publishing anything, and at times without the author's permission: when Simplicio returns from his trip to the moon, he says to his friends: "Well, sir, you shall know what I have seen . . . but then you can find out better from a book that I plan to publish, God willing, unless some publisher from Valencia brings it to light even before I

have finished writing it, and without my help or permission, of course"
(Act 3, Scene 1). Additional social satire (with a heavy dose of
complaints that anyone familiar with Madrid's theatres would be
conscious of) was revealed in Simplicio's tale of life on the moon,
where everything operates backwards:

> Imagine that there everything is backwards, for example: lovers are loyal;
> spouses are faithful; salesmen do not deceive you; soldiers do not vote;
> bureaucrats talk to everyone in a civilized manner; actors have a kind of
> melodious tone which displays all the inflections of their voice; singers have
> one which displays their knowledge and study of the human heart.
>
> (Act 3, Scene 1)

In addition, Grimaldi was himself tiring of the oppressive reliance in
Spain on things French. Could he have been thinking of France when
in this same scene he criticized the Spanish imitation of foreign
customs? "Fashion there is formless: it does not even control medicine.
In eating, dressing, and even in public diversions, the residents of the
moon prefer national things to foreign ones." It is a topsy-turvy world:

> There literature is treated with honor. All talented men are rich, and all rich
> men are men of talent. Journalists speak impartially of the things they are
> capable of judging or remain silent about things they do not understand. . .
> There everything is backwards, my friend, everything is backwards; in short,
> there there are no idiots who write magical comedies. What can you expect?

Nor was Grimaldi immune from sending barbs at his own actors. In
Act 3, Scene 7, when the magician climbs out of the prompter's shell,
Simplicio comments, "Through that hole! What a strange thing!," to
which the magician responds, "Idiot! More than once you and your
friends have found help in that hole . . . More than once surprises have
come out of it." (Larra was similarly caustic about the excessive
reliance on the prompter, and satirized the fact that audiences
frequently heard two versions of the same play, one as the prompter
shouted the lines and again as the actor repeated them.)[69] The rather
limp moral message issued by the magician in Act 3, Scene 8 may have
reflected what Grimaldi perhaps thought he lived by, but it was
overwhelmed in the long run by the play's farcical humor and
spectacle.[70]

Grimaldi's play was not exactly the "original" creation he believed
it to be (". . . not for that can it be called a *translation* in the strict sense of
the word; . . . it is more original than many plays that are sold as such,
since almost all of the things the public has applauded in the dialogue,
and almost exclusively all the comic things that Guzmán does are
original, even though the background in which they are put is not

entirely original"), but it was something considerably more than "plagiarism."[71] In fact, Grimaldi made a number of significant modifications to his source play, elaborating sections to enhance the logical flow of the plot and expanding others for comic effect. He changed details in nearly every scene and added six wholly new scenes to his version (1, 10; 1, 14; 2, 1; 2, 2; 2, 5; 2, 10). He polished and improved the dialogue while at the same time making the play more "Spanish" with the addition of adages, verbal patter and allusions which were in keeping with his projected audience's knowledge and tastes. The most conspicuous improvement was in the figure of the comic hero, Simplicio. In *Le pied de mouton*, Niguadinos is a weak, stupid, passive fellow, but in *La pata*, the blustery foolishness and extravagant cowardice of Simplicio add real depth to his character. As Duffey has noted, "Fourteen of the twenty scenes which are partly or wholly Grimaldi's original work are used to build up the character of Simplicio."[72] By tightening the structure of those scenes, Grimaldi was able to focus this main character more clearly and enable him to carry the weight of the play. In addition, Grimaldi changed the hero's sidekick from a vague squire-like character into a mute, who played against Simplicio's bluster with comic gestures by silently imitating his glib rationalizations. Grimaldi added dance sequences as well, integrating them into the action of the play (as when the three Graces tie up the Cyclopses with garlands of flowers). By adding scenes and concentrating the action and logic of his main character, Grimaldi created a play which was superior both in detail and in overall effect to Martainville's original. His dramatic craftsmanship was keen. "The changes he makes are slight, but they are sweeping in effect, for, by weaving Martainville's random magic effects into a meaningful pattern, they give the play both greater comprehensibility and greater unity."[73]

The importance of Grimaldi's play in the development of the theatre in nineteenth-century Spain can hardly be overestimated. It may not have been "literature" (even he claimed that he didn't aspire to "literary laurels"),[74] but its popularity brought money into the coffers of the theatres and helped to form an audience prepared for the extravagances of Romantic drama. Zorrilla recognized that

At the time of prohibitions, persecutions and repressions, when everything lay lifeless under the weight of universal fear (the revolution fearful of the police, the police of the people, the people of the Government, the Government of itself, and everyone of the king), there was one strange thing that became renovated and regenerated in the strangest manner: the theatre. Everything in Spain had always been like that, unconscious, unexpected, phenomenal, almost absurd. The theatre became renovated and regenerated at the hands of a foreigner, Grimaldi, and by an almost innocent stupidity: *La pata de cabra*.[75]

A more contemporary witness – Bretón – confirmed that *La pata* was a "talisman of all the managements for the past three years for its ability to bring in a paying public, and not only a low class public, who are most inclined to enjoy the magical comedies, but also a well-heeled class of people. In this play there are things to please everyone."[76] Grimaldi's light touch and deft humor created a thoroughly enjoyable confection which sparked the city's interest in theatrical spectacle and managed to "bring the theatre out of its depression."[77]

Grimaldi's play produced excitement, ingenious solutions to difficult staging problems, employment for a host of actors and stage hands, considerable wealth for the director/author, and an audience hungry for spectacle.

Ownership problems and obstacles, 1824–32

Following Grimaldi's first year as impresario (1823–4) and after his failed attempt to extend his contract into the 1824–5 season, control of the theatres shifted back and forth between the City Council and various private concerns for the next dozen years. The Council was naturally always in charge of the theatres, but it preferred to hand over the day-to-day workings of them to individuals or collectives, which might include the actors and their representatives or wealthy local residents who could underwrite the expenses of the Cruz and the Príncipe (or promise to do so). Grimaldi stayed on as stage director.

The acting companies who wrested the theatres away from Grimaldi in 1824 managed to keep control of them until the 1827–8 season, although little had changed as far as the profitability of the theatres was concerned. In the 1825–6 season, the Cruz lost money while the Príncipe made a small profit. The manuscript documents state that with a total intake of 2,094,489 *reales* and a total outlay of 2,070,890 *reales*, there was a profit of 23,599 *reales* (not counting the smaller change in *maravedíes*), but when the general accounting was printed and distributed for public consumption, the figures had changed substantially and the Ayuntamiento was left with a profit of 18 *reales for the year* (February 7, 1826. AV: Contaduría 4-56-1). By the 1826–7 season, losses totaled 117,013 *reales* (March 10, 1827. AV: Contaduría 4-56-1 and 4-57-1).[78] and the King himself became actively interested in what was going on in the theatres and in who was to run them. A crisis was brewing and steps needed to be taken to insure both stable management of the theatres and the maintenance of public morality. Cost overruns, payment of unauthorized bills, inadequate financial records, ticket scalping (punishable by a ten-day jail sentence), reserving tickets for friends, and general disorganization were crippling the theatres. In August, 1827, the Ayuntamiento became seriously concerned with such practices: "The City Council at today's meeting voted to inform the board of directors of the Príncipe Theatre that from here on, beginning today, we shall no longer pay extra expenses incurred by the theatre, unless we are notified well in advance and are presented with proper justifications and receipts" (AV: Secretaría 3-477-28). On November 26, 1827, the King issued another decree – this one very unfavorable to the actors – which stated that "the theatres in Madrid will be given over to whichever individual or collective can offer the best guarantees, or lacking such offers, the City Council will take charge of their adminstration, acting as would any other impresario," and giving permission to whomever takes charge to fire all "useless" actors who had become members of the companies over the years through patronage or nepotism (AHP: Protocolo 23799). The City Council was back in the theatre business, although very reluctantly. An open competition was announced in the newspapers and the authorities hoped that someone would present an application which contained sufficient financial guarantees to enable the city to rid itself of the burden of theatrical management. When at this same time Antonio Silvostri, an actor who had been serving as impresario, was taken ill and was unable to continue in his capacity as actor/impresario of the Príncipe, the Council moved quickly to replace him. It asked Antonio Guzmán to take on the extra duties entailed, but Guzmán, though "thankful," refused, citing his responsibilities as the first *gracioso* (comic) as an excuse to demur (AV: Secretaría 3-477-28). The authorities then named Pedro Viñolas as temporary replacement for Silvostri until January 1828, when it granted permission for the son of a rich businessman from Madrid (and financial backer of the King), Manuel Gaviria, to take charge of the theatres as of Easter Sunday that year.

Gaviria had been involved in the theatre since at least the 1824–5 season, when he may have been involved in mounting operas at the Cruz.[79] Gaviria's petition presented the best guarantees; so he was awarded a five-year contract (Grimaldi had failed in a similar attempt in 1824), but after just one year he turned the theatres over to Cristóbal Fernández de la Cuesta, a man who had been with the theatres for a number of years (he worked for Grimaldi in 1823). Gaviria claimed that it was "his poor health and the attention that he must pay to his other business ventures both inside and outside the capital" which forced him to remove himself from this enterprise, but the fact was that he had lost a substantial amount of money (nearly 400,000 *reales*, according to one estimate)[80] and wished to cut his losses (AHP: Protocolo 23799). Cuesta, nervous that he would get stuck with any losses accrued, insisted that he only provided his name and that the theatres still belonged wholly to Gaviria ("I have done nothing more than lend my name to this venture as an act of friendship and convenience to don Manuel, who still owns the entire business ...") With this history of failure and financial ruin it is small wonder that *La pata de cabra* was looked upon as a "golden calf" when it arrived in February 1829.

For reasons which remain unclear, Grimaldi did not apply for ownership either year ("only don Manuel de Gaviria has presented a petition"). In the 1828–9 season he was director of the Príncipe.[81] Grimaldi was hardly a disinterested party in the negotiations, and while he chose not to compete with Gaviria for control of the theatres at this time, he did side with the actors against him when Gaviria's proposed contracts contained clauses which the actors deemed contrary to their interests. These clauses dealt, not surprisingly, with the matter of retirement benefits and payments to widows and orphans, that is, the exact same matters which had always lifted the actors out of their lethargy and placed them in contention with the impresarios and the Ayuntamiento. In December 1828, Grimaldi himself wrote a "very long and emotional harangue" against Gaviria in favor of the actors, claiming in particular that Gaviria's "draconian severity has caused great indignation since it punishes actors with the confiscation of their legitimately acquired goods ... it punishes the wayward unfairly, and allows any impresario or agent of his, out of ignorance or bad faith, to one day make the most docile, the most sheepish of his actors seem like revolutionaries."[82] Such a position was a radical change from Grimaldi's earlier posture, but at this point it was in his best interest to work with the actors rather than with the impresario. Gaviria remained unmoved. As Gregorio Martín has written in his assessment of the differences between Gaviria and Grimaldi, "Grimaldi had the talent, but he didn't have the money or the temperament; Gaviria had the money but he lacked talent, while the theatre lacked both talent and money.''[83]

The authorities in Madrid were still painfully aware that their theatres paled when compared to the best theatres in the rest of Europe and while they refused consistently to provide the economic support needed to create a truly first-rate theatre or to rein in the oppressive censorship which crippled the repertory, they did just as consistently complain of the situation. They claimed to want their plays to "compete with those of the most brilliant playwrights in Europe" and they bemoaned the horrible conditions of the theatres (lack of comfort, small stage areas and orchestra pit), but they did little except make noises and tentative plans, without ever providing sufficient funding or freedom to the impresarios (AHP: Protocolo 23799). The repertory was expanding slowly and mostly with translations from the French or "rewrites" (for example, of the thirty-seven pieces Bretón wrote between 1828 and 1831, only seven were original plays, and only three of those contained more than one act).[84] As of 1827, there were a scant 328 plays which had received the proper censorship approvals and were consequently allowed to be performed in Madrid.[85] Censorship was the principal problem, of course. Grimaldi knew it and did what he could to circumvent or ignore it. Larra knew it as well, and protested its existence with his usual trenchant satire, but little could be done in the atmosphere of repression and fear which dominated the capital. Since direct opposition to censorship was impossible in the mid-1820s, and everyone was casting about for reasons to explain the consistent losses suffered by the theatres, Grimaldi – and others – fastened on a second culprit, one which they could oppose: the opera.

In Grimaldi's view, a major obstacle against the creation of serious theatre in the capital was the enormous popularity of the opera – often bitingly referred to as the "philharmonic furor" or "music mania" ("musicomanía") – which he thought discouraged the production of serious plays.[86] Operas – especially those by Rossini – had been popular in Madrid throughout the decade and had not only consistently appeared in the repertory but had also earned more money than plays, even allowing for their higher production costs. Grimaldi himself had been involved with them in his first years as impresario and had staged several operas at the Príncipe (part of his initial proposal to the municipality was a promise to bring Italian singers to Madrid, a job he dispatched Fernández de la Cuesta to Italy to do), but he soon realized that such functions were not only not complementary to the creation of serious theatre, but in fact opposed to it. [87] The actors themselves also realized the threat posed by the opera companies and as early as 1823 they had protested that "as long as there is an Italian company in these theatres to give operas, and another company for dance, the Spanish actors will be scorned, paid miserably, made second-class citizens – a fill-in when there are not enough performances of opera – and Spanish theatre, which is already in severe decline, will arrive, in no time at all, at a state of total ruin" (AHN: Consejos 11.411, n. 35). The impresarios and the actors may have opposed these companies, but the public supported them enthusiastically. When the Italian company left Madrid in March 1824, at the end of their contracted period, Spanish singers began to perform Italian operas in Spanish, a custom which lasted for less than two years since the audiences clamored for "real" Italian opera.[88] The arrival in Madrid of Saverio Mercadante's opera company in 1826 satisfied that demand. Several new productions appeared each month. In November 1826, for example, audiences were treated to performances of Rossini's comic opera, *La Pietra del paragone*, his *Il barbiere di Seviglia*, his serious *Celmira* and Marcadante's semi-serious *Il posto abbandonato*, and while their gross receipts were comparatively small (5,786, 5,271, 5,269, 6,385 *reales* each, respectively) they were uniformly higher than any play performed during the entire month (AV: Contaduría 4-136-1). Fernando VII, taking note of the public's enthusiastic acceptance of opera ("the people of Madrid have made clearly known their support of music"), mandated the existence of a resident Italian opera company by Royal decree on November 26, 1827. (AHP: Protocolo 23799.) When Gaviria took over the theatres in 1828, he continued to mount productions of opera at the Cruz.[89] After the arrival of the King's fourth wife, his Italian relative, María Cristina de Borbón, the interest in operatic spectacle intensified even more. As reported in the *Cartas Españolas*, between April and November 1831, nine operas earned a total of more than 510,000 *reales*. The most popular were three operas by Bellini: *La straniera, Bianca e Gernando, El pirata*; three by Paccini: *La vestale, El Condestable de Chester, El último día de Pompeya*; two by Rossini: *Zelmira, La Elisabetta*; and one by the Spaniard Tomás Genovés: *Enrique y Clotilde o la rosa blanca*. We have already seen that of the nine productions which played more than fifty times in Madrid during the 1820–33 period, five were operas and that Grimaldi's own

La pata de cabra was the only real opposition the operas had for audience attention.[90] Surprisingly, Rossini's enormously popular *Il barbiere di Seviglia* was not sung at all in 1829, the year of *La pata*'s debut. This has led Duffey to conclude, rightly, that "Grimaldi was at least temporarily successful in diverting the public's attention from the opera in favor of the spoken drama."[91] Mesonero Romanos suggested that the people's passion for opera was a way of channeling energies which they could not express in political or intellectual matters (which were proscribed or prohibited by the restrictive atmosphere) and that it took on the characteristics of a cult activity:

> Society, restrained and prohibited by the Government from any political aspirations, from any intellectual growth and progress, lacking anything more important with which to entertain itself, had concentrated all its energy in its social life . . . allowing itself to become dominated quickly by the delights of the divine art of music . . . This attachment of Madrid society to music was not, as it is now, the expression of a passing fashion, but a true cult, an enthusiastic devotion to that art which displayed so many illustrious geniuses . . .[92]

This interest in opera spilled over into everyday life, as Mesonero noted, and Madrid imitated the songs, speech, gestures, hairstyles, and dress of the Italian singers. Sides were taken up by the fans of this singer or that. This exaggeration was mocked by Bretón and even satirized by Grimaldi himself in *La pata* ("These fellows are real *virtuosi*," says Juan upon seeing the musicians appear out of the earth in Act 1, Scene 6, "It seems as though there is more talent beneath the earth than on it. I know many singers and musicians who should be buried there for a while").[93] Bretón was more direct and more acerbic. In September 1828, he published a satire in verse called "Contra el furor filarmónico, o más bien contra los que desprecian el teatro español," in which he excoriated the public's enslavement to operatic spectacle. He bitterly criticized those who would memorize arias while showing disdain for poets such as Fray Luis or Gil Polo, or those who would denigrate Spanish plays and actors in favor of foreigners.

> Mas mi cólera, Anfriso, no consiente
> que ensalzando de Italia a los cantores
> al español teatro así se afrente.
>   Tribútese en buen hora mil loores
> a una voz peregrina; y no olvidemos
> que en Madrid hay comedias, hay actores.
>   No sea todo *bravos*, todo extremos
> cuando acata a su reina el pueblo asirio;

y al escuchar a Inarco bostecemos.
      No aplaudamos un *duo* con delirio;
y Calderón y el célebre Moreto
en vez de calmo placer nos den martirio.[94]

He likewise mocked the scramble to get tickets ("Someone loses his cape, someone else a shoe") and the often noted fact that when operas were not on the boards the theatres were empty: "Who does not despair, when there are no operas being performed, at seeing all the seats in the theatre deserted?"

Another line of attack against the opera concerned the low quality of some of its performances (actors in dramas were not the only targets of critical scrutiny). One such complaint appeared in a piece in *El Universal* (April 23, 1834) entitled "Cosas que rara vez se ven en nuestros teatros," which listed as two things rarely seen "A singer who begins his aria without saying a few words under his breath to the prompter and the orchestra" and "A contralto who agrees to play the role of an ancient warrior, be it a Catholic or a Saracen, a crusader or a Babylonian, from the Middle Ages or from the time of the flood, without a favorite tunic adorned with gold or silver tinsel, without a polished and elegant crested helmet with an enormous band of plumes, and above all without delicate silk gloves." Grimaldi could hardly have agreed more.

Most of the individuals seriously involved with the theatres opposed the exaggerated importance which opera enjoyed in Madrid but were incapable of overcoming it and were therefore resigned to its existence. Its popular support, combined with the royal favor it received, made it a formidable opponent, and the fact that the opera companies were attached to the theatres – and under the direct charge of the impresarios – made the relationship that much more compli-cated. Larra recognized the irony of the situation: "As far as the opera is concerned, when it arrived in Madrid with all the pomp and magnificence that it was capable of displaying in our theatres, besides the merit of the novelty it brought with it, how was it possible that it would not win out in circumstances where there were hardly any original Spanish dramatists, and where the very little of worth that our modern theatre possessed was either banned or known by heart by everyone?"[95] There was also direct pressure from the municipal authorities to stage operas – precisely because they made more money than plays. Antonio José Galindo ordered the director of the Príncipe company in 1827 to increase the activity of the opera company, "giving a different opera every day without repeating it for two or more days, picking those which will most please the public." (January 27, 1827. AV: Secretaría 3-477-20). One thing that Grimaldi could not have perceived *avant la lettre*, however, was the contribution of opera to the formation of public taste, the same taste for melodrama and spectacle which would enable Romantic dramas to flourish in the capital. As the popularity of the opera waned, that of Romantic drama increased.[96]

The "philharmonic furor" eventually died down, but not soon enough for Grimaldi.[97] He was frustrated with the seeming impossibility of defeating the "music mania" of the opera, which he thought was gravely prejudicing the development of the serious theatre (he and his co-workers "tried in vain to resist that furious fashion").[98] He was not wrong: Larra, summing up the adverse impact opera exerted on Spanish theatre, wrote in 1836 that the opera had "strangled" the national theatre:

The open reception that the public gave it forced the impresarios to concede to its supremacy, and even to concede that its profits could be a help to its obliging guest. But it didn't happen like that, and soon there were reasons to suspect that the new arrival, with its immense expenses, due to the ever-increasing prices charged by its principal performers and the showy apparatus that it required, would become the fabled viper, and a true strangling vine that embraced the national theatre in order to choke it. This soon became a palpable truism, and even more so when it was realized that its profit did not increase since the costs kept going up . . . Opera, therefore, hastened the death of national theatre in Spain . . ."[99]

Grimaldi's aversion to the oppressiveness of the opera became such an issue that during a new attempt to take over the theatres (three years later, in 1833), gossip that he would eliminate it altogether had to be put to rest. An article in *La Revista Española* assured the people that "We have heard that some individuals are circulating the rumor that during the next season there will be an attempt to eliminate the Italian opera company from the theatres of the capital. This is completely false . . . *there will be Italian opera*."[100] Grimaldi was also tiring of the constant battles with the authorities in Madrid over technical and financial matters, and of the bureaucratic restrictions ("the strict control exercised by the antiliberal government of Ferdinand VII")[101] which suffocated his expansive style.

As a consequence, he decided to escape the vicissitudes of life in the capital by taking a company of actors to the provinces for a year. An opportunity had developed in Seville, and so in 1830 he left Madrid and went south, accompanied by his wife and a small number of close associates. Desfrétières reports that the Mayor of Seville, José Manuel de Arjona (the famous poet's brother), had been looking for someone to take charge of the "education of young actors" in Seville and had originally hoped that Joaquín Caprara would take the position. Grimaldi naturally had more experience in training actors and might have been recruited by Caprara to fill the position. In addition, Arjona had promised to ban performances of opera, a promise which must have proved too attractive for Grimaldi to pass up.[102] Breton, for economic reasons as much as for reasons of friendship and loyalty, went along as resident playwright.[103] Ventura de la Vega, struggling to carve out a place for himself in the theatrical world of the capital, was signed on by Grimaldi as an actor – Ventura had always displayed an interest in acting and Grimaldi recognized his talent – but at the last minute he was detained by government officials who valued him more as a playwright than as an actor. Ventura stayed behind reluctantly, fearing that Grimaldi and Bretón would be angry with him for the last-minute change. Bretón wrote him from Seville to assure him that such was not the case:

... although perhaps I have less reason to repent having given you *certain advice*, than you for not having taken it, you have offended me in believing that I could hold any resentment against you ... Neither does Grimaldi hold any grudge. He remembers your talent more than your inconsistency; not a day goes by that he does not miss you as a person in whom he placed his most shining hopes. The divine Concha also has been very disappointed that you haven't come along. They would both receive you with open arms if you were able to decide to come (mind you, this sentence is not a hint nor does it contain any advice); they both respect you and will be delighted to know that you have written to me. I say this because a sudden flu that struck me last night has me locked up at home and I haven't yet been able to show them your letter.[104]

Carlos Latorre, Joaquín Caprara, Bárbara Lamadrid, the brilliant scenery painter Juan Blanchard, and Mateo Alard (the French actor who played the orangutan in *Jocó*) joined the company, but Antonio Guzmán remained in Madrid to continue his work in *La pata*. He did join his friends during his summer vacation (AV: Corregimiento 1-124-14. Cited by Desfrétières, p. 68). Little is known about their activities during this time in the provincial capital. They performed in plays from their repertory as well as in two new plays written by Bretón (*La falsa ilustración* and *Achaques a los vicios* – this latter banned in Madrid), and took the daring step of staging for the first time in Spain Martínez de la Rosa's tragedy, *Edipo*, also banned by the implacable Father Carrillo.[105] Latorre triumphed as the title character, and it became one of his most celebrated roles. (Latorre "performed the title role with such skill and command that it can hardly be done better. Following that, and in whatever role the distinguished actor has played, it has been believed that his performance as Edipo is considered one of the richest laurels in Mr. Latorre's crown.")[106] They also met two individuals who were to play important roles in their professional lives. One was Mariano Roca de Togores, the future Marqués de Molins and Bretón's eventual biographer. The other was a young actress named Matilde Díez.[107]

Matilde Díez (1818–83) was merely twelve years old when Grimaldi's company met her in Seville, but she was soon to become one of the great stars of the Spanish stage, rivaling Concepción Rodríguez for the public's affection. According to García Llansó, she already knew José García Luna, one of the members of Grimaldi's company in Madrid, from the time of his performances in the city.[108] She was brought to Madrid in 1833 (her "conscription" was protested by the authorities in Seville, but those in Madrid responded: "The best should be in the capital") and her official debut in the capital took place in a role Concepción Rodríguez had made famous – Cristina in *La huérfana de Bruselas* (AV: Secretaría 2-475-26. Cited by Carrière, p. 129). Larra, impressed by her youth and talent, wrote laudatory comments on her in an article of April 9, 1834. He confessed that he had suspected the favorable words he had read of her in the *Diario de Sevilla* were exaggerated, but they were not. "Miss Díez knows perfectly how to modulate and use her voice; her movements are simple and agreeable; her intelligence must be considerable. We do not remember having seen any other actress of her age present herself with such pleasant elegance . . . We judge that she is a valuable acquisition for the theatres of the capital."[109] The sentiments were echoed in *El Universal*, which noticed that she "is gifted with an exquisite sensitivity . . . from the first words that she utters she captures the spectator's good will."[110] As early as that May she was being compared to Concepción Rodríguez: "Miss Díez has been a brilliant acquisition for the company. The public already prefers her to Miss Rodríguez in roles of impassioned emotion: it finds in the young actress more candour, a better voice, more heart. What a shame it is that she tries to imitate the other actress at times, because her performance visibly pales by comparison."[111] Her major triumphs came during the flourishing of Romanticism as she played Preciosilla in *Don Alvaro o la fuerza del sino*, Leonor in *El trovador* (only after Concepción Rodríguez had retired from the role), Isabel in *Los amantes de Teruel*, Clara in Ventura's *El hombre del mundo*, and countless others, where she displayed her mastery of the natural style of acting that Grimaldi had long championed.[112] In 1836 she married another newcomer to Grimaldi's company, the distinguished young actor, Julián Romea.

The sojourn in Seville lasted just one season. Even before it was over, Grimaldi was in contact with Cuesta, the impresario in Madrid, concerning the possibility of returning to the capital. Cuesta, in a letter dated February 18, 1831, indicated his willingness to allow Grimaldi, Concepción Rodríguez and Alard back into the Príncipe company. When the Theatre Commission met on March 1 to make plans for the formation of the company for the 1831–2 season, it agreed to send some money to Rodríguez to underwrite her trip back to Madrid (AV: Secretaría 3-409-9).[113] Grimaldi moved back to Madrid into an apartment on Calle de las Huertas, perhaps in time to witness Rossini's triumphant conquest of the capital during the spring of 1831 (the Italian composer wrote songs for María Cristina which she sang in public; he also directed a performance of *Il barbiere di Seviglia* at the Cruz). The company for the Príncipe was finally formed.[114] In it were Concepción Rodríguez, José García Luna, Carlos Latorre, Concepción Velasco, Antera Baus, Antonio Silvostri, Antonio Guzmán, Bruno Rodríguez, Mateo Alard (as director of the dance company), Ramón Carnicer (as director of the opera company) and Grimaldi (as stage director and manager). Their return was greeted with jubilation by Carnerero in his *Cartas Españolas*. He writes to his anonymous correspondent:

It's too bad that you are forced to be away from the capital, precisely at a time when theatrical performances begin again under the direct protection of the esteemed City Hall. This situation can only produce favorable results, and a simple glance at the lists [of actors] confirms it. Several actors of known merit, who were out in the provinces, have returned to their true center, and even if we had only recovered Miss Rodríguez, Latorre and Caprara, we would have to be very grateful to the enlightened corporation which has restored them to the Madrid stage ... We beg forgiveness of the provinces, but Thalia reclaims them for the capital.[115]

Grimaldi attended the meeting of the Commission on April 2, where it was decided that he would receive a salary of 21,000 *reales* per year – "well, even though he insisted that he be given 22,000"; his wife received 30,000 (AV: Secretaría 3-409-9 and AV: Contaduría 3-182-

2).[116] These were respectable, though hardly excessively generous salaries, at a time when costs were high and payment for services generally low.[117]

As soon as Grimaldi received that year's appointment trouble began to brew. He received a letter on April 18 from Eustasio Nieto y Castaños, the man in charge of the Príncipe's warehouse and contents, demanding payment of the old debt of 5,981 *reales* – a debt left uncollected from Grimaldi's season as impresario (1823–4). Grimaldi ignored the request, as he did the second one (April 25) which contained the threat of legal action. Nieto then wrote to the Theatre Commission, a body which existed to resolve disputes, issue salary advances, hear injury claims, incensed that Grimaldi, while making 25,000 [*sic*] *reales* per year should refuse to pay his debt. The Commission passed a recommendation to the magistrate, Domingo María Barrafón, that the city try to collect the money. It did so by deciding to withhold one third of Grimaldi's monthly salary until the debt was paid off, a decision which was passed on to the paymaster of the Príncipe on June 30 (AV: Secretaría 2-472-61). They began to withhold the money in July (AV: Contaduría 3-182-2). Grimaldi's mishandling of this issue would be one of the factors which cost him control of the theatres for the upcoming season.

Things were not going well at all. The theatres were still losing money and many of the seats remained empty – except, of course, when *La pata*, an opera, or a new piece was being offered. As reported for April, 1831, "The gross for all the seats in the Príncipe Theatre reached 8,800 *reales*; but excepting evenings of Italian opera and the premier presentations of a new play, on most days the theatre remained half empty."[118] (One of the new pieces which Grimaldi staged at the very beginning of the season – April 29 – was his friend Larra's *No más mostrador*. Grimaldi stimulated Larra's interest in the stage and encouraged him to write and translate for it. Larra composed some eighteen works in the six years between his debut as a dramatist in 1831 and his death in 1837.)[119] In April, 1831 the combined loss of both theatres totaled nearly 300,000 *reales* (AV: Contaduría 3-776-13). There did seem to be a general consensus that private managers were overall more successful impresarios and that the theatres offered better performances when they were in the hands of private individuals as opposed to the acting companies or the city authorities. Mesonero, while suggesting that the Cruz was such an abomination that its "capital defects" could only be cured by tearing the entire building down, praised the Príncipe's ability to stage tragedies and operas with "wonderful machinery, appropriate to the scenic demands, being decorated magnificently, and the actors dressed with all propriety and elegance, an area in which the theatres have improved significantly in the past few years, and principally since both theatres have been in the hands of a private concern."[120] Grimaldi's position in the Madrid hierarchy had been strengthened by his success with *La pata de cabra*, by his absence from the capital during the 1830–1 season, and by the loyalty he commanded from the best actors in the Príncipe company. When the City Council once again tried to find someone to take over the theatres for the 1832–3 season, Grimaldi decided that the time was right for him to move up from stage manager of the Príncipe to impresario of both theatres once again.

More takeover attempts

All Grimaldi needed was freedom: freedom from the repressive strictures of the municipality and freedom from the suffocating censorship which kept fresh, daring plays from being written in Spain or performed there. He had proven his ability to gather around him a company of professional actors and to stage with competence and wit those very few plays allowed by the authorities. He had made vast improvements in the technical aspects of those productions, creating at the Príncipe a crew of workers and stagehands capable of mounting spectacular melodramas and *comedias de magia* without accident or embarrassment. He had hired artists (Carnicer in music and Blanchard in painting) whose creations moved Spanish theatre toward the level of achievement in evidence in other European capitals. He himself had contributed two of the four greatest "hits" seen on the Spanish stage in the previous decade (opera excluded) – *La pata de cabra* and *La huérfana de Bruselas*.[121] He had created an audience for melodrama and spectacle, an audience which demonstrated a hunger for new productions and a willingness to support the few that were offered. His friends attested to his deep love for literature and his profound knowledge of it: his conversations at "El Parnasillo" and his readings of texts stimulated comments of admiration and respect, and he was considered to be one of the great intellectuals of his time. Still, he lacked the freedom to move the theatre into the realm of excitement and true creativity where he knew it belonged. His changes had all been internal. Little had changed in the external structures of the theatre world in Madrid between 1823 and 1832. He certainly had little reason to believe that his latest round of demands would be heeded, but he hardly expected the strong opposition and bureaucratic infighting with which his proposals were received.

On January 21,1832, as the City Council was beginning to think ahead to the new season – and to worry that "public funds might have to maintain them" since nobody had stepped forward to take charge of them – Grimaldi sent a nine-point proposal to the Theatre Commission, along with a cover letter in which he reminded them rather pointedly that he was "past impresario of the theatres" of Madrid. As Desfrétières has noted, Grimaldi, after his many years of dealing with the government on matters relating to the Spanish theatre, was not quite as naive or optimistic as he had been in 1823. He knew that the civil authorities had little interest in the "glory" of the Spanish stage and that the theatres were almost exclusively a matter of economics and financial dealings (Desfrétières, p. 76). So he offered to take charge of the theatres for a five-year period, and backed up his words with a statement that he was ready to deposit 200,000 *reales* as an up-front guarantee (AV: Secretaría 2-473-55).[122] He proposed that his only financial concessions be: (1) rental of the theatre; (2) free box seats for a handful of selected political and military leaders; (3) reservation of selected seats for other important personnel until one o'clock on the day of the performance; and (4) payments to two of the charitable organizations supported by the theatres. His list pointedly excluded any additional charitable contributions and the actors' pension benefits, an issue he addressed by stating that the Town Council should pay these directly from the rental fees the impresario paid to that corporation. He thought that the Council should give him full control of the theatres' contents on a buy-back basis, that is, that his rental fee would include ownership of them and at the end of the year the City Council would buy them back from him. He also requested the Council to appoint an intermediary body, a special commission with which Grimaldi could negotiate directly, instead of weaving his way through the usual series of ponderous steps in the theatrical hierarchy.

The Commission was anxious to find a responsible party to take control of the theatres (impending financial losses weighed heavily upon it), but its reaction to Grimaldi's proposal was immediate and hostile. It declared that the terms of his contract "are not acceptable in any way," although it did offer him a chance to amend them. It objected, naturally, to the buy-back arrangement proposed by Grimaldi for the theatres' contents and made a pointed reference to the government's "little faith in being paid back at the end of the contracted period." It proposed as an additional security payment for the use of those goods, to be repaid to the impresario when the goods were returned, as well as an increased security deposit to cover the actors' benefits. The largest contention was, not surprisingly, Grimaldi's attempt to push the charitable contributions and the actors' benefits on the City Council, which, as it had consistently done in the past, refused to hold itself responsible for them. The Commission also picked up that Grimaldi had said nothing about maintaining an Italian opera company and it demanded that he recognize his legal responsibility to do so (it referred to Fernando VII's order of November 26, 1827). Grimaldi's plans, therefore, were opposed on nearly every point, and when the magistrate agreed with the Commission's findings, their decision was returned to Grimaldi on January 28.

Grimaldi responded quickly. Within three days he had drafted both an answer to the Commission's report and a new contract. "I have carefully read the Theatre Commission's notes and I am now even more convinced that it would have been useful and indispensable to have agreed to what I proposed" – that is, the special commission with which he could deal directly. He was rightly frustrated with the "system of notes and counternotes" with which "so much precious time is wasted and difficulties in understanding one another are multiplied." He protested that many of his points had been misinterpreted by the Commission and that face-to-face negotiations would clarify points of contention quickly. Nevertheless, he surrendered to the will of the Commission and put his explanatory statements in writing to be passed back to the members of the board. He was most anxious to take charge of the theatres again. On the matter of the guarantees he anticipated the Commission's objections by offering twice the amount they were requesting (and five times his initial offer): "It seems as though a guarantee of 500,000 *reales* would cover the points raised by the Commission. Fine. Grimaldi then offers one million in order to prove that his business can offer more guarantees than necessary." But he was also shrewdly aware that given the enormous losses that the theatres were still suffering few individuals would – or could – move in to accept the substantial financial responsibilities that being impresario of Madrid's theatres implied, so he pushed for his belief that the City Council should accept at least partial responsibility for charitable payments and actors' benefits. He restated his proposals, noting some important changes: he would take over the theatres for five years, receiving them and their contents rent-free from the City Council and promising to pay for any damage incurred at the end of each year. He would not be responsible for retirement benefits or charitable costs. He reserved the right to hire and fire actors freely and to conscript them from the provinces. He promised to maintain an Italian opera company. And he offered one million *reales* (in property, not cash) as a security bond.

The Commission was not moved by these latest proposals and expressed concern over how to insure that the contents (which included costumes, and sets) would be returned in proper condition and how to insure that the actors' salaries and benefits would be paid if the impresario went bankrupt. Was Grimaldi's "excessive guarantee of one million *reales*" not sufficient? It was not: "the Commission . . . believes that the million offered would not underwrite the goods that will be handed over to the impresario." Both sides maintained intransigent postures and the differences were no closer to being resolved. In fact, the Commission took note that "as much as the Commission has impressed upon Grimaldi the impossibility of having these charges weighing upon the City Council, and as much as he personally has convinced himself of his irresistible power, nothing has been resolved concerning this issue." It seemed as though no progress was being made, but the fact was that each side was inching slowly toward a central ground. Grimaldi conceded several points, accepting additional responsibilities and offering to put a percentage up in cash.

But still the Commission remained unconvinced and on February 8, 1832, it voted to "reject the propositions presented by D. Juan de Grimaldi." Grimaldi, however, refused to admit defeat and returned to the Commission two days later with yet another proposed contract (his "ultimatum"). This back-and-forth series of proposals and counterproposals became a long and drawn-out affair. Flurries of papers and personal meetings (Grimaldi showed up periodically at the Commission's meetings to press his case in person or to clarify points of confusion) continued almost daily throughout February. Grimaldi did some homework and dug up old contracts to prove to the Commission that the municipality had previously underwritten the theatre (in 1807, Carlos IV ordered the city government to provide

143,000 *reales* to support the theatres, which Joseph Bonaparte continued), but the Commission paid scant attention to such arguments. The letters exchanged between the Commission, Grimaldi, and the City Council fluctuated in tone from respectful to accusatory and in substance from significant to trivial. The Commission seemed to resent Grimaldi's attitude, finding him arrogant and improperly appreciative of the "sacrifices" it was making: "The Commission views with shock that the sacrifices it is so generously making have been received with disdain. Its offer to turn over the buildings, goods and props have been viewed with indifference... It is difficult to hear without irritation that the impresario believes himself abused by the guarantee we are demanding" (February 10, 1832; AV: Secretaría 2-473-55; Desfrétières, p. 207). Still, Grimaldi pressed his case relentlessly throughout the month.[123]

Grimaldi turned in a new – his third – contract proposal, with twenty clauses, on February 26. In this proposal he came close to accepting all of the stipulations demanded by the Commission, including the payment of all charitable fees and actors' benefits, although he still demanded use of the theatres and their contents rent-free. The charitable payments were to be subsidized by a contribution from the Town Council of 150,000 *reales* (the Council had proposed this contribution), but Grimaldi still promised to put up the one million *reales* in property as a guarantee and to pay some money in cash as a good-faith gesture. He pressed them to respond immediately, since the Italian opera company was preparing to leave Madrid, and once it was gone it would be difficult to replace it and form a company for the 1832–3 season. It looked as though Grimaldi would succeed, but at the last moment the Commission altered its demands and then moved ahead on the assumption that Grimaldi would accept those alterations (they postponed for a fortnight their decision and declared that in the interim *they* would begin to hire actors for the new season). Grimaldi was shocked ("such an unexpected decision could not help but cause the greatest surprise to the petitioner") and he issued a passionate protest in which he demanded that the decisions be suspended until the conflicts could be resolved (March 3, 1832; AV: Secretaría 2-473-55; Desfrétières, pp. 216–18). He was so angry that he informed the Commission that he had written directly to the King about it: "Such an oppressive condition cannot be ignored and the petitioner not only protests against it as illegal in principle, unjust in its application and immensely prejudicial in its results, but on this very day directs a respectful explanation to the King, not to cause trouble with the City Council, which he respects and about which he speaks in his letter with all due respect, but in order to beg His Majesty to bring this issue to its proper conclusion." A special meeting of the City Council was called for March 5 to address this issue, but on that same day the following notice appeared in the *Diarios de Avisos*:

Since proposals have been made to take over the theatres of the court for a five-year period, the City Council ceding them rent-free to the impresario, with all their goods, vestments, archives and other properties, underwriting him with 150,000 *reales* per year, payable in trimesters for the support of the charges and retirement benefits which weigh upon the theatres . . . the City Council has agreed to announce this proposal to the public and keep it open for a period of fifteen days so that any persons wishing to best it and take charge of the theatres should present their proposals to the secretary's office . .

The City Council had decided to seek elsewhere for an impresario.

At their meeting that day the Council debated the problems caused by the fifteen-day delay and decided to work with Grimaldi on the hiring of the actors, even though the issue of who was to be impresario was not yet completely settled. But by the time the fifteen-day period of grace passed, "nobody had come forth to best it" (March 21, 1832; AV: Secretaría 2-473-55) and it looked as though they would have to approve Grimaldi's petitions. The Commission and the Council reluctantly sent to the King's office the papers outlining the agreements. It asked for royal approval of the contracts, although it pointed out that the 150,000 *reales* which the Council had agreed to pay Grimaldi as an annual subsidy were likely to increase "if the projected business, instead of a profit, shows a loss in this venture." Its recommendation served a dual and contradictory purpose: it seemed to recommend Grimaldi's proposals while at the same time it warned the King's office away from them. The Council feared a no-win situation – it would lose money if it had to take control of the theatres (as it had in the past) and it could lose money if the theatres were given to a private concern (as it had in the past). But the fact remained that there were no other prospects ("after a thousand useless advertisements published with the purpose of attracting petitioners to the management of the theatres"). Grimaldi's long battle to take over the theatres appeared to be won.

As the contract proposals wound their way up through the hierarchy, from the Theatre Commission to the City Council and on up to the offices of the General Protectorate of the Kingdom's Theatres – which reported directly to the King – opposition to them, even to those substantially modified by the Commission and agreed upon by Grimaldi, remained firm. Finally, on April 13, Francisco Tadeo Calomarde, the King's powerful and ultraconservative minister, ordered the Commission to negotiate a new contract with Grimaldi on terms more favorable to the city government and less threatening to the city's coffers.

> After familiarizing himself with the conditions agreed upon between the Council and don Juan Grimaldi, under which the latter would take charge of the theatres for five years, and keeping in mind that this agreement has been based on the state of the theatres in the last theatrical season (which state has changed considerably owing to the recent concessions and decrees that His Majesty has granted the Council in order to alleviate the burdens weighing upon the theatres), the King has decided to order the City Council to negotiate a new contract with Mr. Grimaldi, improving the conditions regarding the guarantees, and sending the final results back to the King.
>
> (AV: Secretaría 2-473-55. Desfrétières, p. 219)

By this point it seemed clear to certain observers – Bretón among them – that Grimaldi would fail in his attempt to take control of the theatres. On the very day of Calomarde's response Bretón published in the *Correo* his observations on the current crisis, noting "it is said that the acting companies have been organized already, and it cannot be doubted that the control of the theatres of Madrid will be kept in the hands of the City Council."[124] But this was not at all clear to Grimaldi, who refused to give up and who responded to Calomarde with some adjustments to the contract, which the Commission read on the 16th; another special meeting of the Council was called for the 17th to discuss them. Each side raised the stakes: Grimaldi insisted that the 150,000 *reales* which the government agreed to use to underwrite the concern be paid up-front and the government insisted that his securities (the one million *reales* in properties) be increased by one third and be properties in Madrid (for easy liquidation should the need arise). Grimaldi was outvoted on both counts: the advance payment was denied and the security bond was raised to 1,400,000 *reales*, a decision confirmed by Calomarde in the King's name on April 20. The King issued an ultimatum that Grimaldi must accept the conditions or the theatres would revert to the hands of the Council for the 1832–3 season. Two days later, on Easter Sunday – the day traditionally set for the new theatrical season to begin – Grimaldi declined the restrictive new terms ("it is impossible to accept charge of the theatres under the terms expressed in the royal order"). The City Council once again found itself in charge of the Cruz and the Príncipe, which it turned over to the control of one of the comic actors from the Príncipe company, Agustín Azcona.

When the Council formed the acting companies in the first weeks of April, decisions had been made (without Grimaldi's consent, naturally) to reduce the companies, and several actors were omitted from the lists. Concepción, struggling with a serious attack of gastrointestinal neuralgia (which caused her to suffer nausea, vomiting, and "violent pains" – the same problems which forced her to take time off in 1826), temporarily left the stage and was not included in the capital's companies that year.[125] Bretón wrote:

Rumors were heard at the beginning of Lent that the two verse companies would be fused into one, an innovation which some approve of and which others vituperate; but according to faithful sources they will continue in the same state as last year, although somewhat reduced. In promotions to main roles we do not know any names other than that of the actor who not long ago made a name for himself in the role of Loredano in the tragedy *Othello* [José Valero], and that of the young Bárbara Lamadrid, of whom we have spoken, who has not yet begun her journey to the capital of Spain; it is probable that she will not delay in doing so and that with her will come someone who can extend the range of old man roles, her father, Jerónimo Lamadrid, already known to Madrid audiences. The list of losses is more significant. It consists of Concepción Rodríguez, Dolores Generoso, Teresa Baus, María Riduara and Lorenza Campos; and Pedro Montaño, José Cubas, José Molist, Gabriel Pérez, Bruno Rodríguez, Santos Díez, and others of lesser status. All of these actors have been placed where it has been possible or convenient to place them, except Miss Concepción Rodríguez, who to universal sorrow has remained at home."[126]

When his proposals failed to meet with the approval of the authorities, Grimaldi, fed up with the bickering and narrowmindedness of the Commission, packed up and took off for the provinces once again, where both he and Concepción performed in plays.[127] Their absence was lamented by the leading figures of the intellectual world of the capital. As Bretón wrote to Juan de la Pezuela, "This theatre is in bad shape these days, because we are missing the irreplaceable Concha Rodríguez and the direction of Grimaldi. Don Juan Aquiles [Grimaldi] got fed up with the City Council, because he wanted to take over the theatres and he almost managed to do so. It's probable that he will succeed next year."[128] They went to Seville for a period of a few weeks (where Concepción received "deserved applause" and was warmly welcomed), moved on to Cádiz by the end of July (where she was again greeted with rave reviews) and then played in Granada before returning to the capital in the fall.[129] Bretón stayed behind in Madrid, but he continued to track Concepción's triumphs in Andalusia and to keep her name before the reading public in Madrid. Their trip home was fraught with difficulty: at one point, while crossing the Guadalquivir River southwest of Bailén, their carriage was overturned by the rushing water and Concepción, Grimaldi and another passenger almost drowned (the two mules pulling the carriage did drown). The majority of their luggage was lost or ruined.[130] They managed to make it back to Madrid just in time to heed the announcement in the *Diario de Avisos* that the Town Council was again searching for a private impresario to take over the theatres.[131]

Undaunted by his previous inability to convince the authorities to change the way the theatres were managed, Grimaldi responded with yet another complicated series of contract proposals. Because of the serious illness of the King, the theatres were closed when Grimaldi returned to the capital in late September, 1832, and they remained closed until October 20, but the municipality nonetheless studied the conditions he presented on October 2 in order to plan for the coming season.[132] The squabbling with Grimaldi began immediately: at its meeting of October 8, it decided that Grimaldi had not submitted his plan in the "proper" form, and it consequently "refused to accept it." But the real reason for the denial, and in fact the real reason for the years of contention between Grimaldi and the authorities, remained buried in one of the responses recorded at a session of the Council on October 16. The reluctance of the City Council to enter into serious negotiations with Grimaldi, or to accede to his wishes on how the theatres should be managed, stemmed from its judgment that Grimaldi's ideas represented a threat to their authority, ". . . which is what is behind the present dispute, it is clear that *it is a direct attack on the authority which properly belongs to the City Council* . . ."[133] They found him pushy, arrogant, and manipulative. Ironically, however, a substantial number of Grimaldi's ideas had been incorporated over the years into the structure of theatre management. The Council's written "list of conditions" for the 1833–4 season contained items which had originally entered the contracts at Grimaldi's insistence and which had been confirmed by royal decrees in the mid-1820s. These demands included the five-year contract, the relatively free selection of actors, the reservation of limited seating for the authorities, the payment of fees to the impresario from any other plays performed in the capital, rent-free access to the theatres, the right to give concerts and/or masked balls during the period preceding Lent, and so on. He also wanted to raise the price of opera tickets, but the City Council feared that with higher prices fewer people would come and the net result would be additional losses. Grimaldi made a number of concessions as well in this new round of negotiations, but still the two sides found it difficult to come to terms. The City Council was in a troublesome, if not impossible, situation: it was terrified of having "the ruinous administration of the theatres" and yet it was suspicious of Grimaldi and fearful of being bested in a contractual dispute. But as Grimaldi was the only petitioner this time around and the Council could not simply ignore his petition or stall too long, the two sides came to what seemed to be an equitable arrangement. As a gesture of good will they got together and rewrote the agreements in person, which they then signed on October 23. Among other things, Grimaldi promised to come up with a surety bond of 1,300,000 *reales* (nearly the amount he had refused to provide six months earlier). Neither side was completely pleased with the arrangements agreed upon, but nonetheless the proposal was sent up to Queen María Cristina – who was conducting official business during the King's illness – for her approval. Finally, and at long last, Grimaldi's tenure as impresario seemed assured.

As these negotiations were in progress, Larra wrote and published one of his most sustained meditations on the state of Spanish theatre. In "Reflexiones acerca del modo de hacer resucitar el teatro español" he issued a call for "a radical reform of the theatres in our country" and reviewed the reasons for the problems which were paralyzing the theatre: poor acting, lack of government support, overemphasis on translations, low payments to authors and the general economic difficulties the theatre owners faced: "It is not enough that there be theatre; it is not enough that there be poets [playwrights]; it is not enough that there be actors; none of these three things can exist without the cooperation of the others, and the union of the three can hardly exist without a fourth and more important element: it is necessary that there be an audience. The four, lastly, depend to a large extent on the protection that the Government can provide them." (*El Pobrecito Hablador*, December 20, 1832.) It was a passionate call for new plays with which to instruct and guide the public ("Who should be, who will be most obliged to begin this great task? We repeat it clearly: the poets. Those who know more have the greatest responsibility"), but he also realized that "they need some support."

He perceived a hierarchy of support, which wound upwards from the dramatist – who should by right be paid royalties for his work (copyright laws did not protect the author's work, as Zorrilla was to find out so painfully after he sold the first copies of *Don Juan Tenorio*) – to the impresario – who should pay the royalties but who, as Larra realized, was overwhelmed by the huge costs of running theatres ("It is difficult to believe the frightening costs that weigh upon the unfortunate theatres"),[134] to the government itself. Echoing Grimaldi's eternal plea, he begged the government to relieve the theatres of the suffocating charges weighing upon them and to adopt a laissez-faire policy toward the impresarios:

We ask, then, that the obstacles and unnecessary observances be removed from the theatre firms; that they be able to govern themselves, as their own bosses, as long as they have viable companies. This will be sufficient to give the theatre an incalculable boost. Then the companies, unhindered and free in their operations, will mark each day with improvements. They will pay their actors – now miserably paid – and their poets – now in no way rewarded – better.[135]

As always, however, such pleas and hopes came to little. New plays would come after the death of the King in September, 1833, but the municipal authorities continued to live in a netherworld of fear – fear of relinquishing control of the theatres to a completely private and free enterprise, and fear of being stuck with them year after year.

In December, 1832, Grimaldi was on the verge of taking charge of the theatres and there was a palpable excitement in the air. But when the contract proposals were approved and passed on to the Queen, it was "always as long as the guarantee proposed by Grimaldi for the security of his contract be as unencumbered and solid as the City Council demands," and it was precisely in the realization of that clause where Grimaldi ran into the obstacle which would block his takeover of the theatres (AV: Corregimiento 1-78-54; Desfrétières, p. 249). The negotiations over this point made the previous ones appear to be troublefree. When the King, recovered from his illness, approved the basis for the contractual agreements in early January, 1833, Grimaldi moved to arrange the promised financial guarantee. He had been requested to come up with the guarantees by the 28th of the month. On that day he asked for a four-day extension – which was reluctantly granted – and by the 30th he had turned in a letter from his backers promising to underwrite the guarantee. Things were moving along so smoothly that the newspapers began to speculate that Grimaldi would once again be the impresario. As early as January 15,

La Revista Española was reporting that "The King has decided to approve by Royal order on the 8th of this month the conditions agreed upon between the City Council and D. Juan de Grimaldi, so that Mr. Grimaldi can take charge of the management of the theatres in the capital for five years, which will begin next Easter Sunday."[136]

Grimaldi's backers were a wealthy couple from Muñoveros in the province of Segovia named Simona del Barrio and her second husband, Miguel Burgueños García, who put up seventy-four parcels of land as the equivalent value of the stipulated guarantee. Simona del Barrio may have been a relative of María Juliana del Barrio, the woman who financed Grimaldi's venture in 1823. The couple from Segovia owned properties valued at some two million *reales* and more than 3,000 head of sheep.[137] The City Council demanded more than mere letters – it asked Grimaldi to turn over the original titles to the properties as well as any documents relating to any mortgages or liens which might encumber those parcels of land. Burgueños and his wife wrote to the Council requesting a further delay in order to get those papers together, steps which would take some time. This request only increased the nervousness of the authorities, who did not put too much trust in Grimaldi anyway: ". . . the City Council suspects that [the guarantees] might be worthless; in which case this respectable corporation – and worse, the government – would suffer a shameful deceit which should be punished so that no one else would ever repeat it" (AV: Secretaría 2-474-7). This fear of a "shameful deceit" at the hands of Grimaldi and his backers kept the Council wary of the repeated requests for extensions which went on for most of the month of February. They remained suspicious of the solidity of the guarantees. The city's lawyers, basing their judgments on laws which went back to the sixteenth century, questioned Burgueños' right to enter into financial contracts, and they filed reports which stated that "neither of the financial documents offers the necessary guarantee to assure the interests of Madrid. . . and in that case, they should be rejected." Grimaldi, however, fought back, and in a letter of February 27 he presented some legal advice of his own, citing chapter and verse of the city's law books in order to persuade the authorities that the guarantees were both solid and grounded in legality.[138] His letter was a forceful presentation of his case, but it was not forceful enough: the Council voted to refuse to accept the guarantees. This was not the end of these contentious negotiations, for the Council, still unwilling to accept charge of the theatres ("wishing that the theatres leave the

hands of the corporation") while at the same time unwilling to turn
them over to Grimaldi on the terms he proposed, passed the whole
matter on to the King's office for resolution, but not without first
insisting again on "the little confidence which Grimaldi inspires in us"
(AV: Secretaría 2-474-7, folios 138–54). The King's decision, handed
down on March 10, was to permit Grimaldi to proceed with the
organization of the new season (get the actors lists together) if he
would pay 200,000 *reales* in advance as a down payment and continue
working to straighten out the problems with the guarantees (AV:
Secretaría 2-480-35; Desfrétières, p. 269). Grimaldi resisted, finding
in the King's order several clauses which could prove seriously
detrimental to him if it turned out that he was unable to take full
control of the theatres, and he asked for further clarification of these
points.

The uncertainty of the situation did not go unnoticed in the press.
Who would end up in control of the theatres? The City Council? The
actors? A private impresario? Larra, in his usual trenchant manner,
satirized the vagaries of the standoff on March 1 in his article, "Yo
quiero ser cómico." He trapped the novice actor who was soliciting his
support into the following dialogue:

"I want to be an actor, and dedicate myself to the theatre."
"To the theatre?"
"Yes, sir . . . Since the theatre is closed now. . ."
"It's the best time."
"Since we're in Lent, and it's the time to hire for the next theatrical season,
I should like you to recommend me . . ."
"Great idea! To whom?"
"To the City Council."
"Really! Is the City Council hiring?"
"I mean, to the management."
"Oh! Is the management hiring?"
"I'll tell you . . . according to some people, nobody knows . . . but . . . for
when it is known."
"In that case, don't be in a hurry, because no one is . . ."

But Grimaldi was in a hurry, although that seemed to have little
impact on the course of negotiations. The case dragged on slowly and
to what must have seemed interminable lengths. There was no more
accord by mid-March than there had been in early January and
mutual suspicion was not diminished by the flood of paperwork and
legal briefs being exchanged almost daily.

Larra was impatient; the City Council was stubborn and fearful;
Grimaldi was tenacious and bold. On March 15, 1833, Grimaldi

enlisted the aid of Juan Bautista Alonso, a lawyer, long-time friend, and member of the *tertulia* "El Parnasillo."[139] They jointly wrote up a long and detailed recapitulation of the case to be sent to the office of the King (AV: Secretaría 2-480-35; Desfrétières, pp. 272–83). In their view the whole issue of the guarantees was a false one, since their purpose was not to pay the actors or underwrite ticket prices or enrich the repertory, but merely to insure that the material goods contained in the theatres (costumes, machinery, sets, curtains, props) would be returned in suitable condition at the end of the theatrical season. They pointed out that such items were really very safe since they would be difficult to hide or sell off or steal ("because the curtains and other furnishings of the theatre cannot be hidden or easily sold and because ultimately the idea is patently absurd that they could be carried off"), even in the unlikely event the impresario had an interest in doing so. They refuted point by point the weaknesses they detected in the lawyers' brief of February 27 and asked that the theatres be turned over to Grimaldi. Domingo María Barrafón, the Mayor of Madrid and Protector of the Theatres, convinced by their arguments (and by the offer of the 200,000 *reales* deposit), recommended to the King that the interim measures be approved. That is, Grimaldi would deposit the 200,000 *reales* in the Banco de San Fernando, take charge of the theatres and continue working to straighten out the remaining discrepancies concerning the guarantees. Yet again it seemed as though Grimaldi had won this long and arduous battle.

Not quite: Grimaldi was having trouble raising the money in cash (he tried to sell shares to investors) and he complained that he had been "the victim of the most audacious felony," struggling with a "catastrophe" (AV: Corregimiento: 1-78-54; Desfrétières, p. 285). He asked for an additional eight-day extension and some relief from the advances he had already paid out of his own pocket (20–30,000 *reales*, according to his calculations) for expenses incurred by some of the members of the opera company. He complained of serious economic hardship and pleaded for compassion "towards a father of numerous children, indignantly sold out," suggesting that if he was unable to reach accord with the municipality he would be reduced to a state of the "most desperate misery." His hysterical words merely confirmed the worst fears of the Council. On March 21, citing the "contradiction in his conduct" and his "bad faith," the Council declared itself free from any contractual responsibility with Grimaldi. The King's secretary agreed, and the matter came to a halt. Within a day the orders went out to begin the formation of the companies, and within a week Burgueños was demanding the return of all his documents (nearly 300 pages) and canceling his agreements with Grimaldi. A last-minute effort by one Manuel Sorzano to take charge of the theatres was rejected, and for the third year in a row the City Council realized its greatest fear and found itself in charge of the theatres.

The initial months of that season, 1833–4, were a financial and artistic disaster. The actors performed poorly and received payment for their services late; the opera company was sloppy and disorganized. It was at this time when Grimaldi acquired the last two actors who would be key figures in the soon-to-emerge Romantic triumph: Bárbara Lamadrid and Julián Romea.

Grimaldi had first seen Bárbara Lamadrid (1812–93) perform in Seville, in 1830.[140] He brought her to the capital in the fall of 1832, where she enjoyed notable successes in the melodramas *La huérfana de Bruselas* and *María Estuardo*. Her greatest triumphs came between 1836 (when she played the gypsy Azucena in *El trovador*) and 1844 (when she played Inés opposite Latorre's Don Juan Tenorio).[141] Her younger sister, Teodora (1821–96), whom Grimaldi had also seen work in Seville, likewise came to Madrid to join the company.[142] Romero Mendoza accused Bárbara of being of the school of actresses who "hiccup and moan," and who always had "a handkerchief in which to catch their quick and copious tears,"[143] but she remained in demand for years.

Julián Romea (1813–68) was destined to become the most famous of all of Grimaldi's actors. His natural style and artistic grace enchanted the theatregoing public, and his intelligence charmed his friends. Romea "made Spanish acting descend from its bewitched sphere of harmonies, rules, cadences and conventionalisms, to a realm of naturalness and to find in life itself its model and inspiration. In this sense Romea was ahead of his time, since with him and after him our stage was killed off by Romantic exaggeration."[144] He and his brother Florencio had studied at the Conservatory of Music in 1831 (under the tutelage of Caprara and Latorre). Two years later, Grimaldi, needing to replace Latorre (who had gone off to Paris for the summer), offered Romea a place in the company. He was twenty years old. The play selected for his debut in Madrid was Ventura de la Vega's translation of Scribe's *El testamento*, first performed by Romea on April 21, 1833 (along with Concepción Rodríguez and Guzmán).[145] Mesonero mistakenly wrote that in the audience that night were the

King and Queen; rumor had it that Fernando commented, "this young man who is in *El testamento* starts where the rest leave off."[146] Larra attacked the play as trivial, but noted the "positive and brilliant triumph of applause with which the audience of Madrid has justly rewarded him on his first appearance."[147] Along with his less gifted brother he acted in many of the most celebrated plays of the Romantic period. He played in *La conjuración de Venecia* (with Rodríguez and Latorre), *Don Alvaro* (with Rodríguez, Guzmán, García Luna and Matilde Díez), *El trovador* (with Bárbara Lamadrid, Rodríguez, Latorre, and Díez; Larra thought he should have played the title role),[148] as well as several of Larra's translations, Martínez de la Rosa's *La niña en casa*, Grimaldi's *La pata de cabra* (as don Juan, in 1834, 1835, 1836 and 1837),[149] and numerous miscellaneous pieces. Later he scored a major hit in Vega's "anti-*Don Juan*" play, *El hombre del mundo* (1845).[150] Romea also sympathized with Grimaldi's literary interests and his goal to improve acting, and was himself the author of a book of *Poesías* (1843) and a *Manual de declamación*.[151] Grimaldi considered him to be a very good poet. As late as 1867, Grimaldi remembered Romea to be

the son of a very highly esteemed businessman, and who in spite of being the heir apparent of a marquis, nevertheless entered the theatre, where he saw a way to serve better his taste for literature in general and for poetry in particular, which he cultivates with success. . . .[152]

A confirmation of the status that Romea achieved early was that he and Latorre were the only two actors included among the literary élite of Madrid at the inauguration of the Ateneo in 1835, and Romea figured prominently in the famous painting by Antonio María Esquivel of the *Grupo de poetas románticos en el estudio del pintor*. In 1836 he married Matilde Díez (two of his sisters made important marriages to high government officials, one to Luis González Bravo and another to Cándido Nocedal) and later went on to become Director of the Conservatory of Music.

Given what we have seen to be Grimaldi's dazzling success at forming an important company, Mesonero's words that Grimaldi "found himself at the head of our stage, and engendered in it extremely important improvements, raised up and supported the great actors, especially Carlos Latorre, Romea and Guzmán; [and] made Concepción Rodríguez into an admirable actress,"[153] takes on richer meaning. Similar sentiments were echoed by Patricio de la Escosura, who credited Grimaldi's lead with changing the very nature of Spanish theatre: "Under his enlightened direction, our then decayed stage transformed itself rapidly, and there shone on it successively Concha Rodríguez, Matilde Díez, Teodora Lamadrid, la Llorente, Guzmán, Latorre, Luna, Romea, in short, the most notable Spanish actors who have flourished during the last forty years."[154] The situation improved somewhat as the 1833–4 season progressed,[155] but additional and even more startling changes were to be seen after April 1, 1834.

4

The Romantic stage

The death of Fernando VII, which forced the theatres to close and the actors to plead for subsistence payments during the period of mourning,[1] ironically brought renewed life to the Spanish stage. Following the King's death in September, 1833, his widow, María Cristina, launched a campaign to liberalize the country, or at least to liberate it from the worst excesses of its restrictive past. The Queen Regent, acting in the name of her daughter, Isabel, appointed new ministers and took steps toward the dismantling of the *ancien régime* and the creation of a more moderate form of government. In January, 1834, Francisco Martínez de la Rosa, an exiled liberal and author of plays which had previously encountered problems with the censors, took office as Prime Minister. He worked with the Queen Regent for the promulgation of his Estatuto Real, a document which annuled many of the absolutist policies of Fernando VII and moved toward the creation of a moderate constitutional monarchy. In June, an outbreak of cholera threatened to close the theatres again and Carlist victories in the north jeopardized the stability of the government.[2]

But on Christmas Day the famous amnesty for all liberal intellectuals in exile was proclaimed, and the country was soon enriched by the presence of thinkers and writers who had been forced to live outside its borders (many in London and Paris) for years. These new arrivals – Espronceda, the Duke of Rivas, Antonio Alcalá Galiano – in combination with the many brilliant men who had stayed in Spain – Larra, Zorrilla, Grimaldi, Quitana, Durán, Vega, Bretón, García Gutiérrez, Carnerero – initiated a period of excitement, radical change and intense debate not witnessed in that country for decades. This is the period generally referred to as that of Romanticism, and the passions generated by the new esthetic were expressed in both literary and political form. As Aristide Rumeau wrote, "We are on the eve of Romanticism."[3] As the 1834 season got under way, a sense of excitement was palpable in Madrid as intellectuals foresaw a veritable regeneration of their literary world. As one reviewer put it: "We shall not end this article without calling attention to the fact that the new theatre season has begun with a new comedy in each theatre, that authors have been given as many free tickets as they want, and that each newspaper has been sent two box seats free of charge. Even if we had no news of the improvements and new ideas that the new management is preparing, just this elegant way of announcing its arrival in literary circles would suffice to make us believe that the time for regeneration is also here for the theatre."[4]

The impresario was Carlos Rebollo, who had solicited the theatres the previous fall for a five-year period; his twenty-two clause contract contained the standard stipulations (AV: Contaduría 1-989-4). Rebollo had won the battle for ownership, and he was the titular impresario of the Príncipe from 1834 until 1836, but it was Grimaldi who, as manager, was the driving creative force behind the brilliant flourishing of the theatre during this period. The new direction taken by the theatres generated controversy, as much by its supporters as by its detractors. Those who supported Grimaldi's innovative plans included several of those individuals who had worked for and with him for years – Larra, writing from his place at *La Revista Española*, Bretón (at *El Universal* and *La Abeja*) and Ventura de la Vega (at the *Gaceta de los Tribunales*).[5]

Larra and Grimaldi

Perhaps the most representative voice of the new Spain was that of Mariano José de Larra. Larra, in spite of his Neoclassical education, his period of flirtation with Fernando's Royalist Volunteer troops and his initial resistance to the excesses of Romanticism, symbolized the difficult yet invigorating years of upheaval which marked the Romantic period.[6] He was the most acute observer of the political, social and literary scene, and his acerbic observations in the daily press provided a running commentary on the hopes and failures of an entire generation of Spanish intellectuals.

Larra lived a love/hate relationship with Spanish theatre. His love for it was deep and consistent, from his earliest incarnation as "El Duende Satírico del Día" (1828) to his suicide in February, 1837. "I have had vehement urges to write about the theatre for a long time," he wrote in "Mi nombre y mis propósitos" (*RE*, January 15, 1833).

He worked both inside the theatre (as a playwright and translator) and outside it (as a critic). He penned translations – an activity which he claimed to loathe – as well as an important Romantic play, *Macías*, and he socialized with the actors, playwrights, poets and politicians who made up the core of Romantic Madrid. His impassioned pleas for improvement and his uncompromisingly high standards earned him the enmity of many of those who saw themselves attacked in his articles, but his devastating wit and flair for satire insured that even his enemies read his articles. Mindful of his readers' responses to his barbs, he frequently turned his gaze upon himself, giving the appearance of accepting public chastisement while skewering his critics. In "No lo creo," for example, he mocked the negative reactions his articles of theatrical criticism engendered (his informant tells him that his critics are out to kill him) by accepting such stern rebukes as, "In the first place, they say that you are partial, that you only praise those who write well . . ." (*RE*, July 7, 1833). His real friends supported him, however, and one of the most formidable of that group of staunch supporters was Juan de Grimaldi.

Grimaldi exerted a substantial influence upon Larra, both in material matters and in matters of literature and art. As we have seen, it was Grimaldi who encouraged him to earn some money doing translations, Grimaldi who "opened the doors of the theatre to him,"[7] Grimaldi who rehearsed and staged *Macías*, Grimaldi who got him his job as critic of *La Revista Española*, Grimaldi who baptized him with his most famous pen name, "Fígaro," and Grimaldi who facilitated his membership in the Ateneo. It was Grimaldi to whom Larra alluded when he wrote, "one of my friends . . . wanted to convince me that we not only had theatre, but that I had talent for it . . . "[8] Their relationship began and grew in the "Parnasillo" *tertulia* at the Príncipe Café, in backrooms at the Príncipe Theatre and across the pages of the capital's newspapers.

Larra's greatest impact on the theatre came from the pen of his alter ego, "Fígaro." Larra began writing for *La Revista Española* (where Grimaldi, as we shall see, was an editor) in late 1832 and inherited the job as head of the section on "costumbres" (theatre criticism and commentary on manners) when Mesonero abandoned it in March of the following year. The demise of Larra's previous publication, *El Pobrecito Hablador* (the title of which he also used as his pen name) left him in need of a new literary persona. The discussions concerning his new name took place among the members of "El Parnasillo."

"Having abandoned the three or four that he had used before, he asked a group of friends, brought together at the Príncipe Café, to invest him with another more expressive and rhythmical name. Several individuals spoke, until the authoritative voice of Grimaldi pronounced the name of 'Fígaro', which Larra adopted enthusiastically . . ."[9] "Fígaro," as is well known, was the main character of a French drama by Beaumarchais, and although Mesonero, among others, objected to a foreign name for a Spanish newspaperman, Grimaldi pointed out that the name had delicious subversive possibilities: Beaumarchais' drama, *Le mariage de Fígaro* (in its Spanish reincarnation titled *Ingenio y virtud o el seductor confundido*), had been banned by Calomarde's censors in 1828 after just one performance, and its title character possessed the quick-witted rebelliousness which became one of Larra's hallmarks. What is more, an opera with a similar title, *Los dos Fígaros*, had likewise been prohibited.[10] In his article, "Mi nombre y mis propósitos," Larra highlighted Beaumarchais' character's qualities as a "charlatan, meddler and an inquisitive soul," while at the same time underscoring his tragic cynicism. The epigraph cites Beaumarchais' Fígaro: "Bored with myself, disgusted with others . . . superior to events; praised by these, blamed by those; helping in good times, putting up with the bad; making fun of idiots, standing up to fools . . . I force myself to laugh about it all in order not to cry."

Larra influenced Grimaldi, too, by providing an objective and steady stream of criticism of the dramas, actors, and performances with which his friend struggled as "dictator" of the stage. We know now, of course, that Grimaldi was not the officially-designated impresario of the theatres, but it was still his voice which was heard the loudest in decisions concerning acting style, repertory selections, stage design, and the overall direction of the theatre. He was "the foremost theatrical producer at the time in Madrid."[11] Grimaldi, "arbiter at that time of Madrid's theatrical scene,"[12] had made himself the most indispensable member of the capital's intellectual élite, with regard to the theatre, and his stimulus became even more important during the years of liberalization which followed the King's death.

Larra knew that the King's passing offered renewed hope for the Spanish stage. A distinguished Royal Commission composed of Manuel José Quintana, Martínez de la Rosa and Lista was named to study the theatres and to make recommendations about their future direction. Larra, ever ready to offer his opinions (whether solicited or not), insisted from the pages of *La Revista Española* that the theatres be returned to private hands. When the Ayuntamiento finally managed to turn the theatres over to a private concern in April 1834 – in fact, ordered to do so by the Minister of Public Works, Javier de Burgos ("the City Council cannot continue with the management of the theatres, which have destroyed the municipal treasury...")[13] – Larra greeted the decision with unaccustomed glee. Other voices were also raised to comment that "happily the new theatrical year has begun under the direction of a private concern, and as such it is in a better position to give a needed stimulus to our drama" and to outline once again the serious defects encountered in the old system. The future was viewed with unbridled optimism: "Withal we can affirm that the managers, convinced that if they do not please their audience they will be put out of business, are working ceaselessly to prepare new and varied performances, more interesting for their merit than for their number; without forgetting the rehabilitation of many plays that had been removed from the stage by a too rigid and whimsical or ridiculous censorship."[14]

The optimism was well-founded. Grimaldi, in charge of artistic direction at the Príncipe, began to stage dramas which would renovate Spanish taste and change the face of Spanish literature forever. The early and immediate smash success of that season was, of course, Grimaldi's staging of the new historical drama, *La conjuración de Venecia*, written by none other than the most important political figure in Madrid, Francisco Martínez de la Rosa. According to *La Revista Española* (April 21, 1834), plans had been made as early as January to stage this play, which it promised would be a highlight of the season. When it was staged on April 23 it was received with general acclaim and it remained on the boards for an impressive thirteen consecutive days.[15] Everything about it excited the critics and audiences: the actors – Concepción Rodríguez, Carlos Latorre, Julián Romea, Antonio Guzmán, Bruno Rodríguez and others of the Príncipe company – received special praise for their skillful interpretations; the sets painted by Blanchard were singled out for their "scrupulous accuracy" and beauty; the daring subject matter (as Larra wrote, "a conspiracy against tyranny will always create enormous interest in the theatre")[16] and the overall production, mounted "with a splendour unusual in these theatres" assured the play's success.[17] Larra, too, recognized the importance of this new undertaking. He praised the impresario's vision and voiced again his hope that original plays would be seen more frequently on Madrid's stages.

We would be unfair if we did not speak of the management. Many times we have indicated the high hopes we had for it, because we knew its possibilities well; however, we were not always believed. We appeal now to experience: tell us when our theatres have seen on stage such splendor and such historical accuracy in a drama; this tribute that the management pays, not to the name of the author – as much as he deserves it – since before taking his exalted position he had already laid the groundwork, but to Spanish theatre, makes us harbor high hopes. Five new sets in one day, and what sets! We can congratulate ourselves for having a painter of perspectives like Mr. Blanchard, and a management which is so protective of our literary heritage. We know that original compositions deserve such attention whenever their nature demands it.

Larra's praise of Blanchard's sets was not hollow flattery or a superficial attachment to spectacle (*that* could be had at the opera). Rather, it was a recognition of the fact that the sets were an integral part of the dramas. That is, the emotional effect of Romantic drama reached the audience through two senses – the visual and the auditory. Antecedents of Romantic drama – melodrama and the *comedia lacrimosa* – heightened the sentimental impact of their messages by staging scenes laden with visual information and by trying to produce tears in the eyes of their audiences (tears revealed the existence of a sensitive heart).[18] Romantic authors refined the melodramatic and tear-jerking elements of these plays but kept the heightened regard for visual impact. Grimaldi and Blanchard recognized this and struggled to maintain the link between visual and verbal theatre. "During this time we find that the theatre firms were very concerned with the effect of the sets, trying to eliminate anything that could destroy it."[19] *La conjuración* opened the theatres' doors to new possibilities.

Francisco Martínez de la Rosa (1787–1862) was hardly an unknown figure in Madrid's theatrical world.[20] His comedies – *Lo que puede un empleado* (1812), *La niña en casa y la madre en la máscara* (1821), *Los celos infundados* (1833) – had been performed with some regularity although little popular success. But the Madrid debut of his translation of Sophocles's tragedy, *Edipo* (1832), enjoyed a run of twenty-one performances[21] and, according to Carnerero, it was a proven money-maker ("*Edipo* makes money)."[22] We remember that it enjoyed a similar success when Grimaldi first staged it, starring Carlos Latorre, in Seville in 1830.[23] Martínez de la Rosa's other tragedy, *Aben*

Humeya, was written before *La conjuración de Venecia*, but did not have its Madrid debut until 1836.

Immediately following the initial run of *La conjuración* the Theatre Commission (Quintana, Martínez de la Rosa, Lista) dispatched its report, which contained some startling recommendations. It suggested nothing less than the complete reform of the theatres, including the abolition of ecclesiastical censorship and the resident censors, the freedom to perform certain plays prohibited in the past decade and (not surprisingly) the transfer of the theatres from municipal to private hands. Censorship was not abolished completely, however. A censorship commission was set up, headed by Nicasio Gallego, Quintana and others to oversee the production and publication of new plays, but the total effect was to lift much of the oppressive censorship which had prohibited hundreds of plays over the past decade from being seen on the stages of the capital's theatres.[24]

As Edgar Allison Peers points out, however, the arrival of Romanticism was neither complete nor sudden.[25] We have already witnessed the Madrid audience's growing attraction to melodrama and spectacle, especially after 1829, and as the 1834 season got under way many of the plays still being performed were translations from the French (Scribe was particularly popular) or rewrites by people like Bretón. But there was a heightened awareness of the new Romantic aesthetic and the theatres mounted a concerted effort to stage new Romantic dramas or to discover the Romanticism inherent in the classics of the Golden Age. The *Diario de Avisos* (October 4 and 6, 1834) defined one of the goals of the new managers as wanting to "show that our theatre has abounded in Romantic creations for over two centuries, pieces not inferior to those which recently have overtaken the French stage..."[26] Bretón's play, *Elena*, contained seeds of the new Romantic aesthetic and after *La conjuración* Larra himself would see one of his own original plays – *Macías* – performed under Grimaldi's direction.

Larra was pleased with the seriousness with which Grimaldi guided the actors through the rehearsals of *Macías*. He had always appreciated the stagings given to his translations ("to him I owed the fact that my first attempts, whether good or bad, were staged") and he was particularly happy that his friend gave *Macías* careful attention. "[To him I owed the fact] that the drama entitled *Macías*, to which I gave all the importance that any author gives his works, was performed and practiced with unusual skill."[27] The play, written in 1833 but prohibited by the censors (it was, like *La conjuración*, an assault against tyrannical aristocracy), did not reach the stage until September 24, 1834. Larra was paid 1,000 *reales* for it by his publisher, Manuel Delgado.[28]

Their friendship remained solid and Larra sought Grimaldi's guidance frequently. The former's sojourn in Paris in 1835 cut him off from the intellectual stimulation of his little group, a fact he wistfully recorded in a letter to Delgado (July 20, 1835):

Try to find out if Grimaldi is angry with me and why; no doubt it is because I have written to him in a very friendly and frank manner; the fact is that he has not answered me.

I ask you to do the same with Vega; ask him if he's upset that I have thought of him so much since my leaving Madrid; tell him that if he comes to Paris I could offer him one of the two beds that I have in an excellent room; . . . there are few things that upset me more than Vega's and Grimaldi's silence; it freezes my blood . . .[29]

Larra, known for his solitary spirit and cutting tongue, had few real friends, and his penchant for writing the truth as he saw it made him an easy target for the hostilities of those he criticized. The *Semanario Teatral* (April 28, 1834) suggested that Larra was trying to keep audiences away from the theatre. After discussing the financial arrangements of the 1834 season, it wrote: ". . . if all the concessions that this article speaks about are true, there will be a yearly profit of 500,000 *reales* for the management, supposing that the theatre is full every day. This supposition would be gratuitous and extravagant when there are Fígaros out there; since they are, we would reduce that figure by half . . ." Larra was also notoriously contentious with his editors.[30] Among his most famous public quarrels was the falling-out with Bretón, the result of petty jealousies and unfortunate allusions to one another in various literary works published in 1835. But its nature was less bitter than critics have led us to believe. By the time of the public reconciliation, which took place on January 30, 1836, the two had made tentative amends, for, as we shall see in a moment, Bretón signed a letter supporting Larra's admission to the Ateneo on the 2nd of the month. Rumeau quite rightly believed, "Because of Ferrer del Río, and in particular because of Molins, an exaggerated importance has been given to this incident."[31] Several accounts of the reconciliation have been told,[32] but the day after the "noble reconciliation" between Larra and Bretón, *La Revista Española* (January 31, 1836) gave a full accounting of it, and credited Grimaldi with taking the initiative toward bringing together two of his closest friends and associates. On the night in question Grimaldi, as was his custom, invited "several people noted for their social position and for their talent" – including Baron Taylor, who at the time was the manager of the Théâtre Français (and who befriended Larra during his months in Paris), Molins, Ventura de la Vega, Carnerero and of course the two principal antagonists – to dine in a private room at the Teatro de Oriente.[33] When Vega offered a cordial toast to his two old friends Bretón and Larra, "both men came forward in the space which separated them, and nearing one another, embraced . . ." The friendship, given a push by Grimaldi, was reinvigorated.

Earlier in the month, Grimaldi was instrumental in securing for Larra membership in the recently formed Ateneo de Madrid. He himself had been present when "all the political and literary notables of the period"[34] met on November 26, 1835 to inaugurate formally the new body. Some weeks earlier, on October 31, Grimaldi had been one of the "special guests" called in to participate in an Extraordinary Session which was meeting to discuss the design of the organization.[35] Larra, who did not return to Spain until mid-December, 1835, was therefore unable to be counted as a charter member, but within two weeks of his arrival his candidacy was presented to the Ateneo by his friend and protector, Grimaldi. Grimaldi penned a short letter on January 2, 1836 which read: "We have the honor of proposing that the Ateneo admit into its body Sr. D. Mariano José de Larra, whose circumstances are well known in this society." He then took it to Mesonero, Bretón,[36] Molins, Gil, Joaquín J. de Osuna, Joaquín Francisco Pacheco and José María Díaz for their signatures, and presented it to the Ateneo the same day.[37] Larra was the first individual proposed for membership following the closing of the charter rolls; a vote was taken at the meeting of January 4 (so new was the process that a voting box could not be found, and a delay was created while the officials sent a runner over to the Royal Economic Society for that organization's voting box). Larra's membership was approved.

Larra eventually became more and more disenchanted with the theatre, more and more frustrated by the petty bureaucratic squabbles which inhibited the creation of a high-quality national theatre. When Grimaldi left Spain suddenly in August, 1836, and the theatres reverted once again to the hands of the actors, no director/manager with sufficient skill or vision could be found to take Grimaldi's place. Larra viewed the situation as desperate and his pessimism was total.

One of his last comments on the state of the theatre in Madrid was published in "Horas de invierno" (*El Español*, December 25, 1836).

Will the theatre be the refuge of our glory? The theatre, without actors or audience, the national theatre, which as a final insult and to the endless disgrace and degradation of the country, is already just a branch of opera and a filler for those nights when the first lady is hoarse? Because it is important to say it; there must exist people who do not know it; the national theatre no longer has a management nor a proper direction; the national theatre has been given over to the management of the opera company, [which] has had the goodness to gather it up moribund from the hands of the actors who can no longer support it.

His daily contact with Grimaldi – one of the few stabilizing forces in his constant battle for excellence and rationality – was over. Slowly, the other pillars which sustained his confidence in Spanish reality (his faith in his country's political future, his relationship with Dolores Armijo, his faith in himself) crumbled around him. In February 1837, he removed the pistol from his infamous "yellow box" and killed himself.

The triumph of Concepción Rodríguez

Concepción Rodríguez's long years of playing hundreds of roles in thousands of productions on stages in the capital and all over the country paid off handsomely as Romanticism gained a foothold in Spain.[38] She had always been rather popular, as we have seen, and had received praise for her performances in the comedies and tragedies staged in the theatres before the King's death (she acted in most of Larra's translations).[39] At times her performances had been received with frenzied acclaim, as Carnerero's comments on her June 1831, performance in Dionisio Solís's *Camila* demonstrate. She had just returned from her year in Seville and the Madrid audiences were delighted with her presence on their stage once again:

It has been a while since we have seen such a complete performance. Caprara, Latorre and Concepción Rodríguez: here is a reunion that could only produce good results. The actress has distinguished herself in an outstanding manner: the applause has been explosive; deserved, very deserved; a true tribute to her sensitivity, her intelligence, and her wonderful ability. If Miss Rodríguez continues to demonstrate such examples of her progress, even though it only be granted from here on, she will be the *diamond* of the Spanish stage. This lovely title, even if granted only from today on, will not be untimely or undeserved.[40]

Carnerero's prediction would be fulfilled: the advent of Romanticism provided her with some of the most moving and passionate characters she would ever have a chance to play.

Her technique and acting style had improved over the years and she had become more comfortable in her roles. She had long since abandoned the artificial posing, copious sobbing and bombastic oratory that passed for acting in Madrid's theatres. "Rodríguez hated the overemotional ambience and was bothered by the intolerable monotony of the verses. She understood that that was not art and if it was, it was only an inferior art; that scenic representation demanded more noble and more human methods."[41] At times she fell back upon the rhythmic cadences of the past ("that measured cadence, that type of sing-song that comes from constantly leaning on the same tone in the endings of the phrases")[42] but for the most part she escaped the pitfalls of her youth. Larra praised her performances in plays such as *Un novio para la niña*, *Siempre*, and *Carolina*,[43] and of her work in Ducange's *El colegio de Tonnington* he wrote: "The performance has been perfect on Miss Rodríguez's part."[44] Grimaldi's staging of the play received mixed reviews – positive comments from his friend Larra ("this drama was well done on stage") and negative notices from Azcona in the *Semanario Teatral* ("the defects of the scenic direction are so numerous and so obvious that they jump out at you"). The *Semanario*, never very favorably inclined to Grimaldi's endeavors, reserved its harshest criticism for Concepción: "All the actors have done their job; but the audience has noticed that the role of Miss Rodríguez belonged to Miss Díez, since it was more in keeping with her age and physiology ... The audience wishes that things be as close to the truth as possible, and Miss Rodríguez is not up to playing young girls any more."[45]

There was some truth in these criticisms and, as Patricio de la Escosura remembered it some years later, much of the blame rested on the intense schedule the actors were forced to play. "First-rate actors, who do not, nor have they ever, abound in Spain or elsewhere, are forced to squander their talents, allow me to say so. I have seen Miss Rodríguez play successively in *Camila*, *Sonámbula*, *Primeros amores*, *Edipo*, *Zorra candilazo*, and work finally, almost daily and in all genres ennobling them all with her admirable talent, but often vulgarizing it, demeaning her artistic talent . . ."[46] Other reviewers were more gracious. *La Gaceta de los Tribunales*, in direct contradiction to the

Semanario, found her to be "the very truth" in *El Colegio de Tonnigton* (especially in the emotional scene in the sixth act when Adela – played by Concepción – dies in her husband's arms). In general she received praise for her work. Even Ferrer, a severe critic of the filth and disorganization of Madrid's theatres and a vocal opponent of the worst actors (he considered the beloved Antonio Guzmán to be "boring")[47] found kind words to write about Concepción. Larra, too, normally an acerbic critic of the wild gesturing and exaggerated miming which passed for acting, consistently praised Concepción's performances. In an otherwise execrable production of Quintana's *Pelayo*, Larra singled out Concepción's acting and extended the praise to her attention to period costumes:

Miss Rodríguez has also been the only one who in the midst of the paucity of facts that exist concerning our ancient dress has known how to approach historic truth. And if the costume she has worn is not pleasant nor pretty she should be praised that much more; few actresses want to sacrifice their good appearance to scenic accuracy and truth; this presupposes a love for art and a great desire to please, more than as a woman, as an actress.[48]

Concepción had not just become better – she had also become more influential. Grimaldi was not the only "tyrant" working in the theatre: his wife possessed the power to postpone or cancel plans for productions which were not to her liking or in line with her current interests. *Ni el tío ni el sobrino*, a play written by Espronceda and Ros de Olano, was a case in point. The play, composed in 1833 but left unperformed due to problems with the ecclesiastical censors, was finally passed by censors at the beginning of the 1834 season. Grimaldi planned to have it performed at the Príncipe in April 1834. But Concepción, along with Antonio Guzmán, refused to prepare for it and it was sent over to the Cruz Theatre for its debut. Espronceda, writing to his collaborator, complained that "I have not been able to get them to do it at the Príncipe, since neither Guzmán nor Concha wanted to do it. Later, the management fixed the day of its debut for some days before *La conjuración*, and Grimaldi did what he could. But the laziness of the actors and their slowness in learning the lines delayed it, which there was no way to avoid."[49] The actors' reasons were logical – they were preparing for the much-awaited premiere of *La conjuración de Venecia* and found it difficult to memorize additional plays – but their actions demonstrated their ability to influence repertory decisions.[50] Its run at the less prestigious Cruz Theatre was undistinguished and the performances by the actors of that second-rate company left Espronceda frustrated.

Everything has been miserable; the times, the Cruz Theatre where they performed it and the audience, which on the first night did not understand the play ... While I have no quarrel with Galindo, who played the role of D. Martín, with Luna who played D. Carlos, or with López who played the colonel, Bravo played the daughter very badly and Cubas didn't know his lines ... Valero, the good actor's brother, played his part as a dunce rather than as a madcap and ruined the role of Eugenio.[51]

Meanwhile, Concepción enjoyed clamorous applause in *La conjuración*, a triumph she no doubt relished for several reasons. First, it indicated her continued acceptance on the stage. Second, it opened the possibilities for new successes in a theatre world not nearly so restricted as the one she had grown up in. And third, it shored up her place as Madrid's "first lady of the stage" at a time when, just weeks before, Matilde Díez's debut had caused a sensation among critics and spectators alike.

For her performances in numerous roles, newspapers and memories were filled with laudatory comments on her superb acting skills. *El Universal* (April 2, 1834) praised her in Bretón's *Un novio para la niña* in these terms: "The performance was good. Miss Rodríguez showed love, innocence, timidity in a way that is never seen except when she does it; in the sixth scene of the second act she pronounced those words of indignation in a way that is never heard except when she says them." Molins remembered her performance in Grimaldi's production of Delavigne's *Los hijos de Eduardo* (October 4, 1835), in which she surpassed the performance given by Mlle Mars, the French actress for whom Delavigne wrote the part.[52] She earned additional laurels for her work as Leonor in Rivas's *Don Alvaro o la fuerza del sino*, one of the most shocking works ever seen on the Spanish stage. Not as popular as *La conjuración de Venecia*, it was nevertheless much discussed.[53] Concepción played the role to perfection, capturing the sweetness of Leonor while maintaining the high passion and intensity of the heroine's conflicts. "Concepción Rodríguez created the role of Leonor ... reciting the verses with an incomparable sweetness and playing the character with unique mastery, not free from ingenuity, but lacking all those elements that can make ingenuity degenerate into an absence of art, into vulgarity and into foolishness."[54] Alongside her were Antonio Guzmán as Melitón, José García Luna as Alvaro, Matilde Díez as Preciosilla, and Julián Romea as Alfonso de Vargas.

Romantic dramas did not bring triumphs for all the actors in the companies. In a not-too-subtle effort to reduce costs and to banish the weaker members of the companies (or those who had passed their peak of usefulness), Rebollo and Grimaldi forced some into retirement by assigning them secondary roles. They banished others to act in the provinces. These acts initiated clamors of protest from the editors of the *Semanario Teatral* (May 26, 1834):

The public notices with disapproval that the direction adopted by the management is moving toward depriving us little by little of many hard-working and well-known actors, who are no doubt being prepared for retirement or for ostracism in the provinces. Miss Baus, the oldest first actress of Madrid, whom one can always recommend for her artistic talents, is seen rarely on the stage. Lately she has been relegated to a secondary role in *El tejedor de Segovia*, a comedy rewritten by Mr. Bretón, and which will probably not make it past its first performance, for reasons which we shall point out when we review it; that is, after its failure. Miss Baus saw this coming: she asked for a copy of the play: she saw that they were trying to humiliate her, and she was determined not to permit it.

Antera Baus shared her fate with Concepción Samaniego, Catalina Bravo, and other minor players. The *Semanario*'s protests fell on deaf ears. Two years later, Larra commented on what he judged to be an "error" committed by Rebollo: "The management made a bad move in our judgment, above all concerning the younger players, because for a business just beginning its run, which had five years to look forward to, it should have been more careful with the young people it was forming. . . ."[55]

Acting was not the actors' only gainful employment. By royal consent they were also empowered to function as ticket sellers, ticket takers, and ushers in the theatres. Each job garnered a few extra *reales* for them and most actors sought some additional work. Concepción was no exception. In April, 1834, she solicited – and received – permission to take over a position in the ticket booth left vacant when the previous holder of it died – a man named Manuel Muntéis (AHN: Consejos 11.387, n. 24). Guzmán, García Luna, and Matilde Díez held similar positions, which were distributed by the Queen Regent on a patronage basis, "in payment for services rendered to the Spanish stage," and enjoyed for life. Even when the individuals moved out of Madrid, or indeed out of the country, they were empowered to maintain these positions, subcontracting them out to resident members of the company. As was to be expected, numerous irregularities occurred with ticket sales and hence periodic decrees were issued in an attempt to eliminate abuses. The actors had to struggle to maintain their traditional rights. As late as 1848, Concepción Rodríguez, Guzmán, and García Luna wrote to Queen Isabel concerning these payments.[56]

Concepción Rodríguez retired from the stage in April 1836, at the height of her popularity, less than four weeks after her stunning triumph as Leonor in García Gutiérrez's *El trovador*. She was thirty-four years old. In *El trovador* she once again played alongside Latorre, Romea, Matilde Díez and, in the role of Azucena, Bárbara Lamadrid.[57] She had reached the top ranks of her profession, but exhaustion and illness (the same nervous tension which she had suffered in 1826) – and four young children – forced her to adopt a less strenuous way of life. She took her final bows before the Madrid audience in *Catalina Howard*, which was played as a benefit for her. Larra, commenting on her need to "retire from the stage because of her diminished state of health," found that "she has convinced us that no one can replace her in good diction and in the surprising truth with which she has played several scenes; her resurrection above all seemed to us to be excellent, as well as the dream scene before the king."[58] Her health had declined seriously. According to her doctor (Manuel Codorniu, the man who treated most of the actors), she was suffering from gastro-intestinal problems which affected her with bouts of dizziness, nausea, vomiting, and "violent pains" (AV: Secretaría 2-476-1). Grimaldi claimed that she had planned to step down in early 1835, but had remained on the stage one more year in order to "follow the repeated insistence of the management" (letter dated February 27, 1836; AV: Secretaría 2-476-1). Ironically, in Grimaldi's view it was the intensity of the demands on her that jeopardized her health, "because the performance of dramas like [Victor Hugo's] *Lucrecia Borgia*, *Angelo*, and others of a similar nature have aggravated the attacks to such an extreme that a cure is unlikely and her very existence is put into jeopardy," and her colleagues García Luna, Latorre, and Guzmán (who became the new owners of the theatres on April 16, 1836, following Rebollo's collapse)[59] concurred.

When circumstances forced Grimaldi to make a rapid exit from Spain in August 1836, Concepción stayed behind with the children. Their family consisted of Clotilde, who was at that time just over ten years old; Odilia, four; and Leopoldina, nine months. In addition,

Concepción was pregnant with Cecilia, born on December 28 of that year.[60] The *Eco del Comercio* (January 1, 1837) expressed hope that she would remain behind, and eventually return to the stage.

We are very pleased to know that our continuous complaints regarding the decadence of our theatres has produced some effect, since the management is trying to correct the defects which have been produced by its disorganized administrative system. We have been assured that Mr. Romea, Miss Díez, and Miss Josefa Valero have already been contracted for next season ... It also seems as though Concepción Rodríguez will be returning to the stage, along with other well-known actors.

But she had intended to join her husband in Paris all along and requested permission to do so (and to have her retirement payments issued there) in February 1837, just days before her friend Larra's suicide.[61] Her petition was approved and she was awarded the right both to collect her pension in Paris and to collect her wages as a ticket dispatcher. In Paris she would personally report to the Spanish Consulate on a regular basis, certify her residence in the French capital and swear that "she is neither under contract in this capital nor does she perform in any of its theatres" (AV: Contaduría 4-171-1). This she did throughout the 1840s, when she collected a little more than 500 *reales* per month.[62] Little is known of her life in Paris. From time to time their old friends came to visit – Latorre in 1838,[63] Ventura in 1853[64] – but her duties as a mother of five (they had a son as well) and wife of one of the most prestigious members of French society occupied most of her time. She died in 1859.

Masked balls and troubadours: Grimaldi's final year in Madrid

The twelve months before his exit from the capital in August 1836, were among Grimaldi's most active ever. He was deeply immersed in producing plays and keeping excitement high in the theatres. He was writing forceful and thoughtful articles for *La Revista Española* (where he was one of the editors), participating in the organization of the Ateneo, working to get Larra into that group and to calm the fires of hostility which had scorched Larra's relationship with Bretón, writing again for the theatre (*Lo que es y lo que será*, performed in December 1835) and enjoying his status as "new father" for the third time. In addition, he worked to bring *El trovador* to the stage and produced a series of masked balls during the pre-Lenten season the likes of which had never been seen in Spain before.

Masked balls had been popular in the capital for years. When the theatres prepared to close for Lent, masked balls were among the few diversions tolerated by the authorities. With the changing spirit and intensification of the Romantic mode, these masked balls took on a new meaning and their popularity increased. Masks and the carnival atmosphere were merged with the Romantic aesthetic, which lent itself to the mystery and duplicity suggested by the mask. "Costumbrista" articles on the masked ball appeared with frequency in the newspapers and short stories were published which used the masked ball as their settings.[65] The Minister of Public Works, Javier de Burgos, had even penned a drama, *El baile de máscaras*, which played in Granada in 1832[66] and Bretón wrote a lively verse story, "Recuerdos de un baile de máscaras," in which he described and satirized the public's interest in this diversion.[67] We need only to remember Act 4 of *La conjuración de Venecia* and Larra's response to it ("The Piazza San Marco, the center of public activity during carnival, is where the fourth act is set. We see several masked conspirators dispersed among the crowd, waiting for the stroke of midnight. There is nothing more clever, nor more dramatic, than an entire act which takes place during the merriment of carnival, when the spectator expects revolution and death to break out at any moment from the carefree and complacent jubilation of a crazed crowd")[68] to witness the appeal such scenes had in certain circles.

In the early 1820s the masked ball was considered a "danger to morals and an incentive to vice"[69]; frequently the excesses generated by the balls had serious consequences for the health and safety of the participants.[70] For some ten years (1822–32) masked balls were banned in the capital, although they were often held furtively in private salons (even the King's relatives attended them without his knowledge or permission). According to Zorrilla, "The King was afraid of them out of fear of conspirators; the authorities were afraid of them out of fear of disturbances; the clergy loathed them out of fear of clandestine retributions against them; but the public went wild for them, because they were prohibited."[71] When they were again permitted openly they were greeted enthusiastically (although they were not always successful)[72] and the authorities issued strict statements regulating the conduct of those in attendance (most of which were blithely ignored).[73]

Even though Grimaldi found himself locked out of direct control of the Príncipe and the Cruz, his instincts as an impresario must have told him that mounting some masked balls in the 1836 season would be a good business venture. In order to capitalize on the frenzy for this type of participatory spectacle, Grimaldi, even as he worked as manager at the Príncipe, planned a series of balls to be held independently at the recently reconstructed Teatro de Oriente (Rebollo was planning his own balls at the Príncipe and the Cruz).

Grimaldi was not unmindful of the conjunction between the theatre and the theatrical nature of these masked balls, which, as we shall see, were reviewed in the daily press as though they were theatrical performances. Tickets could be purchased by subscription, as if they were theatre tickets.[74] The line between life and art frequently blurred during the Romantic period, the one often imitating the other. Grimaldi capitalized on this and elaborated a way to encourage it while at the same time profiting financially from it.

Grimaldi's flair for drama expressed itself in his conception and execution of the masked balls. Not content to put on just another cycle of these events, he made plans to present the most spectacular balls ever seen in Madrid. In January 1836, he asked for and received permission to mount a masked ball at the Teatro de Oriente (which would evolve into the Teatro Real).[75] In a note of intriguing irony the City Council insisted that Grimaldi pay the traditional service fee to Rebollo, impresario of the Cruz and Príncipe, the same fee which Grimaldi had insisted upon, and received, during his season as impresario. He was also asked to put up 1,000 *reales* per dance for the costs of policing by the National Guard, and – a point of eternal contention in the theatres – provide free tickets for certain police officials.[76]

His initial plan consisted of three balls (he eventually gave seven),[77] staged in a salon that would be the most sumptuous possible. In his request to the municipal authorities, written from his bed (he was taken ill some days before), Grimaldi carefully detailed his ideas. He described exactly how many torches he would install, where they would be placed, how and through which doors the guests would enter the theatre, where and how tickets would be sold, how many guards would be needed to control the traffic and to maintain order, where and how the coatroom attendants would be placed and so on. The City Council's traditional resistance to Grimaldi's ideas did not apply to his plans for these balls and the plan was approved with unaccustomed speed. Grimaldi moved quickly to see to the many details of his plan. He had to rent and prepare the rooms, organize the orchestra (Carnicer was hired to conduct), contract the workers, lay rugs, install fourteen magnificent new mirrors, buy and install thirty chandeliers and hundreds of candles, organize the meals and acquire tables, chairs, plates, glasses, silverware, and linens. This all had to be taken care of immediately, since time was of the essence. There was a great deal of competition in Madrid for the attention (and the money) of partygoers. Competing masked balls were being planned at nine other locations (including the bull ring). Madrid was swept up in a frenzy of masked balls, and Grimaldi moved quickly to turn that frenzy into profit: his functions were destined to become the most anxiously awaited ("these so desperately awaited dances"),[78] impressive, and controversial of them all.

Grimaldi rented the Teatro de Oriente, a beautiful building which had been under construction for a number of years and which would, according to *La Revista Española* (January 26, 1836), finally be used for something. ("After six years of work we have the pleasure of seeing the splendid room planned in the theatre for dances and concerts almost finished.") The huge room in the back, designed for painting curtains and sets, and measuring 130′ by 44′, was ideal for public functions.[79] Although one reviewer found the place somewhat "eccentric," it was unusual and exciting and it promised an elegance previously unmatched in the capital. (It was in these rooms that Grimaldi "staged" the reconciliation dinner between Larra and Bretón.)

The first ball got under way on Friday night, January 22, and the dancers partied from 11.00 p.m. until dawn. In order to make a sizable profit and to cover his high start-up costs, Grimaldi took the unprecedented step of charging 50 *reales* per ticket. This was an enormous sum and considerably higher than such tickets had cost in the past. He was free to set whatever price he chose (unlike the rules which prohibited impresarios from raising ticket prices in the theatres) and he calculated that fifty was both necessary and fair. The average cost of a ball ticket until that time had been 20 *reales*; a few had cost as much as 30 and many cost only 8 *reales* per ticket. The sum of fifty *reales* was an audaciously high and risky one. When he announced his prices there was a considerable storm of protest in the press and much resistance on the part of the ticket buying public. Immediately following the first dance, Larra, in an unsigned article in *El Español*, commented with his accustomed irony:

To the inconvenience of going, we have added the inconvenience of getting the ticket: we don't mean to say that it is a Herculean task to find it: there is a good, well-placed box-office and attractive tickets; but if it is not a Herculean task, it is certainly an expensive one. Please note that it is not we who make the observation, but rather we have heard it repeated everywhere, and if all the people going to the ball agree that it is expensive, we don't know who can be persuaded otherwise. This also does not mean that it is expensive relative to the sumptuousness and the appointments of the room, nothing of the sort; it is even worse than what is being said about this, since it is affirmed that it is unconditionally expensive.[80]

Even Larra, an intimate friend and confidant of Grimaldi, thought the price excessive, and he accused his friend of a certain snobbery. He could not understand why the price needed to be so high and suggested that part of Grimaldi's reason was to keep people from having to "mingle with the riffraff." He suggested that if Grimaldi thought he needed to charge such high prices to cover his very high costs, then it would have made more economic sense to sell 3,000 tickets at 25 *reales* each than half that number at double the cost. "This is a question that we shall stay out of because the management will say that, having noted the singular steps taken by decent people in these liberal times in Madrid not to mingle with the riffraff, that is, with the people (as anyone has been able to see ever since there are masked balls), he has established a price which will impede any mixing of this sort."[81] He was probably not far from the mark, but Grimaldi was also motivated by economics, as will soon become evident.

The high price set for the balls did keep many people away and it looked as though Grimaldi's newest endeavor would be a failure. Both the first and the second balls attracted much smaller crowds than Grimaldi had expected. A reviewer at *La Revista Española* (February 2, 1836) noted that the second ball "has been like the first in the few people who attended. It will be a great shame if these balls do not manage to achieve in attendance what they achieve in magnificence. The 50 *reales*; those cruel 50 *reales* are to blame . . . because without a crowd a masked ball, in which confusion, shoving and the shriek of conversation are the very body and soul, is worthless." Grimaldi maintained that the high costs of the elegant surroundings necessitated his high price of 50 *reales* and he insisted that "the price of the tickets will remain at 50 *reales*, since it is absolutely impossible to lower it now or for the coming balls, due to the immense cost of each one."[82] But faced with a sizable financial loss due to poor ticket sales, he did reduce the price for the third ball, scheduled for Sunday, February 7.

The strategy worked. Such expectation and controversy had formed over the first two balls, the reputed elegance of the rooms at the Teatro de Oriente, and the shocking cost of the tickets, that when the price was reduced to 30 *reales tout* Madrid turned out for Grimaldi's spectacle. Some 2,000 revelers showed up for this third ball, creating traffic jams and other problems that neither Grimaldi nor the National Guard had foreseen. As reported in *La Abeja* (February 9, 1836), the reduction in price produced the sizable crowd, "which we calculate to be no fewer than 2,000 people; the salon and the side rooms were, as they say, packed to the gills . . . in a word, it has been the best public ball that has so far been given in Madrid." *La Revista Española* (February 9, 1836) added that "all of the public's indifference changed into a need and a desire to attend." The crush was intense both inside and outside the theatre, and "never has there been seen a greater number of carriages grouped together outside any function." The number of people was from five to twenty times that of normal attendance at any one ball. (Casanova reported that in 1768 two hundred people were considered a sizable crowd for a masked ball.)[83] When few people attended one of the competition's balls two days earlier, *La Abeja* erroneously attributed the scant attendance to "the night of disturbances and alarm" (the dissolution of the legislature by Mendizábal) which rocked the Madrid political establishment.[84] Such figures also contradict *La Abeja*'s statement that "there is less interest in the masked balls."[85] Nothing could have been further from the truth.

Grimaldi's balls became an unparalleled success, but success brought with it its usual problems. Dancing (never at any rate the prime function of the see-and-be-seen masked balls) was out of the question. Larra complained of the horrible mob of people that one needed to push through ("the attendance . . . was such that you could not even walk"),[86] and *La Revista Española* noted that the opulence of the balls was counterbalanced by such disagreeable things as "abundant" streams of wax which dripped down on everyone from the chandeliers, the disorderly heap of capes and shawls which never managed to be stored properly in the coatroom, the lack of adequate seating (the reviewer referred to some people who left at 7:00 a.m. without having sat down the whole night) and the poor and dreadfully slow food service (some people ordered something at eat at 2:00 a.m. and were not served until 5:00 a.m.; other nights, the caterers ran out of food at 3:00 a.m. and guests frequently engaged in bidding wars for the little food that remained). After the sixth dance, held on February 15, Luciano Pérez Acevedo, "El Momo," claimed in *La Revista Española* (February 16, 1836) that since Grimaldi could not fit all of Madrid into the Oriente (he apparently sold many more tickets than he was permitted), he tried to fit the Oriente into Madrid; that is "there were as many people outside the theatre as inside."[87] For "El Momo," the whole function was comparable to Hell itself: "that hell . . . that crush . . . that pneumatic machine . . . that steam bath." Other balls may have received better reviews, but the people came to Grimaldi's.

The newspapers were not the only places where complaints were voiced and reforms demanded. The office of the Civil Governor wrote to the magistrate offering suggestions for the improvement of public order at Grimaldi's balls. In the mind of the magistrate the issue of civil obedience in the capital was related to Grimaldi's functions and depended on the order and calm of the masked balls: "The inconvenience suffered by the people upon entering and leaving the Teatro de Oriente last night and even inside the rooms themselves, caused by the excessive attendance that filled them up, aroused a general impatience demanding a solution, which if it is only fair on the one hand, it is necessary and urgent on the other, in order to insure that public calm not be shattered" (AV: Corregimiento 1-68-59; Desfrétières, p. 291). Decrees were issued in an attempt to establish some order. For example, the magistrate ordered that a maximum of 3,500 tickets be sold (still an inconceivably high number), that persons in possession of counterfeit tickets be arrested, and that any tickets sold in excess of the stipulated number bring stiff fines down on the impresario.

Did such negative comments affect the popularity of Grimaldi's balls? We are surprised to read that the very reviewer who compared them to Hell went on to write that the dance he attended was "without a doubt the most magnificent, the most sumptuous and brilliant dance of its kind ever known in this capital." The people kept coming: Grimaldi's masked balls turned out to be the hit of the season and, as we have just seen, precautions had to be taken against the counterfeiting of tickets (scalpers also did a brisk business). As *El Artista* pointed out, Grimaldi's affairs were not only the best but they were also so chic that it was impossible to accommodate all the people who wished to attend, even when enough tickets were sold to crush people into "every room, every hallway and even all the staircases."[88]

Grimaldi's seven masked balls were elegant, expensive, controversial, and tremendously popular. They set the tone and standard for future masked balls in the capital.[89] That he made money on them, despite his repeated insistence on "the considerable losses which [I have] suffered" (AV: Consejos 11.387, n. 109; Desfrétières, p. 292) can be deduced from several reasons. First, he offered to pay ten times more to the National Guard than was originally asked of him (10,000 *reales* as opposed to 1,000) if the Civil Governor would grant him permission to give an extra ball on Sunday. We know from his contract disputes with the City Council over the theatres that Grimaldi never willingly raised his "contribution" for such activities unless he was forced to do so or unless he perceived a tangible gain for himself. Second, the huge numbers of tickets sold multiplied by the cost of each ticket supposes that Grimaldi could have received between 60,000 and 100,000 *reales per ball*, at a time when his wife's entire *annual* retirement income was only slightly more than 8,000 *reales*. Just five years previously, we know his own salary had been 22,000 *reales per year*. Even presupposing high expenses, it can be surmised that Grimaldi made substantial amounts of money on this endeavor. *La Revista Española* (February 16, 1836) jokingly suggested that Prime Minister Mendizábal could retire the public debt and raise funds for the military by giving a masked ball at the Oriente on the same terms as those given by Grimaldi.

As Susan Kirkpatrick has noted, "the masked balls . . . constituted a supreme event in the social life of the upper and middle classes of Madrid. Perhaps that is why the newspapers of the period commented on the public balls as if they were theatrical pieces."[90] The balls were semi-social dramas presented without a proscenium arch, and the actors were the people themselves. The balls were treated as theatre and their runs were extended if they were hits (Grimaldi originally planned three balls, then five; he added the extras as they became popular and profitable). Grimaldi intensified their theatrical nature during the Romantic period. The vogue for masked balls increased as the Romantic era progressed, but never again would Madrid witness the sumptuousness and frenzy created by Grimaldi's.[91] Larra believed that "El mundo todo es máscaras" (*El Pobrecito Hablador*, March 4, 1833) and, at least in 1836, Grimaldi may have agreed.

During Lent itself, when masked balls were strictly prohibited, Grimaldi organized philharmonic concerts at the Oriente, but it was at the beginning of the new theatrical season when he and his wife shared in one of the greatest triumphs of the Romantic stage – the debut of García Gutiérrez's *El trovador*.

The story of García Gutiérrez's meteoric rise to fame following the clamorous reception of *El trovador* on March 1, 1836, is too well known to bear repeating here. But Grimaldi's involvement in the young author's career is not widely known. García Gutiérrez had arrived in Madrid in September, 1833, determined to become a playwright.[92] He immediately showed one of his first efforts, a comedy entitled *Una noche de baile*, to the manager of the Príncipe Theatre – Juan de Grimaldi – whom he had met at the "Parnasillo." Others at the Parnasillo (especially Larra, Espronceda, and Vega) had read the play and thought it could be produced, but Grimaldi resisted, perhaps finding the play without sufficient merit. However, he did find merit in the play's author and succeeded in securing a job for him on the staff of *La Revista Española*. He also conscripted him for his army of translators and García Gutiérrez managed to scrape out a living with newspaper pieces and translations. When he finally wrote the play that would make him famous, he tried once again to enlist Grimaldi's aid in staging it. "After several unsuccessful attempts that were not well received by the theatrical directors . . . he made the happy decision, inspired by the success of *Macías* and *Don Alvaro*, dragged along by the revolutionary pulse that those two works initiated, of writing a 'chivalresque' drama and calling it *El trovador*."[93] This time Grimaldi agreed and moved to bring *El trovador* to the stage, but it was the acting company which now opposed the idea. It looked as though the play would remain, as had many of his other plays, unproduced.[94] But Grimaldi, in conjunction with Antonio Guzmán and Espronceda,[95] persuaded the company to accept the play as a benefit performance for Guzmán. García Gutiérrez had to be brought back into the capital (in frustration, he had signed up for military service) for opening night. Finally, it was performed and the rest, as they say, is theatrical history. Concepción Rodríguez brought the author out onto the stage for the thunderous applause he received, while the other actors – Matilde Díez, Romea, Latorre, Lamadrid – beamed with pleasure.[96]

Literary Romanticism had triumphed in Madrid and it seemed as though Grimaldi's immense prestige could only increase even further. He was the best-known and most influential producer of his times, organizer of stunningly popular masked balls, author of the still popular *La pata de cabra*, powerful editor of the important *La Revista Española*, "oracle" of the literary figures of his day and a friend to many of the most important people at court. His fortunes seemed secure, but his house of power was made of cards. The liberal politicians and intellectuals who had initially supported the regency of María Cristina had become split over the years into two groups, the *exaltados* (or *progresistas*), who demanded freedom and progress immediately, and the *moderados*, who opted for a more gradual – and in their view, more solid – change. Grimaldi had set his faith in the more moderate approach and had cast his lot with María Cristina. When the rapid change of government in the summer of 1836 swept Istúriz and the *moderados* out of power and threatened the Queen Regent's authority (the famous episode at La Granja, on August 13), Grimaldi's political allegiances forced him, along with numerous others (Rivas and Alcalá Galiano among them), to flee the country. By the end of August, leaving his wife, children, and friends behind, he had crossed the border to return to his native country, France.

Such was Grimaldi's stature that newspapers on both sides of the Pyrenees commented on his movements. In Paris, *Le Constitutionnel* (September 17, 1836) reproduced a letter from Grimaldi in which he noted that news of his arrival had preceded him and in which he made reference to the (he claimed) incorrect assumption that he was acting as a courier between María Cristina and her uncle, King Louis-Philippe of France. He claimed that his recent actions in Spain, and his subsequent departure had no political ramifications whatsoever.[97] His protestations, however, rang false. The flurry of gossip which connected Grimaldi's trip to France to political motives ("Recent French papers speak with great emphasis of the arrival in France of Mr. Grimaldi, whom they suppose to be the bearer of an autograph letter from Her Majesty the Queen Regent, protesting the alleged outrages at La Granja"[98]) had much basis in fact, as we shall see in chapter 5. Desfrétières has pointed out that "the coincidence between the revolt at La Granja and his departure a few days later is still very troublesome."[99] Grimaldi explained his actions unconvincingly. Surely, his proclaimed love for France and desire to return after his fifteen year absence ("I have returned to France because France is my homeland, because I ardently wish to see it after fifteen years of absence") were not so strong as to precipitate the abandonment of his pregnant wife and three small daughters. Grimaldi was an intensely political man who was passionately linked to the Moderate cause. His identification with that cause was likewise well known ("my well known devotion to the cause of the Queen"), and he had publicly defended it in a series of influential articles published in *La Revista Española* in 1835 and 1836, as we shall see.

In Madrid, the newspaper *El Castellano* – indignant with the French suggestion that María Cristina had been coerced into accepting the Constitution of 1812 (!) – picked up the story and gave a brief synopsis of Grimaldi's life in the capital, charging him with being a destabilizing force in liberal Spain. "When Minister Istúriz took over the reins of power to do away once and for all with the last of national freedom, Mr. Grimaldi, echoing a certain faction, wrote those long and famous articles signed 'A' and inserted in the *Revista*, which heaped such venom and acrimony on the Spanish liberal party, and which he maligned and falsely accused of being 'Mendizabalistas' . . ." (*El Castellano*, September 26, 1836; Desfrétières, p. 298). Larra, who had been specifically mentioned in this article, rallied to Grimaldi's defense, but underlined that their relations had been "purely theatrical," never political.[100] He separated himself from the political content of the *Revista* in his days as theatre critic, and wrote that from his literary relations with Grimaldi "was born a friendship which had nothing to do with politics," a friendship which Larra was proud to acknowledge: "I will always be pleased to say to anyone that I am his friend . . ."[101] *El Mundo* (September 28, 1836, reprinted in *El Castellano*, September 29, 1836) also rallied to Grimaldi's defense, but for different reasons: "a 'foreign adventurer' without standing in Spain, would not be the best person to run an errand for the queen of this nation; and the comparison is not only odious, it is *inexact*." Years later – in 1867 – Grimaldi gave his own account of some of the events of these turbulent times, but the matter was never resolved and Grimaldi's intensely political life in Paris, much of it in defense of the Spanish Moderates, leaves his denial of political motives open to serious doubt.

Grimaldi abandoned Spain physically, but never spiritually. His future was intimately entwined with that of his adopted country. Until his death in Paris in 1872 he maintained close political, financial, and intellectual ties to the country which had given him a wife, a family, fame, wealth, and influence, and in which he had invested so much of himself in return.

5

Grimaldi: journalist, historian, diplomat

Grimaldi's passion and brilliance were not limited to his theatrical endeavors. Two other areas, journalism and contemporary political history, occupied much of his time and attention, and his work in them would play a formative role in the shaping of contemporary views of Spanish society. He learned early – perhaps from Carnerero's example – that the press had enormous power to influence thought and he used that knowledge effectively. Grimaldi wrote newspaper articles at three dramatic junctures of Spanish history (1833–6, 1840, 1867) and his writings were read and hotly debated on both sides of the Pyrenees.

María Cristina, Mendizábal and "La Revista Española" (1833–6)

Carnerero ceased the publication of his *Cartas Españolas* in the beginning of November 1832. One week later they reappeared with a new title, a new format and a new board of editors (composed of Carnerero and his brother, Antonio Alcalá Galiano, N. Campuzano, N. Rodrigo and Juan de Grimaldi).[1] *La Revista Española*, destined to become one of the most influential newspapers of the Romantic period, began publication on November 7.[2] It originally was published as a biweekly, then increased to three times per week, and finally on April 1, 1834, encouraged by additional freedoms in the capital (and by additional competition), it began its life as a daily. It appealed to liberal intellectuals who found in its pages stimulating commentary on contemporary issues (as much as was permitted) and the best literary section of any of the capital's papers. Politically, it supported a liberal line which tended to lean toward the Moderates (as did Grimaldi) and when the events at La Granja discredited

135

Istúriz's moderate stance, the newspaper – with its major editors silenced – went out of business.[3]

Within his first year as one of the editors Grimaldi recruited Larra and García Gutiérrez to write for its pages.[4] He also began a series of articles himself which he published under the pseudonym, "A" (his friends called him "Juan Aquiles"). They were occasional articles written over a three-year period and they form no unified whole, although they do reveal the concerns which weighed upon him during these years. The subjects he chose to address – finances and industry, public education, the Carlist War, Juan Alvarez Mendizábal and the Moderate cause – were issues of real moment to Spanish society in the early 1830s and deeply passionate issues for Grimaldi. As a whole, the articles created a foundation of expertise which Grimaldi would later draw upon – and for which he would be publicly recognized – as his career turned toward the political arena in France after 1850. There he was known as one of the most distinguished businessmen, statesmen, and public servants of his day, and he was able to put many of the ideas expressed in the pages of *La Revista Española* into practice.

Grimaldi's voice was judicious, respected, forceful, and intelligent. In print he displayed the same qualities of persuasion, grasp of detail, careful documentation and passion which had charmed his friends and intimidated his adversaries in the theatre. He cajoled his readers, explained his positions and defended his ideas with style and eloquence. His positions were generally moderate, tinged with doses of eighteenth-century rationalism, and unswervingly supportive of María Cristina and her policies. Grimaldi "managed to have enormous influence, not only in the theatre and literature, but also in the political press, engaging in brutal battles in support of the throne of Isabel II and the Queen Regent."[5] Those articles which dealt with matters other than government and the future of the monarchy in Spain – the articles on financial matters, in particular – revealed the thoughts of a man who had achieved success on his own, who, through a combination of innate intelligence, sheer ambition and ceaseless energy had reached the upper ranges of wealth and social acceptability. The same "laissez-faire" attitude which Grimaldi preached so consistently in his contractual proposals to the municipal authorities was displayed in his approach to education and business as well.

He wrote twenty-one articles for *La Revista Española* between January 1833, and August 1836.[6] Some of them appeared as simple letters to the editor ("Dear Editor of *La Revista Española*"), which served as platforms for extended public debate on issues of concern to the populace. More important to Grimaldi than the general reading public, however, was his knowledge that the *Revista* was read by those who formed public policy. Grimaldi could contribute to the debate as well as help to shape it.

All of Grimaldi's contributions to the daily press, both in Madrid and Paris, were published under pseudonyms or completely anonymously. His close friends knew the true authorship of the pieces, but he took glee in confounding his critics and leaving them puzzling as to the individual who hid behind the various masks he donned. As he wrote to Narváez in 1867 (misremembering the year and the newspaper): "At the beginning of 1840 [sic], when I was in Madrid, I published in *El Español* [sic] a series of letters signed 'A', which everyone attributed, which I consider a great honor, to the Count of Toreno . . ."[7] The pseudonym was only a half-guarded secret, however, as *El Castellano*'s article (September 26, 1836) made clear ("he wrote those long and famous articles signed 'A' and inserted in the *Revista*") and as a note appended to the French translation of his article "Inviolabilidad del Rey" ("The Inviolability of the King") confirmed: "'A' was the pseudonymous signature on the articles published in Madrid in the *Revista Española* by its former editor in chief, Mr. Grimaldi."[8] The first article (January 8, 1833) addressed two of the Queen Regent's recent decrees, one of which proclaimed knowledge and education "as the most fecund source of all social wealth" and the other of which created the Department of Public Works (Fomento).[9] Grimaldi, while trying to maintain his anonymity and lend weight to his observations ("I am old . . . my life's long experience . . ."), strongly supported the government's proposed reorganization of the educational system under the guidance of the new "enlightened Magistrate," Minister of Public Works (Javier de Burgos, not mentioned by name in the article).[10] The goal of this reorganization was not knowledge *per se* but rather material well being. He injected a strong capitalistic note into the article, defending a line of argument which had deep resonances in his own personal history. As we have seen, Grimaldi was a man of little formal education who used his intelligence creatively to press for a better life for himself and his family. Consequently, his view of Spain's future hinged in part on what he perceived as necessary and possible, filtered through his own experience.

The man who has in some way cultivated his reason, and who applies to his own personal situation the exercise of clear thinking which he is used to, succeeds in getting the most out of his property, his physical forces, his capital, and whatever nature offers him, and whatever he can manage to plant above and below the earth.

Intelligence – and education – were the path to riches. "People who know the most bring home from the far reaches of the earth whatever riches are not found on their own soil." This was not, as it would appear, a defense of colonialism or imperialism, since Grimaldi emphasized that riches would accrue not by force but by a natural transfer of goods to the most "enlightened" countries: "In those provinces where enlightened thinking is most obvious, there is more agriculture, more industry, a larger population, more wealth, better social habits, less crime, more obedience to the law, in a word, a greater well being for their inhabitants, and greater resources at the disposition of government to provide for the needs of health, security, and common prosperity." This faith in the capitalistic work ethic would remain unshakable in Grimaldi. He argued for, defended, and put into practice these ideas in the years to come.

Grimaldi was a typical nineteenth-century *laissez-faire* capitalist; that is, he argued for government policies which aided the expansion of private economic interests while at the same time arguing against over-regulation or protectionism. His second article (February 1, 1833) addressed the problem of the woolen industry and again argued for open debate on economic matters ("in no way can an economic writer serve an enlightened ministry except by adding to the public debate the discoveries he may have made concerning aspects of this field"). Concern had been expressed in the pages of the *Revista* and elsewhere that foreigners would succeed in usurping Spain's dominance of the merino wool trade. Voices clamored for protectionist measures to insure Spain's continued superiority in that field. Grimaldi argued to the contrary, claiming that dominance in any financial enterprise is the result of open competition and hard work, not protectionism and negligence. "In order to earn more than someone who works intelligently and manages by his skills to make the products of his industriousness worth something, there is no other just and sure way than working harder and more cleverly than the competitor." (We will need to keep these ideas in mind when we discuss later his frantic machinations to insure government intervention on behalf of his railroad proposals, made in letters to Narváez in 1867.) As he had done with his ideas on theatrical reform, Grimaldi cited experiments in Europe (France and England, above all) which supported his case. The old argument which raged in Spain for nearly a century – whether Spain should open her doors to foreign ideas or close herself off and develop her traditions, and which would surface again with deep resonance with the Generation of 1898 – was echoed in Grimaldi's articles on the Spanish economy. He clearly sided with those who wished to open Spain to certain improvements already tried and found successful in the rest of Europe. As far as wool production was concerned, he recommended that Spanish sheep farmers learn to "imitate ... the vigilance and activity of the foreigners who today enjoy a preferential standing in the markets of Europe" – the same advice he had given concerning the theatres.

This enlightened attitude toward hard work and suppression of government protectionism was the dominant note of his next long article, a two-part piece entitled "Sobre la instrucción pública," which appeared on March 19 and 29, 1833. He had learned through personal experience that effort produced benefit, and his economic Darwinism *avant la lettre* supported a policy of survival of the brightest and most hardworking. Perhaps because he had pulled himself up by the proverbial bootstraps, he was vehemently opposed to a proliferation of government funded schools and student scholarships. In his view, general education could best progress if only those who deserved support – demonstrated by hard work and self-improvement ("to acquire a good education . . . one needs to work") – received it. According to this view, those who valued education would benefit from it and as others perceived the benefits of education, they in turn would pursue it and improve their lot. Thus would be created an upwardly spiralling cycle of social and individual benefit. Such beliefs can be inspired and demonstrated, but never forced."Without this practical demonstration schools will be deserted or the only people who will go to them will be children afraid of being punished and adults to fill up whatever number of years they need in order to take their certificate." Not only should the brightest be encouraged and rewarded, wrote Grimaldi, but honors and financial aid should be kept from "all fools and idiots." Even this general public enlightenment was a "market" for Grimaldi, knowledge a "merchandise": "and among the sellers who come to this market, the one who will be most sought out, most looked for and rewarded, will be he who manages to present the most useful merchandise." The article maintained his anti-regulatory pose and called for free market forces in the realm of public education. It contained echoes of fights he had been having with the government about the over-regulation of the theatres for years. In fact, these articles were appearing precisely when Grimaldi was in negotiations with those authorities for control of the theatres.

It can already be inferred from this how far my opinion is from overburdening our legislation, and the concerns of our government, with the formulation of new and multiplied laws, or with the creation of more and more school or non-school committees, which under the plausible pretext of regularizing and directing public instruction for its own improvement and perfection, can produce in it the sad results that guild corporations produced in industry and the arts with their detailed and numbing ordinances. On the contrary, my desire is the complete abolition, or at least a considerable modification, of the regulations that exist today and take up much of our legislative code books.

At the end of May, he returned to this subject for the last time in a three part article entitled "Instrucción pública. Escuelas de primeras letras" (May 22, May 24, and May 30, 1834), where he applied his free market ideas to a discussion of primary education in Spain. His general conclusion, again, was that regulation was the biggest obstacle to the improvement of primary education. He opposed creating schools in every village, since "I ask myself if that school can produce a sufficient number of bright students to justify the work and expense of its creation and maintenance." In other words, would they be "cost effective"? "I think not..." He was full of financial analogies and economic terminology in his defense of "trickle-down" learning, that is, he believed that the desire to learn would increase as the benefits of that learning became obvious. He cited as an example the higher literacy rates on the Cantabrian coast, which were the result, he claimed, not of the creation of more schools and more teachers, but the reverse: "Schools and teachers have multiplied because for years navigation and commerce made these people feel a need to read, write, and count in order to maintain and improve their trade and commercial interests."

These articles were the last that Grimaldi wrote on educational matters, but his interest in education and public instruction, and the expertise he gained through his study of the situation in Spain, earned him a place on France's Commission on Public Instruction (part of the General Council of the province of Jura). He served on the Commission on Public Instruction off and on for nearly twenty years (1851–69).[11]

Grimaldi turned his attention back to politics when the Carlist War began to pose a serious threat to the stability of Madrid's central government. From October 1835, through August 1836, he published fourteen more pieces, all of them concerned with the war, the Queen Regent and her cabinet ministers (mostly Mendizábal). His spirited support of María Cristina was unshakable and his open criticism of her enemies reflected not only his own personal opinion, but that of the *Revista* as well (the masthead of the paper proclaimed it a "newspaper dedicated to Her Majesty the Queen Regent").

We have already seen that his play, *1835 y 1836 o lo que es y lo que será*, written in collaboration with Bretón and Vega and staged in December 1835, presented a corrosive view of the progress of the Carlist War in the north. At the same time as he was writing the play, Grimaldi was composing a series of five articles for the *Revista* which discussed the origins of the conflict, the government's policies and conduct regarding it and the consequences of a Carlist victory. In "Secretos del año 1835 que el tiempo ha de revelar" (October 29, 1835) he posed a series of probing questions about the war, directed at Francisco Espoz y Mina (a liberal general), Valdés (Minister of War), Martínez de la Rosa (Prime Minister from January 1834 to June 1835) and the Count of Toreno (Prime Minister from June to September 1835). There was no discussion or analysis – just a list of seventeen hard questions which he thought demanded attention. He answered some of the questions himself one week later in his next article, "Desengaños de los carlistas" (November 5, 1835), a discursive historical analysis which found the origins of the Carlist War in the Spanish War of Independence of 1808–1814. His rhetoric heated up as he called the Carlists "a handful of egotists," a "Machiavellian, anti-national, usurping party," who had supported "the banishments, the death, the persecutions" which marked Fernando VII's return to power in 1814. He issued a call to unity, exhorting the Carlists to lay down their arms and stand united behind María Cristina and Isabel. "This is one nation," he cried.

The short "Gaceta de Don Carlos" (November 9, 1835) ridiculed the prospectus for a newspaper proposed by the supporters of Don Carlos. Grimaldi criticized this "ridiculous document" as an attempt to "hypnotize the people with a mask of religion," but refused simply to ignore it since "it is necessary to pulverize the evil doctrines by which they mean to mislead public opinion." He called for unity against the Carlist threat again in "A la unión" (November 13, 1835), in particular, unity in the council of ministers and in parliament: "Our representatives need to be firm in their resolve to carry out their weighty charge, but this firmness should now be used only to destroy the common enemy." In the next article of this Carlist War series, Grimaldi speculated on the consequences of a Carlist victory and he returned to his economic point of reference. "La razón," as he titled the article (December 26, 1835), "should be the dividing line between the parties." In this article he suggested that "one of the most infallible thermometers, and a mark of which party is right, is the state of the public treasury," and he proceeded to analyze what would happen to the public treasury if "these blind and cowardly defenders of darkness" won the war. According to him, the treasury and confidence in the national economy would disappear completely. Those who had invested in the Queen's cause, or those who had purchased or inherited state goods during the Constitutional Triennium would lose everything, since fanatics, instead of showing tolerance and clemency in such matters, frequently demonstrate vengeance instead ("we all remember the fateful year of 1823 and those which followed"). Such retributions would fall upon Carlos's own supporters as well, but a victory by María Cristina's supporters would insure tolerance for the vanquished. She would not follow her husband's example of October 1, 1823, "which ruined thousands of families, took away all jobs, and banished the most worthy sons of the nation."

His last article on the Carlists appeared on August 21, 1836, just days before he would begin his journey to France. It combined his concern for the war cause with the recent events at La Granja, where the Queen Regent had been forced to support the restoration of the Constitution of 1812. The Carlists viewed the incident at La Granja as a small victory for them, for it carried with it the potential destabilization of the Queen Regent's moderate cause even though its narrower political consequences (the adoption of a more liberal government policy) were hardly in their best interests. Grimaldi refuted this belief, claiming (rather wishfully, as it turned out) that this occurrence would have no effect on the stability of the government. He did not defend the sergeants' actions; he simply refuted the belief that it would destabilize María Cristina's government.

This impassioned defense of María Cristina resounded through all the other articles published by Grimaldi in the *Revista* in 1836. A previous contribution, written again as a letter to the editor, appeared on May 4.[12] A small debate had broken out (principally in the rival newspaper, *El Eco del Comercio*) concerning the legality of the Queen's decree of May 1, in which she reinstituted public audiences in the Royal Palace. The *Eco* had noticed that there was no legal signature on the document, but Grimaldi's answer to this technicality was that the Queen's secretary was her legal representative and as such his signature constituted the necessary legal basis for the decree. But the real issue, as Grimaldi saw it, was an attempt to proscribe the Queen's rights ("to try to make us believe that the Queen Regent cannot receive in her own house, when and however she wishes, her poor subjects who come to ask her help, without the minister's prior approval!") and he, as always, stood behind her completely.

One of Grimaldi's most interesting articles appeared on July 4, 1836. "Inviolabilidad del Rey. Libertad de imprenta" laid out the growing split noticeable among the country's liberals, who were having trouble organizing themselves into a united front. The conservative liberals (*moderados*) began to articulate goals which were different from the progressive liberals (*exaltados* or *progresistas*). The split had become evident after the return of the exiles in 1834, but the sergeants' revolt at La Granja would make the breach complete.[13] Grimaldi's comments would help to widen the breach. In a blistering attack – not on the reactionary Carlists this time, but on the revolutionary *exaltados* of his own liberal party – he turned to contemporary French history (the Revolutions of 1789 and 1830, and the recent attempt on King Louis-Philippe's life) to warn against the "insatiability of the exalted liberals" and, surprisingly, to argue in favor of censorship of the press.

Press freedom had become a hotly contested issue in Madrid. Several times during the previous years initiatives had been taken to free the press from the restraints of prior censorship and to provide it with a more open forum for political and social debate. Larra, for one, had been a persuasive defender of a free press, but Grimaldi, considerably more moderate than his friend, resisted supporting a bill for total freedom. He preached against Dantonesque excess and warned against the consequences of *exaltado* policy. He believed that the *exaltados* were like spoiled children – one had to tell them "no" once in a while for their own good – but he opposed the "fanaticism [which] frequently stains their doctrines," not the individuals themselves. Grimaldi focused upon the French press as unwitting conspirators in the chaos he perceived in that country. "It is not possible to have an idea of the lack of self-control in the press or in sellers of etchings in the five years following the revolution. Not a single day went by without a new caricature, without a new article, sometimes serious, sometimes ribald, to stir up against the person of the king hate and scorn, ridicule or anger." His comments were to serve as a warning in Spain, where he vociferously defended the Queen Regent against possible attacks of a similar nature. He supported press freedom as long as it did not transgress the boundaries of propriety as concerns the monarchy. The power of the press was subtle and pervasive (something he discovered worked in his favor with his later attacks on Espartero and Guizot)[14] and he called for measures to curb it. He viewed the latest bill introduced into Parliament as too weak, not dealing harshly enough with those who overstepped the limits of decency or contributed to attempts against the monarch (in France, he noted, recent legislation stipulated the death penalty for any "excitation" against the King). His loyalty to María Cristina won out over any journalistic libertarianism he felt as an editor, but his stance was typical of his Moderate posture. When his identification with the Moderate cause forced him out of the country later that year, it was this article he chose to publish in his native tongue in Paris.[15]

Perhaps the most important articles that Grimaldi published in the 1830s were the seven pieces he dedicated to the policies and downfall of Juan Alvarez Mendizábal. Mendizábal's appointment as Prime Minister on September 14, 1835, had been greeted with general acclaim among Spanish liberal intellectuals. He made sweeping promises to end the Carlist War, restabilize the economy and institute numerous administrative and social reforms. Faith in his policies ran so high that he was granted broad powers ("the omnipotence of an unheard of dictatorship," according to Grimaldi)[16] by a vote of confidence in the Parliament in January 1836. Soon, however, that faith began to diminish as it became clearer that Mendizábal was incapable of living up to the promises he had made, and public confidence in him ebbed. Writers and politicians who had once supported him, among them Larra and Espronceda, began to publish attacks on him and his policies. Larra, in particular, felt deceived and wrote a series of corrosive articles detailing his loss of confidence in the Prime Minister.[17] By mid-May, Mendizábal was forced to resign. He was replaced by Istúriz, who was himself discredited following the sergeants' revolt at La Granja in mid-August.

Grimaldi tried to explain the mysterious circumstances surrounding Mendizábal's resignation in an article entitled, "De la dimisión del ministerio Mendizábal" (May 26, 1836). Although he was hardly an eyewitness to the event (as one of his critics scornfully noted in a rejoinder published three days later), he did move in high social and political circles and was privy to some of the details of the resignation (". . . those of us who have had more or less direct contact with certain political circles these days . . ."). His account would be, he claimed, unbiased and truthful: "If the facts we have collected and which we judge to be credible do not deceive us; for that reason we shall not use in the rest of the article the conditional tense since it will only interfere with our narration and which, besides, is unnecessary, since it is obvious that we have not heard directly the conversations cited nor have they been told to us by the participants, but nonetheless as a chronicler of events we can use a straightforward, affirmative language . . ." He wished to recount "the story of the famous resignation" in order to correct several misinterpretations which had been circulating both in Madrid and in the provinces, in order to quell whatever possible rebellious sentiments Mendizábal's resignation might incite. Rumor had it that the Queen Regent had planned Mendizábal's resignation and had delighted in forcing him out of the government. From Grimaldi's perspective, it was crucial to explain the Queen Regent's actions and to demonstrate her strength during this difficult and threatening crisis.

Grimaldi provided a behind-the-scenes look at the events leading up to Mendizábal's resignation. The crisis, precipitated by the Council of Ministers' demand that certain military personnel in the capital be replaced, pitted the Queen Regent's sense of loyalty and authority against Mendizábal's sense of ministerial power.[18] The clash of wills produced a conflict which had potentially far-reaching consequences:

. . . the intervention of one of the co-legislative bodies in acts which are as essentially and exclusively executive as the appointment and resignation of workers, could not be permitted without introducing into the balance of power a real danger which would be threatening to the very freedom within which each of those powers operates in its respective sphere.

When Mendizábal learned that the Queen Regent had refused to accede to the Ministers' demands he visited her at her palace in La Granja and threatened a mass resignation of the Ministers. Instead of giving in to his threat, however, she strengthened her resolve to maintain control of the situation and demanded that they reconsider their decision. For several days the discussions continued and a stream of ministers came and went from La Granja, but María Cristina viewed the issue as one of fundamental governing prerogatives and was loath either to be pressured by the threat of retaliation or to accept the resignations of her chief ministers. "Her Majesty showed on that day a second clear proof that she did not want the threatened resignation to go through."

When a written resignation was handed to the Queen Regent on the evening of May 13, she asked her ministers to reconsider their decision and stated that she would spend some time thinking about the situation. The next day, when she had returned to the Royal Palace in Madrid, Mendizábal ominously informed her that her indecision could precipitate grave and unwanted consequences. Her response, as recorded by Grimaldi, underscored her strength and resolve: "I trust that nothing will happen, as I trust that you will think about the situation you've put me in." Grimaldi indignantly accused Mendizábal of bad faith and of distorting the truth of the crisis: "There is no greater proof of the prudent and inexhaustible patience with which Her Majesty tried to keep the Minister who with such obvious bad faith now wants us to see him as a victim of palace intrigues." When finally the ministers remained implacable in their resolve to resign, María Cristina signed the papers which organized a new cabinet. Mendizábal's bluff had been called and his power came to a (temporary) halt. Grimaldi ended his article with reminders to his readers about the numerous broken promises strewn in Mendizábal's short ministerial career.

Grimaldi's article attempted to demonstrate that the Queen Regent's actions were neither anti-constitutional nor anti-liberal, as some were claiming. He severely criticized Mendizábal, although he kept repeating throughout the whole series of articles that while he abhorred Mendizábal's deceits and wayward policies, "we have never doubted his patriotism, his integrity." (Larra, writing on Mendizábal at the same time, echoed Grimaldi's words: "As much as we have always disagreed with D. Juan Alvarez Mendizábal's style of government and with his financial schemes [and shall continue to do so], we have always praised his honesty and his patriotism . . .").[19] Grimaldi's view of the events has been judged reliable by historians ("The version which has deserved most credence is the account published by Juan Grimaldi . . .")[20] although it did not go uncontested. Mendizábal's version, signed by one "C. de V.," was printed on May 29 in *La Revista Española*, but the editors (i.e., Grimaldi) published it not as it was sent to them, but with the addition of thirteen long notes. "No one will be surprised that we have judged it

necessary to add notes opposing the thoughts that have been sent to us
. . ." His tone remained measured but firm, as was his continued
defense of María Cristina.

His third commentary on the ongoing constitutional crisis concerned the Queen Regent's new cabinet. She had been criticized in the
press for bypassing constitutional requisites, since her new cabinet was
not selected from the parliamentary majority, as it normally was.
Instead, she named a coalition of men who supported her moderate
policies, choices which Grimaldi proclaimed prudent and constitutional in his article, "De la elección de los sucesores del ministerio
Mendizábal" (June 5, 1836). He defended the selection of Istúriz as
logical and natural, a recognition of the confidence that Mendizábal
himself had demonstrated in him on numerous occasions, and pointed
out that "there was no clear majority nor minority in the last
Parliament, and the honest representatives who had Her Majesty's
confidence had voted at times with one side and at other times with the
other, and mostly with the majority . . ."

In the following month (July 1836), Grimaldi continued his
discursive attack on Mendizábal and his passionate support of María
Cristina with a long (over 11,000 words) four-part article published in
the *Revista*. "De la administración del Sr. Mendizábal" (July 12, 13,
19, and 21, 1836) was a response to an article published in *El Español*
(June 26) by one of Mendizábal's supporters and which had
subsequently been circulated (up to 12,000 copies, according to
Grimaldi) throughout Spain. This defense was in itself a response to
an earlier article in *El Español* which criticized Mendizábal's
economic policies. Grimaldi used these pieces as his point of departure
to launch a sustained and detailed critique of Mendizábal's eight
months in office in order to demonstrate that "Mendizábal . . . is a
good man, but it is necessary to show the country that he was a bad
minister."[21]

His sharpest attacks on Mendizábal in these articles centered on the
latter's conduct of economic policy. According to Grimaldi, the ex-
minister's incompetence came from his lack of experience in matters of
politics and statesmanship: "The situation demanded a statesman
and unfortunately only a businessman came forth."[22] Grimaldi
echoed the claims that Mendizábal had mortgaged Spain's future to
bankers in Paris and London and he bitterly denounced the ex-
minister's questionable machinations with government finances, as
well as his hiding behind the shield of the vote of confidence: "Not

without surprise did we see the ex-president of the Council of Ministers maintain that the vote of confidence allowed him to do everything that was not expressly prohibited." He posed a series of questions, probing Mendizábal's alleged "savings," which he found to be based on mirrors and smoke rather than on solid economic principles ("God save us from alchemists, and from people who make money out of mysteries or other superhuman things . . .!") and excoriated Mendizábal for his inept conduct. He recognized, of course, that Mendizábal had carried out certain beneficial reforms, but in his judgment the harm created by the ex-minister's policies far outweighed the little good they did. The benefits that could be ascribed to the period of Mendizábal's ministry (steps to reconcile warring factions in the provinces, for example) were laid at the doorstep of the Queen Regent rather than at Mendizábal's.

Grimaldi's critique of Mendizábal was subtly argued and presented with the appearance of disinterest and objectivity, making it all the more devastating. He argued with force and flair and wielded quantities of facts to support his opinions. He had reentered the debate out of fear that Mendizábal's supporters would succeed in returning him to power: "That party is trying hard to resuscitate the Mendizábal administration, because with it it expects to triumph, and since in such a triumph we view our freedom in danger, it is legitimate – necessary – to combat it." He prided himself on the enormous influence of these articles (". . . I left him ruined forever," he boasted in a letter to Narváez [November 12, 1867. RAH: Narváez, 56]), but his fears were justified and the articles unwittingly planted the seeds for his own destruction: Mendizábal would remember the articles when he returned to power in August as Finance Minister, after the fall of Istúriz. As the historian Gómez Aparicio has written, "*La Revista* was one of the most energetic and effective victors over Mendizábal during his time in power and one of the papers which contributed most to his downfall: Alvarez Mendizábal never forgave it, and that is, perhaps, one of the primary reasons for the disappearance of *La Revista*, defunct a few days after the 'Revolt at La Granja' and the formation of a government in which Mendizábal was Finance Minister. In its issue – the last one – of August 27, 1836, it declared that 'due to difficulties with the printer we find ourselves in the difficult situation of not being able to continue publication' and added immediately: 'Let this short explanation suffice for those who want to attribute to other causes the absence of an issue this morning.'"[23] Grimaldi, his political position severely compromised (and his life even perhaps in danger), fled the country.

Espartero, the radicals and "La Presse" (Paris, 1841)

As a supporter of the Queen Regent and the Moderates, Grimaldi witnessed with dismay the activities in his adopted country following his departure. The promulgation of the radical Constitution of 1837 jeopardized the stability of the Queen Regent's government, for it fragmented the various political factions even further and opened the way for the increasing influence of the most powerful general to come out of the war, Baldomero Espartero. The Carlist War, while eventually won by the defenders of María Cristina and Isabel, exacted a heavy financial and political toll. Espartero, named Duke of Victory for his decisive role in the defeat of the Carlists, used his immense prestige to intimidate the Moderate coalition in parliament,[24] and eventually to intimidate the Queen Regent herself. In a confrontational meeting between the radical Espartero and the moderate María Cristina in Barcelona in July 1840, it became clear that the regency of María Cristina was in serious jeopardy. By October of that year Espartero had named himself regent and María Cristina was forced to abdicate and to leave the country.

María Cristina went to Paris where she was greeted by old supporters (first among them, Grimaldi) who vowed to organize a resistance campaign and to work against the radical usurper, Espartero. María Cristina received support from the July Monarchy of her uncle, King Louis-Philippe I. Grimaldi had been working all along for the Queen Regent and had accepted numerous "assignments" for her from Madrid during the 1837–40 period.[25] The group in exile marshaled French support, as well as that of two of Espartero's Moderate enemies, Ramón Narváez and Leopoldo O'Donnell. The rest of Grimaldi's life would be marked by the fortunes of María Cristina, Narváez, O'Donnell, and the moderados.

Grimaldi's major contribution to the Moderate conspiracy to return to power was the publication of a series of articles, similar to those he had written against Mendizábal, but this time directed at Espartero. "Etudes biographiques sur Espartero" appeared in the Paris newspaper La Presse, in six long installments (June 29, July 2, July 5, July 8, July 14, July 18, 1841). Their success led Grimaldi to publish an updated and expanded version in book form entitled

Espartero. Etudes biographiques nécessaires á l'intelligence des faits qui ont préparé et déterminé la dernière révolution d'Espagne.[26] He maintained his anonymity, but left clues for the attentive reader ("Having spent fifteen years in Spain, in a position perfectly independent from men and things [that is, not formally aligned to any one political party], the author has studied the country carefully" [p. vi]).

The Espartero biography provided Grimaldi with the opportunity to continue waging his war against the progressive liberals who had unseated the Queen Regent. It had a two-fold purpose: 1) to shape French opinion concerning the contemporary political scene in Spain, and 2) to subvert Espartero's prestige and therefore call into question his legitimacy. Years later, in a letter to Narváez, he bragged that they had achieved the desired effect: "You know what happened to Espartero, on this side of the Pyrenees, after the biography I published in *La Presse*." (November 12, 1867; RAH: Narváez, 56.) In *La Presse* Grimaldi recounted the stormy and meteoric rise to power of Espartero, his conduct during the civil war and the events culminating in María Cristina's abdication. He used a wide range of sources, both printed (the contemporary press, the memoirs published by Córdoba and Aviraneta)[27] and private (friendships, personal observations, private documents ["We have here before our eyes a copy of this long and important document . . ."]). Among those sources figured personal testimony by some of the principal players in the drama: "In intimate and frequent contact with the principal political and military champions of this battle, he has been able to express his judgments with a clarity rarely found in these documents" (pp. vi–vii). It is very likely that two of those sources were the Queen Regent herself and Narváez, both of whom were in the French capital during this period and both of whom shared a driving commitment to the defeat of Espartero. Grimaldi's admiration for Narváez, which would become closer and stronger in time, was already sharply delineated in this study of his antagonist, Espartero.

As Grimaldi depicted him, Espartero suffered from the double weakness of inaction and indecision, combined with a dictatorial streak which made him – after neutralizing the influence of Narváez and Fernando Fernández de Córdoba – "stronger than government, opinion and laws . . ." (p. 28). Grimaldi painted him as voraciously ambitious, repressive, and brutal. His heavy-handed policies jeopardized the war effort and his penchant for conspiracies made him not only troublesome, but dangerous. Grimaldi's intentions were clearly polemical, but he marshaled an impressive array of facts to support his arguments, and his own personal history (as a soldier and business-man able to make quick decisions) colored his view of his antagonist. For Grimaldi, Espartero's success was more the result of good luck than talent or hard work. In the political arena, his actions were similar: "We shall see him in war as in politics continually avoiding confronting difficulties, while looking for a way to turn them away rather than attack them; in any case, positioning himself so that their solution becomes the responsibility of someone else (if it is bad), and only benefits himself (if it is good)" (p. 12). He sought to prove that the credit given to Espartero for the end of the Carlist War was misplaced, that Espartero's public actions were mere posturing ("pure acting") and that the great success at Vergara was not a success at all which could be attributed to the General: "The glory of the denouement of Vergara is far from belonging as exclusively to Espartero as he would like it said" (pp. 53–4).

Grimaldi also provided important details concerning the Queen Regent's fateful trip to Barcelona. It was not undertaken, as reported by Espartero's supporters, as a refuge and eventual step toward the abdication of her throne, but simply to follow doctor's orders that Isabel be treated for some childhood infirmities in the hot baths in Valencia – as she had done the previous year ("Certainly the trip could not have been more legitimate, more innocently motivated." p. 74). Her subsequent meeting with Espartero in Zaragoza revealed the general's "Machiavellian intentions," for he demanded, among other things, that she dissolve her cabinet and replace it with individ-uals of his choosing. When she resisted, as she had done when similar demands were made of her by Mendizábal at La Granja several years earlier, Espartero offered his resignation. This time, however, unlike that parallel incident at La Granja, she refused outright to accept it and Espartero won the confrontation. But not until he finally pronounced against her did she abdicate her throne. "The plan succeeds. The queen abdicates. Espartero is head of a provisional regency. The Moderate parliament is dissolved" (p.89). Grimaldi ended this discussion with a quotation from his theatrical past:

Espartero, in his constant protestations of disinterest, has fairly often sworn that what he aspired to most, as the price of his services, was to become one day the leader of his country. But Espartero is Spanish, and he could well have thought, along with Lope de Vega, that in Spain, the best leader is the king.   (p. 91.)[28]

Translated sections of *La Presse*'s articles caused a furor when they were published in Madrid, and Espartero's supporters organized a campaign against them. The most direct combatant published a thirty-six page pamphlet entitled *Espartero: Contestación a los seis artículos que con este título ha publicado el papel francés La Presse, y han sido traducidos por algunos periódicos de esta corte* (Madrid: Omaña, 1841). The purpose of this response was, of course, to defend Espartero against the scurrilous attacks of the French newspaper, "[which] with less than noble intentions, reveals an obvious longing to denigrate him" (p. 3). The author of this pamphlet was forced to recognize that *La Presse*'s articles contained "a basis of truth" and "a brilliant flash of . . . insight" (p. 27) but in his view the conclusions drawn by the author of those articles were nearly always false. He objected strongly to the depiction of Espartero as "possessed of a system of subversion and political tumult, which he supported in a Machiavellian manner by his elevated position and by the truly formidable revenues which he had at his disposal" (p. 25). In addition, this publication painted Espartero as an innocent victim of a popular uprising against the Queen Regent, an unwilling recipient of popular trust who reluctantly accepted leadership of the country. The Madrid pamphlet was as much a partisan document as was Grimaldi's, but it contained more opinion and less evidence ("We are not nor have we ever been close to the source of secrets of this type" [p. 25]) and it resolved nothing. Grimaldi did not even consider it worthy of a reply.

Within two years Espartero had demonstrated his inability to control the various factions of his own party. Skirmishes in the provinces undermined his government's stability. Moderate generals (Narváez in particular) fought together with the Progressives against the central government in Madrid. The Narváez faction predominated militarily and a coalition of Moderate leaders forced Espartero into exile in the summer of 1843. (Grimaldi returned to the subject of Espartero twenty-seven years later in a series of anonymous "Lettres Espagnoles" which he published in the *Mémorial diplomatique* in Paris).[29] By May, 1844, Ramón de Narváez was named Prime Minister of Spain. The Moderates had returned to power and Grimaldi's political and social prestige enjoyed a new upward surge.

Grimaldi: diplomat, conspirator and éminence grise

Narváez would dominate Spanish politics until his death in 1868. In numerous ministries he carried out policies which moved gradually but inexorably from centrist-moderate to conservative, and these latter policies contributed to the decline and ultimate downfall of the monarchy of Isabel II, the Queen whom he had fought for decades to defend and protect. María Cristina's relationship with Narváez was affected by her deep concern over the marriage of Isabel, one of the central issues of Spanish politics during the mid-1840s and which ultimately became a pan-European obsession. Lack of consensus within the Moderate ranks created periods of dangerous instability. The Queen (Isabel had been declared of age in 1843) dismissed Narváez in January, 1846, but by October, 1847, he was back in power. It was during his third ministry, from 1847 to January, 1851, that Grimaldi achieved additional prominence in Paris and solidified his relationship with the Prime Minister.

Grimaldi, from Paris, served the Narváez ministry both publicly and privately and remained an acute observer of the Spanish scene. (We shall see in the next section that his last public battle was fought once again to defend the Moderate cause, and as before it was played out anonymously in the pages of the daily press.) Little is known of his activities in the mid-1840s, although it can be supposed that he spent much of his time seeing to his investments and business ventures and consolidating his social standing in Paris. During this time he was also active in the life of Salins-des-Bains, a small town (population 7,112) in the province of Jura, where he invested in the tourist industry (the thermal baths) and, later, in the railroad.[30] He maintained homes in both Salins and Paris, and kept in close contact with the officials at the Spanish Embassy – where Concepción had to go each month in order to collect her retirement benefits and to sign an affidavit testifying to her residence and lack of employment in the French capital – and with the Spanish government. In May 1848, immediately following the Spanish defeat of the international revolutionary movement and the proclamation of the French Republic, he was named Spanish Consul in Paris.[31] He was fifty-two years old.

His post in the consulate in Paris was more honorary than specific. It was an unpaid position, but Grimaldi was motivated by prestige and by his political nature to accept it. At first he had some difficulty taking over the post, since the French government – the nascent Republic – refused to notarize the papers of a man so famed for his allegiance to the institution of the monarchy. Isabel II perhaps felt it necessary now more than ever to fill the position, which had gone vacant for a decade, in order to have a strong contact in the French capital. The case was stalled in the bureaucracy throughout the rest of the year and not until Grimaldi appealed to the Spanish Secretary of State (the Duke of Sotomayor, who soon became the Spanish Ambassador) and to his friends in the French government did the authorization become official (February 1849). In March 1849, in order to reinforce his position and to help overcome the embarrassment of the delay, he was named honorary member of the Royal Order of Carlos III, "exempt from all fees, since he is a foreigner" (MAE: Legajo 125). Even at that he was not able to take charge of the consulate until December of that year. The position was not that of General Consul of the Spanish government to the French government (a position attached to the Embassy) but rather a "private consul," a personal emissary of the Queen charged with limited responsibilities only within Paris. For Sotomayor's successor at the Ministry of State, Grimaldi's position was purely honorary, carrying with it not only no salary, but no budget either. Grimaldi, who had willingly accepted the fact that it was an unpaid position, could not accept that he was not granted the same operating budget that other consuls received and in letters which carried echoes of similar conflicts he had had twenty-five years previously with other government officials concerned with the ownership of Madrid's theatres, he protested that his high operating costs ("rental of a place for the office, which should be in keeping with the prestige of the appointment, salary of the doorman, fuel, normal printing costs, desk . . .") should be underwritten with the same 6,000 *reales* received by the other consuls. His enemies intervened and the request was denied.

As private Consul, Grimaldi's duties were unspecified. He served as a liaison between the Queen and French officials – a conduit of information concerning activities and attitudes in the French capital. His contacts in the French business and social worlds made him an invaluable source of inside information and his allegiance to the Spanish Moderates (especially Narváez) made him a valuable ally abroad. More openly, he worked as an agent for the Teatro de Oriente, setting up contracts for French actors, dancers and opera singers to work in Madrid.[32]

As Narváez became more dictatorial and therefore more vulnerable to opposition from both progressive liberals and the staunchly moderate factions of his own party (opposition in parliament was particularly vocal and his best ministers frequently undercut his authority), he lost favor with the Queen's family as well. Isabel's husband, the generally weak and ineffectual Francisco de Asís, was instrumental in forcing Narváez to resign in January 1851. He was replaced in the ministry by Gonzalo Bravo Murillo. In April 1851, the Queen accepted Grimaldi's resignation as Consul.

Narváez retired to Paris, where he was warmly greeted by Louis Napoleon, the president of the French Republic. "The president of the French Republic, Louis Napoleon, receives the recently arrived General Narváez with demonstrations of great affection: he invites him to his table; he has him accompany him in a solemn public occasion to review the troops of Paris; he honors and praises him at every public opportunity."[33] The historian Jesús Pabón rightly wonders what formed the basis for the seemingly impossible friendship between a representative of the triumphant revolution in France and a representative of the restored monarchy in Spain. His answer speculates on a five-person drama played out between the two capitals and provides a special glimpse into Grimaldi's activities during the late 1840s and early 1850s.

According to Pabón, Grimaldi served as one of the chief intermediaries between Narváez, who was anxious to determine the political status of the new French President, Louis Napoleon. Grimaldi, after returning to Paris from an enforced absence due to illness in November 1849, held a meeting with one of Louis Napoleon's confidants, Léon Faucher, then Minister of the Interior. He recounted the meeting to Narváez by letter, informing him that he viewed Louis Napoleon as "a friend of Spain and Spain's present government."[34] In that same letter he informed Narváez that he had delicately broached a subject which Grimaldi and Narváez had discussed previously in Madrid, that is, "the scarce financial resources of this President" and Narváez's offer of financial and military aid to help shore up the faltering government of Louis Napoleon. Faucher demonstrated keen interest in the offer.

Grimaldi also met with Louis Napoleon himself concerning this possible alliance between Narváez and the head of the French government. The meeting was long, frank and cordial, and centered upon Louis Napoleon's difficulty in arranging credit to pay off some outstanding debts. He could not turn to the French bankers (Rothschild, Fould, Holtzinger) for help, since such a public display of economic instability would precipitate a crisis which the government could not withstand and, in addition, Louis Napoleon refused to become beholden to his country's bankers. Grimaldi asked, "So what can be done to pay the debts, to avoid a scandal . . .? Turn to private credit? The President cannot do that" (November 20, 1849; Pabón, p. 267). Louis Napoleon finally decided that Grimaldi could help him avoid a crisis and stabilize his situation.

In conclusion what was decided in order to help the President out of his current difficulties, was that I alone could offer a solution. I alone, because since I am the purest Napoleonist in France, I am not involved in the political arena nor do I have business interests with the government. I alone, because the friends whom I'll have to turn to for the necessary funds are *foreign friends* who, rightfully, will be able to count on the President's favor, but who won't exact a fee for services rendered.

The "foreign friends" were Narváez, of course, and another figure who played a key – though secretive – role in Spanish politics, the Duke of Riánsares. Riánsares (Fernando Muñoz) was María Cristina's secret morganatic second husband, and he served as the courier of Grimaldi's letters in his frequent trips between Paris and Madrid. His main interest was the accumulation and protection of his private fortune, but he naturally sympathized with the Moderates and therefore willingly entered the negotiations with Grimaldi, Narváez and Louis Napoleon.

How much did Louis Napoleon tell Grimaldi he needed from Narváez? "He told me that in order to get *completely* out of trouble he needed one million francs, half of it as soon as possible . . ." Grimaldi strongly recommended that Narváez accept the suggestion to bail out Louis Napoleon: he foresaw "incalculable political and private advantages which the present situation offers the Spanish Government." He offered to be the conduit of the transaction ("I should keep on being the only intermediary") should Narváez agree. On November 30, by return post to Grimaldi, the Prime Minister of Spain agreed to the proposition and revealed that he had instructed Riánsares and the Minister of Finance (Bravo Murillo) to release four million *reales* (one million French francs), but to do so secretly. Narváez's correspondence shows that he took the issue up with only a select group of his council of ministers, who decided that the best way to carry out the arrangement was through a private intermediary in order to avoid embarrassment or scandal should word leak out that Spain was interfering directly in the internal politics of her neighbor to the north. Riánsares sent a packet of information to Grimaldi. At the moment the dossier reached Grimaldi's hands, he and his son were about to leave for the theatre. Grimaldi quickly scanned the materials "under the light of a stairway lantern" and, realizing their urgency, rushed to Louis Napoleon's house ("my neighbor") to tell him the news and to set up an appointment with him for the following day (December 10). Grimaldi, believing that the matter was settled, went off to the theatre where he glanced over the rest of the dossier. But as he read more closely he realized that there would be a delay in securing the loan and, troubled by his precipitous statement to Louis Napoleon, he left his son alone in the theatre and rushed back home, "to immerse myself without any distraction in the ocean of thoughts that overflowed in my head."[35]

Grimaldi worried – with reason – that the French president would react negatively to what would appear to be a broken promise. Just hours before their appointment on December 10, the postman delivered two letters to Grimaldi, one from Faucher and one from Narváez (via Riánsares) in which the Spanish general confirmed that a delay was inevitable ("at this time, I cannot do it the way I had indicated"). Grimaldi was stuck: he had made a rash promise to Louis Napoleon and within one hour he would be faced with an embarrassing situation. "In my hand rested the ability to conclude or not the negotiation of the loan to my neighbor." When the meeting took place, Grimaldi acted with the same grace and quick wit that had always characterized his behavior. He assured the president that the loan would go through, insisting merely that there would be a two-week delay and, as a sign of goodwill, handed to him 100,000 French francs *of his own money*. And in good business practice, he required a receipt.[36] At this point, Grimaldi wrote back to Narváez (he included the receipt) to propose a banking solution to the loan problem, but Narváez rejected the idea of involving even Belgian bankers since "everyone would know that this operation had taken place, and the money would not go into the Treasury, and there would be questions" (December 30, 1849; Pabón, p. 274).

It is not known whether the entire four million *reales* ever found their way to Louis Napoleon, but in 1850 Grimaldi was honored with membership in the Legion of Honor by the French president, and Pabón speculates that Louis Napoleon's lavish treatment of Narváez in early 1851 implied "a huge debt of gratitude on the part of Louis Napoleon."[37]

Grimaldi's resignation as consul in 1851 was linked to Narváez's resignation as Prime Minister and to Louis Napoleon's public display of sympathy for the ousted Spanish leader. Sotomayor, the Spanish Ambassador in Paris, had helped to organize Narváez's welcome. He received Narváez upon his arrival in Paris and arranged a meeting between him and Louis Napoleon, who, shortly thereafter, organized a dinner to celebrate Narváez's arrival. To the dinner were invited "all the Spaniards of distinction who were in Paris." In the days following this event Narváez was treated as visiting royalty, much to the disgust and discomfort of the Spaniards in Madrid who had orchestrated his resignation. As a consequence of his involvement in the Narváez affair in Paris, Sotomayor was summarily relieved of his duties.[38]

Grimaldi had also appeared on the outskirts of Paris to greet his old friend Narváez on the day of his arrival and was surprised to find Sotomayor there ("... I found the Ambassador, with whom, however, I had not arranged such a meeting") (March 10, 1851; RAH: Narváez, 10). He took an active part in Narváez's welcome, not only by attending many of the functions given in his honor but also by hosting a party of his own, attended by many of the most important Spanish and French notables in Paris. In offering his resignation, Grimaldi pointed out that the "modest title" of Consul added little to his considerable social standing and nothing at all to his financial status and he launched a spirited defense of Sotomayor and of Narváez. This subtle criticism of his dismissal angered the Queen, who accepted his resignation, but found the tone of this and subsequent letters to be inappropriate. She refused to store them in the official palace files.[39] Grimaldi gave a copy of his letter to Narváez, which revealed his evident disappointment and bitterness with these developments.

But Grimaldi had proven himself such a loyal supporter of both Narváez and Louis Napoleon that this episode was only a temporary setback. Soon he found himself appointed to the General Council of the province of Jura and showered with honors and recognition. In 1854 the marqués de Pidal, who at that time was charged with carrying out the Queen's business arrangements in Paris, attempted secretly to name him consul again (with Isabel's permission, of course; the Queen "has been very satisfied with the zeal with which he has carried out his consular duties" [May 4, 1854; Desfrétières, p. 309]), but word of his impending appointment leaked out and he was unable to take up the position.[40] Grimaldi understood the opposition very well. Even though he considered himself as much Spanish as French ("a good Spaniard by heart if not by birth" [March 10, 1851; RAH: Narváez, 10]), the other Spanish consuls in Paris viewed it as an affront to their honor and prestige to have to work under the direction of a foreigner. "Your Excellency can imagine the disgust produced among the current consuls, among whom are numbered Potestad, Segovia, Prat, Tovar, Gavarrón and others as distinguished by their long careers as notable by their good service, seeing themselves suddenly placed beneath the orders and direction of a foreigner, who does not even belong to the foreign service, and whose education and knowledge of the world, however vast they may be, cannot in any way make up for the special and practical knowledge demanded of such an important and delicate position" (Letter dated at the Royal Palace, May 6, 1853; MAE: Personal, Legajo 125, num. 6071). Grimaldi had heard similar arguments used against him in Madrid thirty years earlier by the actors who opposed the installation of a "foreigner" as their boss.

Even though denied any official position in the Spanish government, Grimaldi kept a close watch on the political situation in Madrid and served as an advisor, commentator, and business contact to the numerous Spaniards who came to the French capital. He was also a financial representative for certain English interests in Paris.[41] Although at times he fantasized about leaving Paris to retire to Spain (the Count of San Luis, head of the last government of the Moderate decade – 1853 – asked Ventura de la Vega to find out "if it is certain that [Grimaldi] plans to quit business, liquidate his assets, and retire to Seville"),[42] he kept himself busy with his business dealings, with maintaining his social position and with his duties at the General Council of Jura. In April 1854, he was granted another of the highest honors conceded by the Spanish government – the Gran Cruz de Isabel la Católica – and he apparently enjoyed the fruits of his wealth and prestige. Asenjo Barbieri tantalizingly wrote to Vega, "If it weren't for the fact that I don't like to commit to writing certain hot stories, I would tell you what I have discovered about Grimaldi. Father Claret was right when, referring to a certain saint, he said that man's excess continues as long as he can move his eyelids . . .! I'll tell you in person some details that will make you howl . . ."[43]

The General Council of Jura was an administrative body charged with overseeing the details of public works for the province. Grimaldi had conducted business in Salins during the 1840s and had reached such prominence there that he was elected as a representative from that town to the General Council in 1851.[44] He kept his relationship with Salins alive for years, being constantly re-elected to the Council and receiving several honors from it. He served as Mayor between 1864 and 1867, and was credited with making a number of "significant urban improvements" to the town.[45] He also used his banking skills in his position as President of the Salins Mutual Aid Society and was credited with spending much of his own money on the improvements he instituted in Salins. His annual re-election to the Council was always unanimous until 1865, when a challenger threatened his hold on the position. He had been in Madrid on business and received a letter from a contact in the area urging him to return to be present for the campaign and election. He refused to go, declining to "suffer the humiliation of being a mere candidate." He won anyway (September 10, 1867; RAH: Narváez, 56). On the Council he typically did not content himself with merely attending meetings and doing nothing – by the second year of his service to the Council he was named President of it by Louis Napoleon (soon to be named Emperor Napoleon III with the declaration of the Second Empire).[46] In 1853, the Emperor reappointed him to the same position. In his second presidential address he thanked the Emperor for the honor conceded him, stressed his long-standing allegiance to the Napoleonic cause ("my whole life's devotion to the Napoleonic dynasty") and demonstrated once again that he was indeed "a good Spaniard at heart" by commenting on the Emperor's recent marriage to a Spanish noblewoman (Eugenia María de Montijo, the beautiful Countess of Teba) and pointing out the long line of Spanish/French dynastic marriages which had helped to stabilize relations between the two countries.[47] He was considered to be the "most eminent orator" on the Council.[48]

His political duties in France did not keep Grimaldi from continuing to attempt to manipulate public opinion about Spain. Throughout the rest of his life he made frequent trips to Spain on business (both financial and political) and he remained in close contact with the leaders of the Spanish government, in particular Narváez, who in 1856 had been put back in power with the help of an old ally, General Leopoldo O'Donnell. His main interest was to shore up the popularity of Narváez and to insure that attacks on him were countered as quickly and as effectively as possible. He maintained a close watch on political commentary in the French press and kept Narváez closely informed about French opinion regarding his rule. Many examples of his protective attitude are to be found in his correspondence with Narváez, never before studied, and with which we will deal in the next section. For now, it will suffice to cite Grimaldi's letter to Narváez (November 22, 1856) commenting on an article published in the *Messenger de Bayonne* (September 23, 1856) which subtly criticized Narváez. Grimaldi clipped out the article and sent it to Narváez along with a letter recounting Napoleon III's displeasure with "a newspaper favored with an indirect subvention through judicial advertisements, that would be worth 2–9000 francs a year, that would disagree with imperial policy by attacking a foreign statesman thought so highly of by the Emperor." Grimaldi, using his prestige and position in the General Council of Jura, could put pressure on such papers (one of the paper's officials was a man who "owes me his official position and many other favors" and the editor was a personal friend) to make sure that such articles were not repeated. Years later, in another letter to Narváez (November 1, 1867) he bragged that he had been able to pressure the *Messenger* to do his bidding and that he could do it again, this time with one Emile Louit, a rich businessman who owned the *Journal de Bordeaux*. He attempted to convince Narváez that buying favorable press coverage was in his best interest:

Louit . . . has offered to place in his paper letters from Madrid if they are sent with an agreed-upon return address. A great deal of advantage can be had from a newspaper near the border because those newspapers are read attentively by the papers in Paris, which look in them for news of the bordering country, and they distrust them less than sources they drink from here, even if those sources come in the most golden cups. I was very successful a few years ago with the *Messenger de Bayonne*. It can be done again with the *Journal de Bordeaux*.

Grimaldi even provided Narváez with the agreed-upon signal: "All you need to do is send what you want to insert to *Monsieur Emile Louit, armateur, 21 rue Judaiques, Bordeaux*, and put on the front of the envelope a cross +."[49] As we shall see, Grimaldi's belief in the efficacy of newspapers to form public opinion received ample confirmation in late 1867 when he launched a bitter polemical attack against the great French historian, François Pierre Guizot, from the pages of the *Mémorial diplomatique*.

During the 1850s and 1860s Grimaldi worked assiduously on the Council on a number of projects, lending his expertise in business and administration to various commissions. One of his major interests was education, a subject which had occupied his attention in Madrid in the early 1830s (see the *Revista Española* articles). He served on the Commission on Public Education for five separate years and was instrumental in writing and publishing several position papers calling for reforms. He also served on the Finance Commission, the

Commission on Postal Service, the Commission on Local Roads, the Commission on Navigation, the Commission on Agriculture and finally on one of the commissions most directly related to his personal financial interests, the Commission on Railways (1859, 1864, 1865).[50]

The decade of the 1850s was a period of rapid development of the railways in Spain and Grimaldi became interested in expanding his considerable fortune by investing in this newly profitable enterprise. In 1855 the promulgation of the Railway Law, which offered incentives for domestic and foreign capital investment, gave fresh impetus to the creation of railway lines.[51] The Rothschilds and other French concerns invested heavily in railway projects (it has been estimated that by the end of the century French capital controlled over eighty per cent of the Spanish railway system)[52] and many of the decisions concerning the conduct and development of the Spanish system were made not in Madrid but in Paris by, as Grimaldi wrote, "the principal houses of Paris, interested in the Spanish railway industry."[53] Concessions, important to the profitable development of railway lines, were prized commodities handed out and controlled by the Spanish politicians and were frequent sources of abuse and scandal.[54]

In France, Grimaldi had constructed some 126 kilometers of railway lines in his province of Jura, connecting several of the industrial areas with the Swiss frontier, and often – in the words of one of Jura's officials – at considerable "personal sacrifice."[55] He prided himself with this improvement of provincial life and industry. By 1867, Grimaldi's interests had turned toward the railways in Spain and centered on the line from Gerona to Venta de Sales on the French border. He pressed his project for additional concessions publicly through the Minister of Finance and privately through Narváez. With the exception of the Irún–Hendaya segment in the western section of the Pyrenees, none of the Spanish railway lines connected with those in France. Grimaldi sought to end this isolation of Spanish goods by focusing on an eastern connection to the European railway system. He made several trips to the Spanish capital to lobby for the contract, realizing the great benefits to be extracted from a successful line, but deeply concerned by the counterproposals being advanced by his competitors (English railwaymen). He was suspicious of the English businessmen and begged Narváez not to deal with them without consulting him first. On November 7, 1867, he wrote to Narváez:

I have noticed that several Englishmen are wandering about with counter proposals on Sales. I trust that D. Manuel [Barzanallana, Minister of Finance] will not lose sight of my proposals, and that he will not make a decision without hearing me out. I will be very sorry if my propositions fail; I have placed great hopes in them and expect them not only to bring me honor but also to bring benefit to Venta de Sales and be a true service to the State.

A few days later (November 12, 1867) he repeated his position: "I have received several letters from Madrid trying to alarm me with the arrival of some Englishmen who are attempting to give proposals concerning Salinas to the Ministry of Finance. The surname of the main petitioner is a bad sign: he is named *Gibb*, which in English means *nuisance*, or deceit . . . I'm not moved by such news, as I have written to Mr. Barzanallana, since I do not believe that the Minister will deal with these recent arrivals without first hearing the man who raised the question initially and who has more capital than anyone to carry the project through."[56]

He seemed confident that his money and his connections would win the necessary additional concessions for him, but when the budgetary crisis of 1866–7 generated a backlash against foreign investments, Grimaldi, for an added measure of security, began in October of 1867 to publish a series of articles on the Spanish economy in the *Mémorial diplomatique*. These articles, entitled "Finances de l'Espagne," were published anonymously, but we know Grimaldi to be the author from information he revealed in his letters to Narváez ("Today's *Mémorial diplomatique* contains an article of mine on the Spanish treasury . . ." "In the meantime I have placed today in the *Mémorial* an article on 'The Spanish Treasury,' which contains the statistics that you were so kind as to send me," etc.).[57] In five articles, Grimaldi supported a recent Spanish plan to enable regional and local interests to enter the financing of the railway lines by raising money by national subscription (twelve year bonds).[58] A decree issued by the Narváez government on October 20, 1867, outlined a reorganization of the national debt and called for a new bond offering of five hundred million *reales*. The restructured financing would affect the railway investments: "You often hear that it is necessary, indeed urgent, to accept the conditions proposed by the railway companies; they will make deals that will insure that Spain will have money and means to credit, etc. On this point the exaggeration has no limit. They will persuade some, they will make others doubt, and in the final analysis, the supreme law of supply and demand, the situation, carefully chosen to produce effect, will do the rest. All doubts, commentaries and vacillations cease. We shall be judges and arbiters of the railway question; . . . the Treasury will come out of the situation counting only on the country's resources."[59] In these articles, which he mailed out for publication in London and Amsterdam as well, he argued in favor of forcing the Spanish government to honor previous and pending commitments, but praised the government's willingness to float a public debt to increase credit available to those who had an interest in the future of the railroad. The purpose of the articles was not merely to keep the French business community informed but also to advance his own interests by influencing policy in Madrid. A translation of the November 21 article, "which we believe to be of major interest given the current situation," appeared in Madrid in *El Español* (November 27, 1867). It was Grimaldi's belief that the move toward a subscription needed to be studied carefully in France, "given the enormous capital which our compatriots have invested in that country, either in State bonds or in stocks in the railway companies, capital that surpasses one billion four hundred million francs." He confidently saw Barzanallana's reorganization plan as the best way to protect that investment and he publicly praised Narváez for orchestrating a "financial Renaissance" in Spain.

The lessons Grimaldi had learned during his battles with the city authorities over the ownership of the theatres in Madrid many years before were not lost on him as he maneuvered for these latest favors controlled (again) by the government. He argued and cajoled, flattered and threatened, using every means at his disposal in order to convince the Spanish bureaucrats that his proposals would bring real benefits to the country. He called upon influential friends and placed opinion pieces in the press in order to persuade the authorities to favor him with the desired concessions.

Several months later (March 1868) he was back in Madrid on business to lobby for his interests in the Gerona–Venta de Sales railway line, but he was suddenly taken ill and forced to deal with Narváez, not in person as he had planned, but by letter. He had hoped that the services he had rendered to Narváez and Barzanallana in Paris would be remembered ("I hope Mr. Barzanallana will listen more attentively, more favorably, after he has read the *Spanish Letters*" [October 24, 1867; Narváez, 56]) but he was startled by a report he read in *El Español* which seemed to threaten his hold on the Gerona–Venta de Sales line. "They've just given me a fright with the news . . .

that the Minister of Finance is about to present to Parliament a projected law concerning the railway line from Gerona to France, a project based . . . on the wishes expressed by the representatives of the provinces in question." He was stunned that Barzanallana would formulate new policy "without having heard one of the most interested parties, the most informed party, the most practical party, the principal party to the proposal," that is, Grimaldi himself and his investment/construction company. Even though he was sick in bed, he begged Narváez to facilitate a meeting (with Narváez present) between him and Barzanallana, who was scheduled to meet with industrialists from Cataluña and Valencia. It was such an urgent matter that he offered to show up on a stretcher, if necessary: "Still laid out in bed, I think I can come up in three or four days at most, to wherever you tell me so that the Minister of Finance can hear me out, with you present (if you will grant me this favor). But if the matter is so urgent that such a delay seems too long, I am ready to come by stretcher, being moved, not by private interest (I swear it) but by my proven and unalterable loyalty to the government presided over by you" (March 18, 1868; Narváez, 56). His construction company had not yet finished the line (it is possible that the system had not even been begun yet), but he asssured Narváez that his company could complete the work much more quickly than any competitors (two years as opposed to five or six) and that it would provide immediate employment for some ten thousand laborers (a significant promise during a period of economic retrenchment, high unemployment, and declining railway construction).[60] In addition, he hastened to add that his participation in the project would insure that "not a single penny of public money will be spent," whereas the plan put forth by Barzanallana implied an investment of "several million" by the government. Three days later Grimaldi felt stronger but not yet able to attend meetings. Narváez favored him by inviting his daughters, who had accompanied their father to Madrid, to join him in his box at the theatre, but the records of the correspondence between the two men ends on March 21, 1868, and the final outcome of Grimaldi's pleas remains unknown.[61]

Narváez was stricken with a serious pneumonia at the end of March and was dead by April 23. His death, along with the political and economic chaos which ushered in the September Revolution in Madrid and the exodus of the Queen, put an end to Grimaldi's influence in the Spanish peninsula. Grimaldi returned to Paris, where he died four years later. As for the railway line, it began service on January 20, 1878.[62]

D. *Narváez, Guizot and "Le Mémorial diplomatique" (Paris, 1867)*

We have seen many examples of Grimaldi's dedication to Narváez and the Moderate cause in Spain, a loyalty which began with his earliest support of Narváez's "moderate liberalism" (September 27, 1867; RAH: Narváez, 56), became strengthened when they met in Paris in the early 1840s (in 1866 Grimaldi wrote to Narváez, "You know how constantly passionate in your support I have been during the twenty-five or twenty-six years I have been your friend . . ." [July 15, 1866; RAH: Narváez, 56]), and lasted unchanged until death claimed the Duke of Valencia in 1868. He served him as courier, business and political contact in the French capital ("this letter has been long and I cannot permit myself to steal more time away from the business you are doing for me" [September 30, 1867; Narváez, 56]), Consul, and, as we shall see, chief propagandist abroad. Grimaldi's service to Narváez – which he claimed to be purely altruistic – produced benefits for both men: Narváez obtained an articulate and passionate supporter of his policies abroad and Grimaldi received important contacts, business and private favors ("you were kind enough, not long ago, to grant me special favors which I have not forgotten, which I do not and will never forget" [July 15, 1867; RAH: Narváez, 56]) and gifts (cigars, art objects) (September 10, 1867; RAH: Narváez, 56). Grimaldi was not, however, a puppet for every Narváez official wishing to have his views trumpeted abroad. He did receive and publish articles from other ministers (González Bravo, for example) but he frequently refused to place in French newspapers articles forwarded to him from Madrid which he deemed too sloppy, hostile or seditious (see letter dated October 10, 1867; Narváez, 56). At other times he rewrote pieces sent to him for publication.

Grimaldi was an excellent agent for Narváez. His wealth and prestige gave him access to the highest government officials and he was privy to many "insider" decisions in the court of Napoleon III. He could shape the debate concerning Spain both inside and outside the Spanish capital. He could quote conversations between the likes of the Emperor, the King of Prussia, and the Emperor of Austria to Narváez on matters which concerned the Spanish government (see, for example, his letter dated October 25, 1867; RAH: Narváez, 56). We shall see that his own view of Spanish history carried enormous weight in Paris.

In the mid-1860s, the monarchy of Isabel II was undergoing what would prove to be the last of its many crises. The economy and the pillars of institutional support began to crumble around the leaders of the Moderate party and the subsequent period of instability threatened the foundations of the Spanish government. When Narváez returned to power yet again in 1866 (following O'Donnell), Grimaldi wrote to him immediately, offering his services "either in the press or for any report or financial business, since you know that I am in a position here to do some good in either area" (July 15, 1866; RAH: Narváez, 56). His chance to serve Narváez again came following the publication in mid-1867 of the eighth and final volume of Guizot's *Mémoires pour servir à l'histoire de mon temps* (Paris: Michel-Lévy, 1858–1867). In this volume Guizot occupied himself at length with the question of the Spanish marriages of 1846 (Queen Isabel II and her sister, Luisa Fernanda) and of the continental machinations which raged through the months and years preceding them. Guizot (1787–1874), a near contemporary of Grimaldi's, was a noted and influential historian and politician who had served King Louis-Philippe I in various ministries in the 1840s and whose intransigent policies helped to touch off the February Revolution of 1848 in Paris. In chapter 45 of his *Mémoires* ("The Spanish Marriages: 1842–1847") he drew upon his experience and his personal correspondence with major political figures to attempt to explain the complicated negotiations which surrounded Isabel's marriage to her cousin, Francisco de Asís, the future Duke of Cádiz, and to explain his own involvement in those negotiations.

Interest in Isabel was of course interest in the Spanish crown. A dynastic struggle raged through the courts of Europe, played out in numerous diplomatic meetings, behind-the-scenes plans, private dispatches, and public displays of concern. Jockeying for power began as early as 1841, following María Cristina's abdication of the Spanish crown and arrival in Paris. The chief antagonists in the struggle were the various factions in Spain, most of whom were anxious to avoid another civil (Carlist) war; France, eager to maintain a Bourbon on the throne of her neighbor; England, interested in gaining a foothold through marriage in Spain as well as an ally against her traditional antagonist, France; and Austria, intrigued with the possibility of regaining long lost influence on the Spanish peninsula. The principal players included the numerous lines and groupings of the ruling Bourbon family – Isabel herself; María Cristina; María Cristina's sister, Carlotta; her uncle, Louis-Philippe, King of France; her brother, the King of Naples; and their various offspring – as well as the political and diplomatic leaders of England (Queen Victoria, Lord Palmerston, Lord Aberdeen), France (Louis-Philippe, Guizot, Ambassador Bresson) and Austria (Prince Metternich). The negotiations were difficult and delicate, and any missteps could have hurled Europe into another protracted war over the succession to the Spanish throne.

Guizot's long (238 pages) account of the complex negotiations emphasized France's "neutrality" in the matter. He contended that France sought to maintain its policy of non-intervention (as it had done during the Carlist War) but concern for the marriage of the Spanish queen forced it to become involved. Guizot, as foreign minister to Louis-Philippe, quoted extensively from his private correspondence (especially the letters exchanged with the French Ambassador in Madrid, Bresson) in order to uphold his view of a reluctant France, selflessly sacrificing its own political interests to a broader European interest in peace.

Naturally, the British bitterly opposed the prospect of Louis-Philippe's son, the Duke of Aumale, on the Spanish throne, fearing that such a marriage would close them out of the corridors of European power. María Cristina had suggested this possible liaison to her uncle early in 1844.[63] Other prospects – María Cristina's Italian nephew, the Conde de Trapani; her Spanish nephew, Francisco de Asís; Leopold, a German cousin of Prince Albert of England; or the son of Fernando's brother Carlos – were all considered at various times and rejected. Spain, in the meantime, was becoming sensitive to what it considered outside meddling in its internal affairs.

These frenzied negotiations were being played out against a backdrop of a series of changing ministries in Madrid. As Guizot saw it, Espartero's fall and the subsequent rise of the Moderates brought with it serious instability in the Spanish capital. Various ministries came and went (Olózaga, Pidal, Serrano) and came again, and pressure was exerted upon the Queen to force her into accepting the hegemony of the Moderates in Parliament and the ministries. Guizot quoted one of his sources to the effect that in 1843 Olózaga physically forced the thirteen-year-old Queen to sign a decree dissolving the

Cortes ("She had responded negatively, and then he had taken her forcibly by the arm, and putting a pen in her hand, he said to her: 'You must sign.' She was afraid and signed it.")[64] and that Narváez was behind it in order to get the Moderates into power ("... this intrigue, similar to those which he had already discovered, was conducted by General Narváez, and had as its aim to put power in the hands of the Moderates").[65]

Guizot's major source of information from the Madrid of Narváez was Ambassador Bresson. He discussed the return to Spain of María Cristina (she arrived in Aranjuez on March 25, 1844) and the two major issues facing the government: the young Queen's marriage and the proposed constitutional reform. Narváez's choices for cabinet ministers included Alejandro Mon (a Narváez supporter who eventually abandoned him), Pedro José Pidal, and Francisco Martínez de la Rosa (whose plays Grimaldi had staged in Seville and Madrid in the early 1830s). In addition, the Duke of Rivas, author of *Don Alvaro, o la fuerza del sino*, was ambassador in Naples (and involved in the negotiations concerning Trapani's possible claim for the Queen's hand). Narváez supported the choice of one of Louis-Philippe's sons, either the Duke of Aumale or the Duke of Montpensier, but when Aumale married an Italian princess and Montpensier was thought a better match for Isabel's sister, Luisa Fernanda, the round of negotiations whirled on. Guizot and Bresson criticized Narváez for what they judged instability ("General Narváez had not long maintained the balance which was little by little reestablishing itself in him; when his passions are excited, he is no longer himself nor does he control himself")[66] and quoted María Cristina as comparing Narváez to his enemy, Espartero: "It is Espartero, she told me, it is the same demands; he wants to reach the same goals."[67]

It was this depiction of Spain as a bumbling oligarchy and of Narváez and María Cristina as indecisive and manipulative leaders that galvanized Grimaldi into action. He read Guizot's last volume with rising anger and consulted with Narváez about a possible response. But how to do it? It was clear that a frontal attack on Guizot would be impossible, since certainly Narváez himself could not undertake it and Grimaldi, a known and avid supporter of the Spanish general, would be discounted as a partisan observer. Together they developed a plan – which involved secrecy, substantial amounts of money, the *Mémorial diplomatique* and huge doses of hand-rubbing glee – to counter Guizot's version of the recent events in Spain.

Grimaldi was seventy-one years old when he embarked upon this final chapter of his life as a political correspondent. He conceived of a way to rebut Guizot's accusations: he would place – anonymously – in the *Mémorial* a series of long articles which answered Guizot and which presented a more favorable portrait of Narváez than the one painted by the French historian. As he later explained to Narváez:

I have done it because a friend of mine, who does not know of my participation in the *Cartas Españolas* [the series in the *Mémorial* was entitled "Lettres espagnoles"], told me a few days ago of the good effect which the rectification has had on the grossly false idea that many people had of you as little more than a parvenu sergeant, notable only because of your military courage and the energy of your character. That is why I have tried to return to you your real features, as I said at the end of my first letter: a gentleman by birth, by nature, by ideas, by manners, well versed in all the sciences which show that without them military art is no art at all; a political man, a statesman, orator, etc., etc.   (October 17, 1867; RAH: Narváez, 56)

Grimaldi also saw these publications as an extension of the quasi-biography of Narváez he had begun with his book against Espartero in 1841, a continuation of his public defense of the leader of the Spanish Moderates: "I feel fortunate to be able to finish the work that I began with the biography of Espartero, and a thousand thanks to you, my general, for having thought of me for this purpose" (October 24, 1867; RAH: Narváez, 56).

Initially there were five articles planned (September 10, 1867; RAH: Narváez, 56), which he soon extended to nine ("I trust that the sixth letter, which is the longest and most important and comes out today, will enjoy the same success as the others. There are three remaining" [October 24, 1867; RAH: Narváez, 56]), but only seven were actually written and published. They appeared as "Lettres espagnoles" in weekly installments in the *Mémorial diplomatique* beginning on September 19, 1867 (there was a two-week delay between the last two). From the very start Grimaldi planned to publish them in book form as well, as he had done with the Espartero biography: "I am not writing newspaper articles, but a book, a serious book, a book for the future; the importance of the subject matter will suffice to overcome the obscurity and inadequacy of the writer" (October 17, 1867; RAH: Narváez, 56). He had hoped that Narváez would work with him in updating the book and adding notes ("we can correct whatever needs to be corrected and add whatever notes might be necessary" [October 24, 1867; RAH: Narváez, 56]) but the book was never published. Grimaldi took on this assignment with the utmost seriousness and viewed himself as a historian, not merely an apologist for the Narváez regime. He organized his ideas, collected data and attempted to present a coherent and forceful argument to counter Guizot's formidable influence. More was at stake that the mere protection of Narváez's image abroad; the opposition in Madrid was strengthening daily (led by Juan Prim's conspiracies against the Prime Minister). In Paris, as he wrote in the first published letter, "the majority of our colleagues considered a general revolution on the other side of the Pyrenees to be imminent and inevitable."[68] Privately, he confessed to Narváez:

I need to tread cautiously in the collection and use of my materials. My responsibility is a daunting one when one considers the prestige of the illustrious protagonist of my story and the colossal, if assailable, reputation of my adversary. You cannot imagine the quantity and variety of books and documents which I have been studying for the past two months. Each article, by itself, considered as literature, seems minor, but each word has been carefully thought out and the collection of them arrives at the printers only after having been thought about long and hard. I plan to read three different proofs of each printing and correct any mistakes before they are printed, because I am a follower of Boileau in that I am convinced that the "difficult ease" supported by him (following the dictates of Horace) can never be achieved if one does not follow this precept: *subject your work to one hundred corrections.*   (October 17, 1867; Narváez, 56)

He expected his "Lettres espagnoles" to be read in the highest circles of French and European society, particularly in the corridors of government ("it would be useful for them to be read abroad and in the different chanceries of Europe . . ." [October 24, 1867; Narváez, 56]), an expectation which was fulfilled. As he reported to Narváez in late December of that year, the owner of the paper, Louis Debrauz de Saldapenna, received word that "those letters have attracted the special attention of the Emperor [Louis Napoleon], of all the ministers, of the diplomatic corps . . ." (December 26, 1867; Narváez, 56).

The "Lettres espagnoles" were read assiduously and commented upon, but still, nobody knew who had written them or how they had come to be published in the *Mémorial diplomatique*. Grimaldi reveled in his anonymity and enjoyed playing his cat-and-mouse game with those who tried to establish the articles' authorship ("The digression on the governors has in addition a special goal, which is to send off track the snooping of those who are scurrying about trying to find out who the author of the letters is (and there are many who are trying to find out)" [October 10, 1867; Narváez, 56]). There was some suspicion that Narváez was involved, a suspicion which Grimaldi tried to deflect by criticizing some of the General's actions ("They can't keep saying that you are behind it when they see that there is criticism in the author's observations . . ." (October 10, 1867; RAH: Narváez, 56). Even by the end of the run the mystery still hung in the air: "Mr. de Moustier [the new chief of the French Foreign Office] has said . . . that they must be the work of someone involved in public business at a very high level (Poor souls! How far off they are!)" (December 26, 1867; Narváez, 56).

The story of how the articles came to be placed in the *Mémorial diplomatique* reveals intimate details of the political and financial dealings which connected Grimaldi to the Narváez enterprise in Spain. The *Mémorial diplomatique* began its life in Paris as a semi-official political organ of the Austrian Emperor, Maximilian, in the 1850s, but slowly lost its importance as the Emperor's influence with Napoleon III declined. When Prince Metternich arrived in Paris as Ambassador in 1859 he became interested in reviving the newspaper by taking charge of its political reporting and by linking his interests with those of the Marquis de Moustier, at that time Napoleon III's Minister of Foreign Affairs. But Louis Debrauz de Saldapenna, the owner of the paper, resisted Metternich's advances by telling him that he had made other commitments which could not be renegotiated until January 1, 1868, and turned to other quarters for support. Those "other commitments" were his negotiations with Narváez and Grimaldi, although Debrauz lied to Metternich and denied any Spanish connection.[69] Grimaldi quoted Metternich's conversations with Debrauz: "'With whom are you dealing?' the Prince asked. 'With the Spanish government?' 'No, sir,' answered Debrauz. 'That's what I had thought,' said the Prince, 'because for a long time the *Mémorial* has been entirely Spanish, too Spanish, more than what Mr. de Moustier approves of . . . you are wrong if you think you can do business with the Spanish government.'" In order to have open access to the pages of the *Mémorial* (and to keep Metternich out), Grimaldi contemplated buying into it, underwriting the placement of his articles against Guizot with money forwarded to him by Narváez. The owner of the paper wanted 15,000 francs per year to subsidize the articles and in addition he advanced the possibility of selling a half-interest in the paper to Narváez-Grimaldi for 70,000 francs (beginning January 1, 1868), the first annual installment of 15,000 being

accepted as a down payment toward the purchase. Grimaldi placed
this proposal before Narváez in early September, reminding him that
the Emperor "reads attentively and with pleasure every issue."
Narváez became intrigued with the idea and spoke to Barzanallana
about the possibility of releasing the equivalent of 10,000 French
francs per year to support the plan: "I have spoken with Mr.
Barzanallana about underwriting the *Memorial diplomático* and I have
decided to write to Mr. Borrajo [a Spanish diplomat working in Paris]
to have him give the paper 10,000 francs, which will be paid every year
as a subsidy" (Undated letter [mid-September, 1867]; RAH:
Narváez, 56). He wanted to provide an even larger subsidy, "but you
are aware of our problems, the scarcity of our available funds."
Grimaldi was charged with making the final arrangements in Paris as
soon as possible, for Narváez was anxious to read his articles ("I hope
you'll send me your published letters as soon as possible"). Grimaldi
recommended a cautious posture concerning the proposed purchase
of half-ownership, but was likewise anxious to begin placing the
articles defending Narváez against what he considered to be Guizot's
impertinent attacks.

Debrauz, the owner of the *Mémorial*, temporarily agreed to
Grimaldi's offer of 10,000 francs, but pressed his request for more
money and for his offer to sell them a half-interest in the paper. He was
being pressured from other quarters, most notably by one Mr. David –
"a market speculator who rents out his pen," according to Grimaldi –
but he was more interested in attracting Narváez and Grimaldi as
investors than Mr. David.[70]

In the midst of these negotiations, the first of the "Lettres
espagnoles" appeared (September 19, 1867). Debrauz introduced the
anonymous author of the "Lettres espagnoles" to the readers of the
Mémorial as "a writer deeply involved in the events which for forty
years have occurred in the Peninsula, and having close relations with
the principal political figures in his country." The "Lettre" created
such a stir ("it has caused a disturbance") that booksellers and kiosk
owners descended upon Debrauz's offices and forced him to publish
an additional 500 copies of that day's issue (see Grimaldi's letter dated
September 19, 1867; RAH: Narváez, 56). "That's great," declared
Grimaldi. Narváez, in a telegram sent to Grimaldi's home address,
approved the increase to 12,000 francs.

Grimaldi's first "Lettre" contested Guizot right from the start by
questioning the truthfulness of his account. He attacked the French

historian's penchant for taking Ambassador Bresson's word as gospel, which Grimaldi often interpreted as a compilation of snap judgments and opinions rather than factual accounts of the events transpiring in Madrid during the time of the negotiations concerning Isabel's marriage. He mocked Bresson's claim that he was privy to insider information, especially when those claims were made within eight days of his arrival in the Spanish capital: "Good God! What an eagle's eye the new ambassador has! He has seen everything from all sides in a week, in a week which was hardly enough to receive or make his first official visits."[71] The "Lettre" once again demonstrated that Grimaldi considered himself in many ways to be more Spanish than French (he even wrote from the perspective of "*we* Spaniards, who are . . .," etc.). It exuded an inverted xenophobia which had little tolerance for criticism of Spanish customs, people or (particularly) Moderate leaders. He included several personal anecdotes to counter Guizot's view of Spanish roads as dangerous and overrun with brigands, which led him into a discussion of the effectiveness of the Civil Guard, the creation of which he mistakenly credited to the ministry of Luis González Bravo.[72] In his "Lettre" Grimaldi also pointed out that he had traveled extensively in Spain and had never been robbed; the only time he had been robbed was during a trip in France.

He ridiculed Guizot's depiction of the Spanish aristocracy and claimed that the Spaniards, "the most democratic people in the world," harbored an ancient and Christian democracy which allowed non-aristocratic sons of poor parents to rise to positions of wealth and influence. He mentioned examples from Fernando VII's time (Calomarde, Villela, Cardinal Inguanzo of Toledo) but he could just as easily have mentioned his own example – a foreign-born soldier who through quick wit and hard work rose to achieve substantial wealth and influence at the Spanish court. His defense of the "little guy" – the humble individual who has risen to the top – confirmed his belief in the efficacy of the Spanish constitutional monarchy. He resented Guizot's depiction of the Spanish people as backward, intolerant, and fanatical.

One additional example he provided also echoed his own situation and brought him to write of a past world he had known so well – the Spanish theatre. The example was that of a Spanish actress who in 1822 married a nobleman with little interference from State or society ("this marriage did not shock anyone"), a tolerance which he claimed would never have been permitted in France. With nostalgic gauze over his eyes, he defended Spain's fair and open treatment of actors, as opposed to a more restrictive French treatment of them. But he knew what he was talking about: he praised the fact that in Spain actors received Church rites (and were even buried in their own chapel), while he criticized Napoleon's refusal to honor his friend, the great actor Talma. He also observed that King Louis-Philippe never gave honors to the teachers of voice and declamation, whereas in Spain men such as García Luna and Romea had received numerous honors from the reigning monarchs. Much of this view was utopian wishful thinking, of course, but it did underscore Grimaldi's position that Guizot and Bresson were not capable of judging Spain or of seeing it with unbiased eyes. They were victims, he contended, of generations of French authors and painters who had always distorted Spanish reality, creating an "imaginary Spain" – Beaumarchais' "Spain of Figaro."

Grimaldi immediately sent a copy of his first "Lettre" to Narváez, who proclaimed it "magnificent" for its undercutting of Guizot's "pedantry" and Bresson's "lies." Narváez demonstrated keen interest in the next installment (September 24, 1867; RAH: Narváez, 56). That second "Lettre" appeared on September 26, and the next day Grimaldi bragged to Narváez that "they are making much – very much – noise here" and that both Napoleon III and Eugenie received copies of each issue (September 27, 1867; RAH: Narváez, 56). He also informed Narváez that he was keeping María Cristina's husband, the Duke of Riánsares, up to date by reading him sections of Guizot's *Mémoires*. Riánsares, one of the key figures in the marriage negotiations, doubtless provided valuable information to Grimaldi for his rebuff of the French historian.

The second "Lettre" addressed the Narváez issue more directly than the first. In order to establish the facts surrounding Narváez's resignation on February 11, 1846, Grimaldi led his readers through a mini-biography of the Spanish general, offering an extremely positive view of Narváez's family background, youth, career as a soldier (Grimaldi claimed to have read Narváez's personal dossier in the Ministry of War), student days, and overall character. The portrait painted by Grimaldi was detailed, sweeping, and beautifully composed, if colored with an abundance of bright hues. He went over the details of Narváez's period of semi-exile, followed by his rehabilitation by María Cristina and his rapid advancement in the Spanish army during the Carlist War, and praised him specifically for remaining cool and firm during the Sergeants' Revolt at La Granja. By refusing to allow his troops to join in the revolt, Narváez came to the attention of the Moderates and received the Queen Regent's strongest support.

Narváez's enthusiasm for Grimaldi's "biography" of him remained high, as did his contempt for Guizot's "vanity and bad faith" (September 30, 1867; RAH: Narváez, 56). In his letters to Grimaldi he accused Guizot and Bresson of deceit, hypocrisy, greed, and treachery:

Guizot criminally intercepted the correspondence of several people in order to find out what was happening even in their private lives; and what can we say about Mr. Bresson! Given that those letters may be true, he lied in them like a desperate man maltreating those who praised him daily; he even begged favors for his wife, crosses for himself, rewards for his Minister, grandeeships for his son, and he feigned friendship with the woman whom he was betraying in secret.   (September 30, 1867; RAH: Narváez, 56)

His letters also proffered small rectifications of fact which Grimaldi could incorporate into future installments or into the book he planned to publish.

The letters' popularity continued ("the publication is continuing to garner great favor" [October 3, 1867; RAH: Narváez, 56]) into the third "Lettre" (October 3, 1867), which continued the discussion of Narváez's activities during the Carlist War and repeated many of Grimaldi's old accusations concerning the conduct of Espartero during those days. In this installment Grimaldi traced Narváez's period of disgrace (he had been stripped of his honors and leadership of the army by Espartero), his period of exile in Paris and his subsequent return to Spain with the rise of the Moderates. He never lost sight of his goal and promised that his next "Lettre" "will address head-on the errors brimming from the pages dedicated by Mr. Guizot to the question of the Spanish marriages."

The fourth "Lettre" was in many ways the strongest, for it listed Narváez's string of successes during his 1844–6 ministry, successes which added up to, as Grimaldi saw it, "the complete reconstitution of the State."[73] His point was to demonstrate that by the time the negotiations for Isabel II's marriage partner began in earnest, Narváez was already an accomplished statesman and an energetic leader, not the bumbling neophite suggested by Guizot. Narváez applauded Grimaldi's attack on Guizot and foresaw that the French historian would be "more prudent" in his future writings as a result of Grimaldi's articles (October 13, 1867; RAH: Narváez, 56). The reasons for his fall from power were analyzed in the fifth "Lettre" (October 17, 1867). Grimaldi investigated Bresson's interpretation as reported by Guizot (that Narváez's interest in money was one of the primary reasons) and launched a spirited attack on the inconsistencies and duplicities in Bresson's letters to his boss in Paris. He concluded that Bresson's view of things was intentionally false and he reacted angrily that Guizot, who as a historian had the duty to preserve the historical record with some accuracy, distorted it with such indifference.[74] As Grimaldi explained it, not only were Narváez's actions honorable and justified, but Guizot and Bresson knew this perfectly well:

But in the final judgment, what were the reasons behind the resignation which put a sudden and unexpected end to the first ministry of Narváez? ... I will prove to you, in my next letter, that they were multiple, that they were obvious, that they were all serious, and that Mr. Guizot and Mr. Bresson knew them perfectly well.

Narváez continued his close watch on Grimaldi's articles, praising them and adding bits and pieces of information as he deemed necessary. He attempted to steer Grimaldi away from certain areas[75] or the criticism of certain friends (Mon and Pidal in particular).[76]

The sixth "Lettre" (October 24, 1867) focused on Bresson's interpretation of the crisis of 1846, which Guizot reported as having been manufactured by Narváez "under the vain pretext that the throne is in danger" (Bresson's words). Grimaldi presented in this article a Narváez who surprised many of his French readers – an old liberal, a man committed to the defense of liberty (for his enemies in France and England he represented the forces of absolutism and bloody strong-arm tactics) who had not been toppled from power but who had resigned for the good of the state. He angrily caught Bresson admitting to having conspired against Narváez during his time in the French Embassy and then distorting the facts surrounding his actions. And Guizot merely repeated it all as historical fact: "And that's how history is written," remarked Grimaldi with evident sarcasm. Yet Grimaldi was not forthcoming about his own sources and documentation. He claimed to have had access to private conversations from "an old friend." But this "old friend" was Narváez himself, a fact that Grimaldi was at pains to suppress, as he explained in a letter to his correspondent in Madrid:

It was said that the resignation could not be avoided and they interpreted it to be an act of true mental derangement. I had to prove the opposite; ... I have prided myself in not leaving open any suspicion of contact between you and the letters' author. Searching among public documents that preceded the quarrel which made you resign, I couldn't do less than center upon one which Guizot himself had used . . .   (October 31, 1867; RAH: Narváez, 56)

What turned out to be the final "Lettre" (although Grimaldi projected it to be third from last) appeared in the *Mémorial* on November 7, and again, in Grimaldi's words to Narváez, "they have liked it very, very much here" (November 7, 1867; RAH: Narváez, 56). It dealt with the very short second ministry of Narváez in 1846 and with Guizot's charge that Narváez surrounded himself with his friends (Pezuela, Burgos, Egaña). It also answered Guizot's charge that María Cristina accused Narváez of turning into another Espartero, an accusation which Grimaldi found particularly loathsome. We know his claim that "we write without passion, without self-interest" to be wholly disingenuous, but the force of his defense of Narváez and the cool control he exercised in laying out his arguments provided an important counterweight to the Guizot-Bresson version of Narváez's place in recent Spanish history. Narváez himself thought this seventh article to be "better than the rest" and he declared himself satisfied with having "confided in you the rebuttal to Guizot, because it is certain that no one else would have done such an outstanding job" (November 9, 1867; RAH: Narváez, 56). Grimaldi's decision to postpone the last two "Lettres" until he could consult with Narváez more directly resulted in their never being written (or at least published in the *Mémorial*). Grimaldi and Narváez praised themselves for having successfully depicted Guizot as a liar and a traitor:

I've managed to paint him as a liar; I've said he has no heart. Now I shall say that he conspired his entire life; . . . that he was a traitor to the First Empire that hired him; a traitor to the Restoration that treated him so well; a traitor to Louis-Philippe who even placed himself in his inept and unfaithful hands, and even more I shall show that his reputation as a journalist is misplaced, that it always lay and continues to lie in the most incredible ignorance as far as what type of liberalism Europe needs, led astray by him and his evil doctrinal school in pursuit of a freedom completely inadequate to Europe's social needs, etc.   (November 12, 1867; RAH: Narváez, 56)

He had fully intended to complete the other two "Lettres" but his declining health kept him from fulfilling his promise to Narváez and Debrauz. His recent illness ("Considering the state of my health which permits me to continue the course of the 'Lettres espagnoles' which the *Mémorial diplomatique* has edited . . .") was the reason that the last two "Lettres" were never written. In fact, he had been confined to his bed with a painful attack of the gout, unable to get to the Bibliothèque Imperiale to check his facts on Guizot for the next installment (see letter dated November 22, 1867; RAH: Narváez, 56). His recovery was slow; in mid-December he was still complaining of his terrible "pains" and he was not yet fully recovered by the end of the month, although he did want to continue with the "Lettres." Debrauz wanted him to continue them as well since they were selling papers: "Debrauz has been here this morning to lament this new interruption and at the same time to congratulate me for the general impatience with which the continuation of them is awaited at the highest levels [of government]" (December 27, 1867; RAH: Narváez, 56). But the fact is that the last two were never published, and Narváez and Grimaldi moved on to different matters.

One of those other matters was the death of General O'Donnell, which occurred in the first week of November. O'Donnell had been an early ally of Narváez (and an enemy of Espartero) and his decisive role in the suppression of the revolutionary left in 1856 insured Narváez's return to power that year. But O'Donnell moved away from support of Narváez and toward the alliance of Moderates and Progressives called the Liberal Union, which dominated Spanish politics from 1856 to 1863 (he served as Prime Minister from 1858 to 1863).[77] His death, as reported to Grimaldi by his correspondent Narváez, "will no doubt have a great and long-lasting effect on Spanish politics" (November 7, 1867; RAH: Narváez, 56). Narváez predicted the demise of the Liberal Union. Grimaldi received an article on O'Donnell from his sources in Madrid that he was to translate and insert in the *Mémorial*, but he did not like the tone of the piece and decided to write his own. He immediately took pen in hand ("The day after tomorrow I will publish in the *Mémorial* an article which I sent off last night entitled 'O'Donnell'" [November 12, 1867; RAH: Narváez, 56]) to provide a thumbnail biography of O'Donnell for the readers of the *Mémorial* (November 14, 1867) and to repeat Narváez's prediction that "With O'Donnell dead, so is the Liberal Union." The article was a masterpiece of deft criticism. Under the guise of praise, he made it clear that O'Donnell's leadership was inferior to that of Narváez. He openly criticized O'Donnell's role in establishing the hated Espartero in power in 1854, but he kept in mind that O'Donnell was more of an ally than many of the other military leaders of the time. When reports published in a journal in Paris, the *Intérêt Public*, painted O'Donnell as

a liberal turned reactionary (November 27, 1867), Grimaldi responded with a short follow-up to his "Lettres espagnoles" and depicted
O'Donnell as an early anti-constitutional royalist.[78]

At this same time – mid-November – problems began to develop
with the 12,000 franc subsidy that Narváez and Grimaldi had agreed
some months earlier to pay Debrauz. For reasons that are unclear,
Grimaldi was asked to return the money to Cuadra at the Spanish
Embassy. Narváez insisted that it was merely a bureaucratic slipup
and ordered Cuadra to hand over the funds to Grimaldi once again,
which subsequently were paid to Debrauz. Debrauz wrote to
Grimaldi at the end of November, reminding him that it had never
been decided whether the 12,000 francs "should be considered as the
price for placing the articles in the *Mémorial diplomatique*, at the cost of
40 cents per line . . . or whether the 12,000 francs are only the first
installment toward half ownership in the paper . . ." (November 28,
1867; RAH: Narváez, 56). Metternich was still interested in the
paper, but Debrauz hoped that Grimaldi would buy into it. He
planned to increase circulation, publish three times per week and
thereby improve his profits. Grimaldi, in turn, sent Debrauz's letter to
Narváez and recommended that they withhold their answer until
Grimaldi could talk personally with Narváez during a trip he was
planning to take to Madrid as soon as his legs had recovered from his
crippling attack of gout. He professed to have a secret plan which
would give them access to the paper without costing them any money:
"I shall explain to you some ideas and plans which can keep the
newspaper at our complete disposal without costing the government
anything" (December 5, 1867; RAH: Narváez, 56). Part of that plan
included a gradual financial takeover of the paper with Grimaldi
making himself administrator. But Narváez, saddled with enormous
political and financial problems at home, balked at the idea and
instructed Grimaldi to inform Debrauz that the 12,000 francs were to
be considered a subsidy for the "Lettres espagnoles" and nothing
more. They would not buy ownership of the *Mémorial*. Grimaldi
reluctantly agreed with Narváez's orders and counseled Debrauz on
what he should do about Metternich and Moustier. That agreement
stipulated that Metternich and Moustier would pay the paper's
subsidies and direct the *Mémorial* in 1868, but since Debrauz would
still own the paper, his agreement to insert any of the Grimaldi–
Narváez pieces remained in effect.[79] But Grimaldi never gave up his
hope of taking charge of this "important forum from which one can

speak to all the governments of Europe" and contemplated rounding up a group of investors to buy the *Mémorial* and use it as a "base of operations" (December 26, 1867; RAH: Narváez, 56).

Grimaldi continued his work as an agent for Narváez charged with inserting "proper" articles on Spain in the *Mémorial diplomatique*. Many of the pieces he received from Madrid had to be drastically rewritten before they could appear in the *Mémorial* and it was Grimaldi who took it upon himself to rewrite them. "L'Espagne et sa politique en Europe," a two-part article by a Mr. Emile Collas, published on December 27, 1867, and January 2, 1868, appears to be one of the last items "rewritten" by Grimaldi. His interest began to turn again to railways, and in March 1868, he was in Madrid lobbying his friends there for support, as we have seen.

The health of both men was declining: Grimaldi suffered a recurrence of his painful gout which forced him to return to his elegant house in Paris without concluding his business (March 15, 1868; RAH: Narváez, 56) and Narváez contracted pneumonia, which killed him by the end of April. Grimaldi's final years were spent in Paris at his house at 30 rue de Miromesnil, in the company of his son and daughters. He continued his work with the General Council of Jura through 1870 (roads and public instruction) and was promoted to the rank of Officer in the French Legion of Honor.[80] He died at the age of seventy-six on February 4, 1872.[81]

6

Conclusion

Juan de Grimaldi's adult life seems to divide into two discrete segments. One segment covers the time he spent in Spain as theatrical impresario and stage director, years which are marked by his activity preceding and during the advent of Romanticism. The other covers the time he spent in Paris as a businessman, newspaperman, and social figure. But the two segments intersect not in any point in time but rather in a posture – an attitude – for Grimaldi's divergent talents nearly always shared one thing in common: his love for Spain. His love for Spain manifests itself in a love for complex negotiations, surprising spectacles, diplomatic mysteries, behind-the-scenes plots, and circuitous intrigues. Grimaldi's attention to Spain focused upon few of the characteristics identified by other French observers. He cared little for the colorful *costumbrista* Spain described by numerous French travelers to the peninsula and wasted no time searching for the flashing eyes and tambourine cadences which attracted so many northern Europeans to this stubbornly independent country. Not only did he observe Spain; he absorbed it. He imbibed its language, its literature, its politics, its social climate. Although his stay in the Iberian peninsula was of brief duration (1823–36) when compared with the length of his life, he became, in many ways, more Spanish than French ("a good Spaniard at heart").

How was it that a foreigner, a soldier who came to Madrid with the invading forces of the French army in 1823, managed to carve out a place of such distinction in the Spanish theatrical and political worlds? Grimaldi did more than any other single individual to shape Spanish theatre in the first half of the nineteenth century. When he got to Madrid he saw a business opportunity in the theatre, although the recent history of Spanish theatrical endeavors should have warned him away from such an enterprise. He took over a failing business. Spanish theatres were saddled with enormous costs and overhead expenses, stifled by an ignorant ecclesiastical censorship and destabilized by a contentious group of untrained and self-centred actors. The previous impresarios had gone bankrupt and the repertory consisted of rehashed and rewritten "classics" of Golden Age theatre and silly imports. The city government, which owned the two principal theatres, tried to protect everyone's interests (everyone but the impresario, that is): they needed to protect their financial investment, or at least try to minimize the drain on their resources that the theatres represented; they needed to protect the actors' retirement benefits; they needed to protect the public's morals; and they needed to protect national "glory" (whatever that was). The result was an over-regulated, underdeveloped theatre which cost everyone money and pleased no one.

Grimaldi sought to change all that. He had an uncanny ability to seize an opportunity and to turn it to his own advantage. He immediately entered into disputatious negotiations with the municipality concerning his takeover of the theatres. He recognized that he would be forced to honor certain past commitments, but he insisted on several significant changes in the structure of theatrical regulation which he considered essential to the health of the enterprise. He realized that if he was to have good plays and quality translations he would have to commission them himself, and so over the years he enlisted the aid of Bretón de los Herreros, Ventura de la Vega, José María Carnerero, Antonio García Gutiérrez, and Mariano José de Larra to write original plays and to translate the most popular French comedies and melodramas being seen in Paris. During his tenure at the Cruz and Príncipe (mostly the Príncipe) Grimaldi expanded the Spanish repertory to include historical dramas, continuations of the Moratinian comedy, and the best of French theatre.[1] He even composed plays himself, some translated from his native French (*La huérfana de Bruselas, Lord Davenant*), one written in collaboration with his friends Bretón and Vega (*1835 y 1836 o lo que es y lo que será*), and one hybrid "adapted" translation which became the most popular play performed on the Spanish stage in the first half of the nineteenth century (*La pata de cabra*). He perceived the problem of creating an audience as well as a repertory of plays and a good acting company. *La pata de cabra* was designed for that purpose and it surpassed even his own ambitious dreams.

He also realized that he would need to train the actors to perform in these plays. His original idea of establishing an acting school never became a reality, although it had some influence upon the creation in 1831 of the Conservatory of Music, where acting was taught by and to members of the company. Over the years he brought into his company and trained all of the luminaries of the Spanish stage: Concepción Rodríguez (whom he married in 1825), José García Luna, Antonio Guzmán, Carlos Latorre, Matilde Díez, Teodora and Bárbara Lamadrid, and Julián Romea. He created real repertory companies, groups of skilled actors and in-house dramatists and translators who worked together to make their enterprise into an exciting and successful venture. As early as 1825 he was being credited in Paris with "the dawning of the dramatic resurrection" of Spain.[2]

Grimaldi was responsible for staging the most important plays of the Romantic period and he did so with a professionalism previously unknown in Spanish theatres. He improved not only the acting and the repertory but also the technical aspects of the theatre – sets, lighting, stage machinery, interior design – which played key roles in the acceptance of Romantic dramas in the capital. By the time the colorful, often exaggerated Romantic dramas reached the hands of the stage director, the actors and the theatres were prepared to perform them with seriousness and skill. Years of training and performances in French melodramas, years of practice with the complicated scenery of plays like La pata de cabra,[3] and years of preparing the audience to expect decent and interesting plays opened the way for the arrival of La conjuración de Venecia, Macías, Don Alvaro o la fuerza del sino and El trovador (all staged by Grimaldi). For this reason he has been called "a diligent and comprehensive impresario, without whose support it is almost impossible to think of Romanticism in the Spanish theatre."[4] Interestingly, although Grimaldi was not the impresario (meaning the individual in direct charge of the theatres) for the entire 1823–36 period (he was more often stage manager), he is remembered as being the impresario, which gives evidence of his lasting impact on theatrical memory.[5]

Grimaldi's struggle was not easy. He was thwarted at every step by the government's restrictive policies, by censorship, and often by the actors' fears of being disenfranchised and losing the considerable influence they wielded in the theatre (they helped to select the company and decided which plays they would or would not act in). He was not always triumphant in the myriad individual skirmishes he waged with those in power, but he remained tenacious, clever, manipulative and aggressive, and he ended up winning the war:

during his time as the chief proponent of the professionalization of the Spanish stage, the theatre in Madrid was irrevocably transformed. He added little to the canon of lasting drama, but his contribution to the theatre itself was unmatched in his day.

His authority spilled over into other areas of Spanish life and letters. He was considered to be a key figure in Madrid's intellectual élite, a man so respected that the leading literary figures of the day gathered around him to hear his views on Spanish and European literature. He talked to and cajoled, charmed and humored, persuaded and bullied his friends. He read pieces aloud to them with eloquence and energy ("What an instinct he has to discover theatrical effects where no one except him suspected they existed! . . . Again, the fear that I shall be accused of partiality and idolatry forces me to keep silent. I shall only add that to hear him read a play aloud was as enjoyable [if not more so] to people of taste, as seeing it performed on stage," gushed Bretón)[6] and debated the merits of contemporary literature at places like the "Parnasillo" *tertulia* at the Príncipe Café.

His immense charm and dramatic presence brought him to the attention of the Spanish aristocracy. Fernando VII, a fanatical devotee of the *comedias de magia*, provided access to members of the Spanish court. Grimaldi became a confidant, then a passionate supporter, of María Cristina and the Spanish monarchy. He served them well: intelligent, urbane, ambitious, literate and wealthy, Grimaldi became the perfect voice of the Moderate cause in the peninsula. From his position at the newspaper *La Revista Española*, he championed the policies of María Cristina and the Moderates against the *exaltado* progressive views of individuals like Juan Alvarez Mendizábal.

His taste for political polemic increased as María Cristina's position was besieged by Espartero's liberal band. After his own hasty retreat from Spain in 1836 he continued his war of words against the Queen Regent's enemies by publishing a clever and forceful attack on Espartero in the Parisian newspaper *La Presse* in 1841. In Paris he worked closely with María Cristina and the leaders of the Moderate opposition, mainly Ramón María Narváez (later Duke of Valencia), to restore the Moderates to power. Once that goal had been achieved, Grimaldi served the numerous Narváez ministries first as special consul then as minister of propaganda without portfolio in Paris, charged with placing articles in the newspapers of that capital which reflected favorably on the Narváez government in Spain.

His last and most contentious sally in favor of Narváez took the form of a series of articles he published against the French historian and politician Guizot, in 1867. Guizot's negative view of the early Narváez ministries, especially regarding the complicated machinations surrounding Isabel's marriage in 1846, rousted from Grimaldi a hostile polemic aimed at countering the Guizot view. Grimaldi prided himself on his ability to take on and defeat adversaries in the polemics he initiated: "Until now I have been favored by fortune in the lively polemics I have entered: I have always made it impossible for my adversaries to issue a suitable reply. I am never as courteous as when I am cutting someone down" (November 12, 1867; RAH: Narváez, 56).

In France he also served the government of Louis Napoleon (later Emperor Napoleon III) as a member and sometime president of the General Council of Jura, where he took charge of studying educational, administrative, and public works issues throughout France. He hobnobbed with the French élite, discussed issues with the leaders of the government and at one point lent a considerable sum of money to Louis Napoleon in an attempt to stabilize his fledgling republic. But his service was always colored by his loyalty to Narváez, with whom he corresponded for years and whose every move he watched and defended.

Grimaldi was witty, imposing, exciting, observant, and contentious and he managed, with very little formal education but huge doses of ambition and tenacity, to catapult himself into the highest echelons of two very different societies. He spoke and wrote French and Spanish with equal facility, and read English as well.[7] His sizable fortune began with the profits from the astonishing success of his play, La pata de cabra, and grew through smart investments, innovative business ventures, hard work, and constant manipulation to receive favorable treatment from those in power. He quickly rose in influence and prestige and ended his life in possession of numerous honors granted by the Spanish and French governments. His energy and animation attracted attention and followers (at seventy-one he still prided himself on the "youthful blood that still burns in [my veins]," a boast supported by his hectic business schedule [November 12, 1867; RAH: Narváez, 56]). His power and knowledge attracted loyal friends.

Antonio Buero Vallejo depicted Grimaldi in his play about Larra, La detonación (1977), as a man committed to "new times, new blood." This is particularly true of his activity on behalf of the Spanish theatre, but his commitment to the Moderate cause left little room for "new blood." Still, his constant drive, opportunistic manipulation of circumstances and cleverness made him, in Bernard Desfrétières's words, a "master of intrigue."[8] Grimaldi's life and career hinged upon his ability to adapt to circumstances and then to triumph over them. What emerges from our study of Grimaldi is the portrait of a man who, in its broadest implications, held a key place in the history of the theatrical and political world of nineteenth-century Spain, a world of passion, repression, fight for dominance, and unrelenting conflict. Juan de Grimaldi served many masters during his long life and prosperous career, but ultimately he served just one – himself. He survived and triumphed. He was indeed a "master of intrigue."

Appendices

Appendix 1. "Cargas que sobre sí tienen los teatros"
(Bernardo Gil, 1820)

(1) Razón circunstanciada de las cargas que tiene el teatro de la Cruz, y el gobierno ha mandado satisfacer siempre a los autores.

ANTIQUISIMAS

Al hospital de Antón Martín.	9,835	2 *maravedíes*
Al del Buen Suceso.	9,835	2 *maravedíes*
Colegio de Niñas de la Paz.	11,000	
Al hospicio (por contrata) a razón de 50 rs. por representación suponiendo 330 en un año.	16,500	
A los actores jubilados, viudas y huérfanos, a razón de 345 rs. y 12 mrs. cada día del año.	126,050	30 *maravedíes*
A un Escribano de teatros.	550	
A un alguacil (cuya vara compra el Ayuntamiento, y le paga la compañía) 8 rs. cada representación.	2,640	
Al alcaide del teatro (cuya plaza provee el Excelentísimo Ayuntamiento, para la guarda del edificio, y le paga la compañía) 16rs. cada día del año.	5,856	
A la guardia de infantería y caballería 47 rs. cada representación.	15,510	
Cuatro sillones para el escribano y alguaciles de que preside.	13,200	

OTRAS CARGAS MODERNAS

Por el alquiler del teatro al año	41,600
Al establecimiento de la galeria por contrata a razón de 106rs. y 1/2 por representación.	35,145
Partido de 10 rs. a la virgen de la Novena para su culto, que ha importado cada año de los últimos.	10,000

Ración de 12 rs. por representación para la
virgen de la Novena y la enfermería de los
actores.   3,960

Se hacen dos funciones también para estos
objectos, y se entrega el producto libre de
gastos que un año con otro importa.   5,000

El señor Arquitecto mayor de la villa
disfruta una luneta principal en cada
representación.   000

Otra luneta principal para el médico que
puso el gobierno poco hace para
satisfacerse de las enfermedades de los
actores.   000

El mismo Excelentisimo Ayuntamiento
tiene reservado el palco grande que
ocupan SS.MM. y AA. cuando se
dignan concurrir al teatro, cuyo palco
ocupa cuatro de los comunes, y tres
de los de la villa, que también
disfruta gratuitamente.   000

No se incluye el palco de la presidencia, ni
las lunetas del oficial de la guardia y
el ayudante de la plaza.   000

                                    Total   306,682

(2) Estado que manifiesta las cargas que sorbe sí tiene el teatro del
Príncipe en la hipótesis de 330 representaciones al año con las
ordinarias y extraordinarias.

Alquiler del teatro.	45,000	
Hospital de Antón Martín.	9,835	2 *maravedíes*
Buen Suceso.	9,835	2 *maravedíes*
Colegio de Niñas de la Paz.	11,000	
Galera: por 330 representaciones a 106 1/2 rs. cada una.	35,145	
Hospicio: por las mismas a 50 rs. cada una.	16,500	
Escribano de teatros.	550	
Alcaide, a razón de 11 rs. diarios, año natural.	4,015	
	131,880	4 *maravedíes*

Es carga de la compañía nueve palcos
que ocupa el del Rey y los dos palcos
de villa, que regulados por una mitad
que debe ser, un día que pueden
ocuparse con otro que no, esto es, la
mitad de las 330 representaciones.   89,100
También es carga, la que
espontáneamente se han impuesto los
cómicos por instituciones antiquísimas,
y por repetidas Reales órdenes, para
pago de jubilaciones, viudedades y
huérfanos de los mismos 345 rs. y 12
mrs. diarios, que multiplicados por 365
dias del año asciende a la cantidad de   126,050   30 *maravedíes*
Reducidas a una suma las tres expresadas
ascienden a   347,031

Appendix 2. Royal Order Concerning Conduct in the Theatre (1826)

Bando. Manda el Rey Nuestro Señor y en su Real nombre los Alcaldes de su Real Casa y Corte: Que para evitar los desórdenes que puede producir la inobservancia de las providencias dadas para la Policía de los Teatros, tal vez por ignorarse o estar ya olvidadas, y con el objeto de que jamás se desmienta el noble carácter y decisión que ha tenido siempre esta M.H. Villa en favor de las buenas costumbres, manifestándolo así en su compostura, tranquilidad y buen orden, tanto en acciones como en palabras, se renueven los Bandos publicados en los años anteriores y se observen los capítulos siguientes:

I Los concurrentes a los Coliseos, sin distinción de clase ni fueros, no proferirán espresiones, darán gritos ni golpes, ni harán demostraciones que puedan ofender la decencia, el buen modo, sosiego y diversión de los espectadores, bajo la pena al contraventor de ser destinado irremisiblemente por dos meses a los trabajos del Prado con un grillete al pie por la primera vez, y cuatro por la segunda; y en caso de reincidencia se le aplicará al servicio de las armas; si los contraventores fueren de otras circunstancias se les impondrán cincuenta ducados de multa por la primera vez, ciento por la segunda, y por la tercera se les destinará al Presidio.

II Con el objeto de que sea más exacto y puntual el cumplimiento de esta providencia se distribuirán Subalternos de Justicia que observen, estén a la vista, y den cuenta de los que se desordenaren en los Teatros, para poder resolver su prisión y castigo.

III Las Comedias u Operas se empezarán a la hora que se anuncie en los carteles; y los coches han de entrar para arrimar a los Coliseos por las calles señaladas al tiempo de principiar y de acabarse la Comedia, colocándose ínterin dura en las que se acostumbra, formando una sola fila, quedando el del Alcalde en el primer sitio para que pueda hacer uso de él en cualquiera ocurrencia.

IV En la calle de la Cruz no se detendrán los coches a las puertas de las casas más que el tiempo preciso para entrar en ellos, o apearse sus dueños, por lo que impiden el tránsito de los que salen de la Comedia, debiéndose colocar y esperar en la calle de la Gorguera y Carrera de San Gerónimo.

V Al entrar los hombres al patio, grada, tertulia, galería o luneta, guardarán el debido orden y sosiego, sin incomodarse unos a otros, ni causar confusión, sin embozo, y advertidos que para las gradas, tertulia, aposentos, galerías y lunetas no se permitirá gorros por ser justo que haya lugares distinguidos para los que concurren con mayor decencia.

VI Luego que el primer Cómico salga a las tablas, hasta el fin de la representación, se quitarán el sombrero y sentarán los asistentes sin excepción alguna, para no impedirse la vista unos a otros, y al que así no le acomodare puede escusar la concurrencia, buscándose las comodidades sin agravio de tercero, ni turbar el orden público y la atención que se merece.

VII No se gritará a persona alguna ni a aposento determinado, ni a Cómico, aunque se equivoque, por ser contra la decencia debida al público, y un agravio para los que hacen en su obsequio lo que saben y pueden, con deseo de agradar, y que suele improporcionar sus progresos en este modo de vivir.

VIII Las mujeres han de guardar la misma compostura y moderación en la Cazuela.

IX En ningún aposento podrá haber persona con el rostro cubierto de cualquier modo, cuidando los acomodadores de advertirlo, y que no se pongan los aposentos en cabeza de personas supuestas.

X No se repitirán los bailes, tonadillas, ni otra especie de cantos y diversión que se disponga para recreo del público, a fin de que así no se hagan molestas y demasiado largas las funciones, ni grave a los espectadores ni a los actores, causándoles una detención y trabajo con que no contaban.

XI No se permitirá bajo pretexto alguno que los actores y actrices después de retirados de la escena vuelvan a salir a recibir aplausos, bajo las penas contenidas en el artículo primero al que interrumpiese la representación con palmadas, voces u otra demostración.

XII Desde que se abren los Teatros para la diversión hasta que se cierran no se puede fumar de puertas adentro en ningún sitio del

Coliseo, ni introducir hachas encendidas con ningún motivo ni pretexto, bajo la multa de diez ducados o diez días de Cárcel por la primera vez, doble por la segunda y triple por la tercera.

XIII   A los actores no se les puede arrojar al tablado papel, dinero, dulces ni otra cosa, cualquiera que sea, ni se les ha de hablar por los concurrentes, ni los Cómicos contestarán ni harán señas.

XIV   También se prohíbe el hablar desde el patio a las mujeres de la Cazuela y el hacer señas a los aposentos u otro sitio.

XV   Ninguno podrá pararse a la puerta de la Cazuela y lugar por donde entran y salen las mujeres, aunque sea con motivo de esperar a la que sea propia, hermana o conocidas, pues esto deberá hacerlo en parajes más desviados del Coliseo y en que se convengan respectivamente, para libertarlas de los riesgos y desórdenes advertidos alguna vez, y que causa la multitud de gentes que se junta con semejantes pretextos.

XVI   Por esta misma razón, y también por lo mucho que incomoda al paso y ofende a la decencia pública cierta clase de gentes que se observa detenida con frecuencia en los portales de los Coliseos y frente al de la Cruz, se prohíbe el que nadie pueda detenerse allí ni a la distancia de treinta pasos más tiempo que el preciso para tomar los boletines, entrar en el Teatro o en las casas de dicha calle, bajo la pena de diez ducados de multa por la primera vez, veinte por la segunda y treinta por la tercera; y en su defecto de un mes a los trabajos del Prado por la primera contravención, dos por la segunda y tres por la tercera, sin perjuicio de proceder a la averiguación de la conducta y destino de semejantes gentes, a fin de tomar contra ellos la providencia que corresponda, sobre cuyo punto se celará muy particularmente, valiéndose del auxilio de la tropa en caso necesario.

XVII   Si contra toda esperanza hubiese alguna persona de alto empeño o carácter que contraviniere a estas reglas se dará cuenta al Señor Governador del Consejo para que lo ponga en noticia de S.M.

XVIII   Sin embargo de estar mandado repetidas veces el que no se revendan los billetes para evitar las estafas que sufre el público, se renueva esta prohibición; en la inteligencia de que al contraventor, además de perder los billetes, se le exigirán diez ducados de multa, o en su defecto sufrirá diez días de Cárcel por la primera vez, doble por la segunda y triple por la tercera.

XIX   Se prohíbe a los encargados del despacho de billetes reservarlos para determinadas personas en perjuicio de los que con anticipación acuden por ellos, y se manda: que todos los que se les entregan los despachen precisamente por la puerta destinada al efecto, reservando sólo los de orden y no otros para persona alguna, bajo la pena de privación de destino, al que no podrán volver sin orden espresa de S.M.; y para que esta justa providencia tenga cumplido efecto tomarán los Alcaldes de Corte, y en especial el del Cuartel, cuantas medidas juzguen oportunas, haciendo los registros, informaciones y justificaciones necesarias, y admitiendo las que se les ofrezcan en el asunto.

xx Observadas puntualmente estas prevenciones y mandatos en que todos los concurrentes son interesados, tendrá el público en los Teatros una diversión tranquila y decente, sin daño ni incomodidad, a proporción de la que permitan sus haberes y puestos que elijan, y habrá el decoro y moderación correspondiente a unos actos públicos que sirven a todas las clases del Estado desde la ínfima hasta la más elevada, y el respeto y veneración debida a la Justicia y sus providencias que tan acreditado tiene el pueblo de Madrid.

Y para que llegue a noticia de todos, y ninguno pueda alegar ignorancia, se manda publicar por Bando, y que de él se fijen copias impresas en los parages acostumbrados de esta Corte, autorizadas por D. Juan Diego Martínez, Escribano de Cámara y de Govierno de la Sala. Y lo señalaron en Madrid a primero de Setiembre de mil ochocientos veinte y seis.

Appendix 3. Magical effects in *La pata de cabra* (1829)

Additional tricks – Act 2 (See chapter 3):

14.   6   Don Simplicio pulls a four-yard long sword out of a sheath only three-quarters of a yard long.

15.   8   At a picnic table don Simplicio cannot get any wine to pour out of a full wine bottle.

16.   8   A piece of bread sails from one side of the table to the other as don Simplicio tries to grab it.

17.   9   Don Juan and doña Leonor are standing on the balcony of the house when don Lope demands that they come down. Don Simplicio and don Lope grab the bars on the windows of the first floor in order to climb up to capture the lovers. Suddenly, the window bars (with Lope and Simplicio attached to them) rise to the second floor while the balcony descends to the ground level. Juan and Leonor walk away.

18.   9   As the previous effect is taking place, the police officers are suspended three feet in the air.

19.   18   The room in which Simplicio rests while he guards Leonor contains portraits of Lope's family members. As he yawns, so do the portraits.

20.   18   When Simplicio puts out the second candle he is carrying, the first one automatically relights itself. When he extinguishes this one, the other spontaneously relights. This is repeated three or four times.

21.   18   The cap he is wearing blows up to the size of a balloon and he floats away.

22.   18   As Simplicio floats over the countryside, Cupid flies in the opposite direction in his carriage with Juan and Leonor.

Act 3:

23.   1   After Simplicio's rescue, as the townfolk move to carry him back to Lope's house, Simplicio suddenly disappears from the stretcher, "sinking down into the ground."

24.   4   After Juan loses a fight with Simplicio and a Cyclops, he and Leonor are chained to posts which rise up suddenly from the ground.

25.   5   Cupid appears out of one of the Cyclopses' clubs.

26.   5   Cupid touches the edge of the sea with one of his arrows and out of the sea rise three Graces, riding a mother-of-pearl shell pulled by three swans.

27.   5   Cupid touches the posts to which Leonor and Juan are chained and the chains disappear.

28.   5   Cupid changes the shell into a magnificent Greek ship, manned by a host of cherubs.

29.   6   The ship changes into a frightful sea monster which belches flames.

30.   7   As Simplicio waits near a cave, an enormous arm reaches down and scoops him several feet into the air.

31.   7   Flames shoot out of the earth as Simplicio tries to escape.

32.   8   A horrible Cerberus appears to block Simplicio's way.

33.   7   A magician who "is alternately four and seven feet tall" appears to Simplicio, and as his cloak opens we see not a body but " a revolting skeleton."

34.   8   The magician disappears in a roar of flames.

35.   10   A cloud rises and lifts Simplicio and Lope up with it.

Appendix 4. Bretón de los Herreros reviews *La pata de cabra*

(1) From *El Correo Literario y Mercantil* (September 2, 1831)

Ha vuelto a ponerse en escena este singular espectáculo, talismán de todas las empresas de tres años a esta parte para atraer a los espectadores, y no espectadores solamente de bota y garrote, que son los más inclinados a las comedias *de magia*, sino también de fraque y levita, y galones y plumas. Función es esta donde hay para contentar a todo el mundo. ¿Gusta Fulano de magníficas decoraciones? Allí verá una selva admirable; verá las desiertas rocas del Pirineo cubiertas de eterna nieve, con tal perfección pintada, que dan intenciones de tiritar mirándola; verá las horrorosas oficinas de Vulcano y las dulces glorias de Cupido, y cual compiten en ambas riqueza del colorido con su composición tan ingeniosa como filosófico; verá en fin en todas ellas la mano de un artista distinguido, y se unirá a nosotros para tributar justos elogios al profesor D. Juan Blanchard. ¿Es amigo Citano de transformaciones y brujerías, y alguaciles colgados, y novios chasqueados, y tutores aburridos? *La pata de cabra* satisfará sus deseos. ¿Quiere Mengano de un poquito de baile y de jaleo, y de jota y de pantomima? Nada de esto echará de menos. ¿Desea Fabio ver en las tablas mujeres constantes a toda prueba ya que no las halla en el mundo? Ahí está Leonor, que es la flor y la nata de la fidelidad. ¿Apetece la novelesca y *lunática* Dorotea pasear su espíritu vaporoso por los espacios imaginarios? Siga al intrépido aeronauta D. Simplicio en su viaje a las regiones de la luna. ¿Se inclina D. Teofrasto a las sutilezas de la alegoría? Será servido. ¿Es aficionado D. Zoilo a picantes alusiones y sentenciosos epigramas? Preste atención, que en el diálogo no faltan. ¿Es tentado a la risa el bonacho y mofletudo D. Inocencio? Oiga los chistes y aun las sandeces del insigne Bobadilla, Majaderano y Cabeza de Buey. En una palabra, esta es función para todos; es un cajón de sastre; una enciclopedia dramática, donde se saca muy bien el jugo a los reales y maravedíes que suelta un prójimo en la sobada ventanilla del despacho de billetes. Pero, señor, ¿quién tolera tantos desatinos? dirá algún cejudo Aristarco circunvalado de volúmenes griegos y de unidades y peripecias. Ahí está el mérito, le responderemos. En la *Pata de cabra* se desatina, porque este es el elemento de semejantes dramas; pero se desatina con talento; y para culpar a la infinidad de gentes de todas clases, principios y condiciones que han asistido a este espectáculo, tan prodigioso número de veces repetido con el teatro lleno, sería forzoso negar al pueblo de Madrid su fino discernimiento y su acreditada ilustración. Cuando se anuncia *La pata de cabra*, el más rudo de los espectadores sabe muy bien que no va a ver una obra clásica de literatura, que no va a ver una comedia, si vmd. quiere; va a divertirse y a reir poderosamente por espacio de tres horas; asiste a una función teatral que halaga sus sentidos, prescindiendo por aquella noche de teorías y clasificaciones. Aunque por lo dicho esté dispensada de una severa análisis *La pata de cabra* preciso es decir que algunos de sus diálogos son algo prolijos; pero conocemos que no pueden menos de serlo para dar lugar a los preparativos de nuevas mutaciones y juegos de maquinaria, algunos bastante complicados. Los actores trabajan bien. El papel de la linda Leonor está desempeñado con gentil donaire; el tutor ejecuta el suyo con inteligencia; el nuevo D. Juan no desagrada, y el gracioso lo es tan de veras retratando a D. Simplicio, que haría reír a Heráclito y a Jeremías. Y ya que viene a cuenta y se acercan los días de feria, sépase que *La pata de cabra* se vende impresa en los despachos de billetes de ambos teatros y en la librería de Escamilla. He dicho.

(2) From *El Correo Literario y Mercantil* (November 19, 1832)

Este singular espectáculo atrae nuevamente la extraordinaria concurrencia, que nunca ha dejado de favorecerle en las repetidísimas representaciones que de él se han hecho desde el año 1829, en que se verificó la primera. Para darle en la actual repetición al aliciente de la novedad no ha perdonado gastos ni desvelos la comisón del Excmo. ayuntamiento. No solo han sido retocadas las decoraciones y reparada toda la maquinaria, cuyo deterioro, y no la inasistencia del público, hizo que se suspendiesen en el año próximo pasado las representaciones del célebre melo-mimo-drama, sino que le adornan al presente otras varias decoraciones nuevas no inferiores en mérito a las antiguas, y otras también del profesor D. Juan Blanchard. Todas ellas han sido con mucha justicia aplaudidas, y sobre todo ha parecido tan linda la que se muestra en el final del acto segundo, que es lástima por cierto goce de ella tan pocos momentos el espectador. La que acompaña al sacrificio de la cabra al principio del acto primero es una creación muy propia del genio distinguido y de las luces que han dado tanto crédito al Sr. Blanchard. Aquellos grupos errantes de visiones, espectros, ensueños, pesadillas y cuantos horrores y desconciertos traza la humana fantasía al través del sueño y de las tinieblas, causan un efecto sorprendente, y dan un prestigio verdaderamente mágico a la misteriosa ceremonia que en torno suyo se ejecuta.

También el servicio de la maquinaria, aumentado y perfeccionado considerablemente, honra mucho a su director D. Mateo Sierra. Se verifican con mucha exactitud y como por encanto todas las mutaciones, y entre ellas las hay sumamente complicadas, como la del final del acto segundo.

Un solo juguete se suprime ahora de los ya conocidos: el de dar vueltas D. Simplicio asido a la puerta de la granja, que en dicho acto segundo ha servido de asilo a D. Juan y a Leonor. Lo echamos de menos, no por el mérito que en sí pueda tener, sino porque al fin hacía reír al público, y en esta ocasión le hubiera indemnizado en algún modo del disgusto que le han causado ciertos diálogos asaz prolijos, que, sin duda para dar tiempo a disponer la gran mutación que sigue, y en ella la cual juegan tantos muebles, ha sido forzoso ingerir. Pasa demasiado tiempo sin haber nada de magia desde que los alguaciles hacen piruetas en el aire hasta que la posteridad de D. Lope, no ya el auditorio, bosteza con D. Simplicio. Tanta conversación en un drama de esta especie y en ausencia del héroe no podía menos de fastidiar. Pero vuelve este a presentarse tan donoso como siempre: la brujería recobra su imperio, y el público su buen humor, tanto más cuanto que esta escena se refuerza con una multitud de estatuas y retratos, que aumentan el cómico terror de Majaderano, produciendo luego la hermosa trasformación que hemos insinuado.

Otras varias novedades ofrece esta función: el haberse dado más aparato y autoridad al baile y faenas de los cíclopes; la aparición de dos enormes reptiles vomitando llamas; el haber crecido prodigiosamente el elástico dios de las riquezas, cuyos descomunales brazos movidos a guisa de inmenso telégrafo han divertido mucho, etc. En una palabra, este coloso dramático, felizmente rejuvenecido, campa de nuevo sobre la escena con muy fundadas apariencias de producir muchos doblones, y de dar sendas cuchilladas a cuantos dramas líricos o rezados se le pongan por delante.

Appendix 5. List of works approved for performance
(1827)

Nota de las piezas dramáticas que se hallan censuradas y corrientes
para su ejecución en los Teatros de esta Corte.

Antes que te cases mira lo que
  haces
Amantes y celosos todos son
  locos
Amor médico
Amar por señas
Amor y la intriga
Aradin Barbaroja
A secreto agravio secreta
  venganza
Amantes de Teruel
Amantes engañados
Aburrido
Amanda
Arca de Noé
Anillo mágico
Asesinos en la posada de
  Adrests
A falta de hechiceros lo quieren
  ser los gallegos
Astracán
Abre el ojo
Avaro
Aviso a los casados
Astrólogo fingido
Atalia
Amigo de la razón
Anillo de Giges

Aguador de París
A cual más loco
Ademar y Adelaida
Abate L'Epée
A suegro irritado
Ayo de su hijo
Amor al uso
Amantes llorones
Anciano y los Jóvenes
Amigo íntimo
Asombro de Jerez
A la vejez viruelas
Alba y el Sol
Amante jorobado
Abuelo y la nieta
Aparición y el marido
Alcalde de Zalamea
Buen hijo, o María Teresa
Blanca y Montcasin
Baron de Felchein
Banda y la flor
Carpintero de Libonia
Celoso confundido
Carlos y Carolina
Compromisos sin saber de qué
Cobrar en vida lo gastado en su
  entierro
Corrección maternal

Contrabandistas
Corsarios de amor
Cardillac
Café
Cierto por lo dudoso
Cuatro Naciones
Convidado de piedra
Cristina de Suecia
Casualidad contra el cuidado
Catalán Serrallonga
Coloso de Rodas
Carlos el Temerario
Conde de Saldaña
Celos con celos se curan
Caballero Canol
Celosa de sí misma
Cadete o el Preguntón
Caballero o mozo de café
Caballero Bayardo
Casamentero
Costumbres del día
Caprichos de amor y celos
Cabeza de bronce
Citas
Cárceles de Lamberg
Cuantas veo
Cid, tragedia
Celoso por fuerza
Cuadro
Comedia casera o los poetas
Califa, opereta
Calavera corregido
Carcelera de sí misma
Caballero a la moda
Castillos en el aire
Cid campeador
Confidente casual
Cuento de la liebre
Dama sútil
Duque de Viseo

Dos yernos
Dama duende
Delirio paternal
Dos ayos
Dos Mendozas
Desquite
Deber y la naturaleza
Dos sobrinos
Dos sargentos
Dama coronel
Dos primas
Doña Inés de Castro
Dido
Don Berenguel
Desdén con el desdén
Don Gil de las calzas verdes
Duque de Pentiebre
Dos matrimonios
Dama labradora
Dido abandonada
Disensión fraternal
Delincuente honrado
Darlo todo y no dar nada
Duque de Craon
De fuera vendrá quien de casa
    nos echará
Desafío
Duque de Belmar
Español y la francesa
Esposa delincuente
Escuela de los maridos
Enfermo de aprensión
Eugenia
Escuela de los viejos
Embustero engañado
Entrometido o la máscara
Eccio triunfante
Esteriores engañosos
Enriqueta y Adolfo
Esclava de su galán

Escuela de la amistad
Ermitaño del monte Posilipo
Erivan
Filósofo casado
Familia a la moda
Falsos hombres de bien
Fénix de los criados
Familia pobre
Funeral y baile de máscara
Filósofo fabulista
Fulgencia
Florentina
Fernando III el Santo
Flora o el diablo mujer
Gemelos
Gerarda y Dorotea
García del Castañar
Galería de novios
Gabriela
Guerra abierta
Huerfanita
Hombre de tres caras
Hijo abandonado
Hombre agradecido
Hermanos a la prueba
Hermano legítimo y natural
Hombre singular o Isabel de
  Rusia
Herrerías de Maremma
Huérfana de Bruselas
Hombre de la selva negra
Honor da entendimiento
Hombre pardo
Inocencia y la intriga o el robo
Indulgencia para todos
Ifigenia y Orestes
Industria y la suerte
Juventudes de Enrique V
Jenwal y Faustina
Jugador

Joven de 60 años
Janina destruída
Jueces francos
Juan labrador
Juicio de Solomon
Joven rifado
Leñador escocés
Lo que son mujeres
Lo que son criados
Lugareña astuta
Lugareña orgullosa
Lujo e indigencia
Luis IX
Lord Davenant
Lucrecia Pazzi
Llave falsa
Lechugina patética
Lágrimas de una viuda
Hombre gris
Llegar a tiempo
Luisa o el padre Juez
Madrastra
Marido según las circunstancias
Mocedades del Cid
Mejor alcalde el Rey
Médico a palos
Mayor Palmer
Mañanas de abril y mayo
Melindrosa
Matrimonio tratado
Mágico de Salerno, 1ª parte
María Teresa o el buen hijo
Montañés Juan Pascual
Madre rival
Máscara reconciliadora
Mari-Hernández la gallega
Moza de cántaro
Minas de Polonia
Marta la piadosa
Mujer prudente

Media noche
Montañés sabe bien donde le
 aprieta el zapato
Mendigo
Moscovita sensible
Mujer de dos maridos
Lindo don Diego
Misántropo
Monteros de Espinosa
Maestro de la niña
Más ilustre fregona
Mal hospital
Mujer celosa
Margarita de Estraffor
Molino de Quebens o aventuras
 de Tequeli
Más heróica piedad más
 noblemente pagada
Mágico catalán
Mágico Salerno
Mágico y el cestero
Novia impaciente
Natalia y Carolina
Nino
Naufragio o los herederos
No siempre los jóvenes se
 burlan de los tutores
Numancia, tragedia
No puede ser guardar una
 mujer
Niña de Gómez Arias
Opresor de su familia
Oscar
Otelo
Pastelero
Parecido en la corte
Peligros de una corte
Pages de Federico
Prueba feliz
Pablo y Virginia

Presumida y la hermosa
Pelayo
Pobre pretendiente
Para vencer amor
Por ocultar un delito
Príncipe y el villano
Pretendiente con palabras y
 plumas
Por la puente Juana
Por el sótano y el torno
Pauli o corsos y genoveses
Picarillo en España
Pintor fingido
Palmis y Oronte
Pedro el Grande Czar de
 Muscovia
Padre avariento
Panadizo de Federico II
Por su Rey y por su dama
Pedro el Grande o el
 emperador carpintero
Padre criminal
Quinta de Paluzzi
¡Qué de apuros en tres horas!
Quijote y Sancho Panza
Rechazos
Rey valiente y justiciero
Reconciliador
Romeo y Julieta
Rey Eduardo III
Ruinas de Babilonia
Reconciliación de los dos
 hermanos
Recompensa del
 arrepentimiento
Remordimiento o la capilla de
 Glenston
Rico hombre de Alcalá
Sueño
Solterón

Suegra y la nuera
Sueños hay que lecciones son
Secretario y el cocinero
Sepulcro en las ruinas
Seductor enamorado
Sensible carcelera
Sobrino fingido
Socorro de los mantos
Serrana de Escocia
Sin una vez llega a querer la
más firme es la mujer
Secreto a voces
Seguir los libres a un tiempo
Sueños de José
Selva de Hermanstad
Tal para cual
Tres maridos
Triunfo del Ave María
Títeres
Tetrarca
Tener que casarse sin tener con
quien
Tellos de Meneses
Tres sultanas
También hay secreto en la
mujer

Todo es enredos amor
Triunfos de valor y honor en la
corte de Rodrigo
Tesoro
Tirano de Hungría
Tocador de órgano
Vano humillado
Ver y creer
Viajes de Segismundo
Viuda generosa
Valle del torrente
Viejo y la niña
Viejo de la montaña
Vecinos
Vicente de Paul
Vampiro
Víctor o el hijo del subterráneo
Verter
Villano del Danubio
Valeria
Washington
Un loco hace ciento
Urraca ladrona
Un momento de imprudencia
Zeydar o la familia árabe

Madrid 26 de mayo de 1827

El Corregidor interino Juez Protector de los Teatros del Reino
Antonio José Galindo

Faustino Domínguez
Secretario

Appendix 6. Grimaldi's letter to *Le Constitutionnel* (17-IX-1836)

Nous avons souvent averti nos lecteurs de se tenir en garde contre la tendance de la correspondance ordinaire de Madrid. Une assertion de cette correspondance vient de donner lieu à la lettre suivante, publiée par un journal du matin:

Monsieur,

Arrivé à Paris avant-hier, j'ai su aujourd'hui que la nouvelle de mon voyage m'y avait précédé, et qu'on me supposait, dans quelques journaux, chargé d'une mission auprès du Roi des Français, et porteur d'une lettre autographe adressée à S.M. par son auguste nièce, la Reine Régente d'Espagne.

Cette supposition blesse par trop toute vraisemblance; car une mission de nature si délicate, si elle avait été jugée nécessaire, n'aurait pu facilement arriver à la connaissance des correspondans qu'ont à Madrid les journaux français, et beaucoup moins encore le contenu de la lettre autographe dont parle ces correspondans. Tout absurde qu'est pourtant la nouvelle, mon silence pourrait lui donner quelque poids. Un devoir d'honneur m'oblige donc à la démentir, quelque soit d'ailleurs ma répugnance à occuper de moi le public.

Que mon dévouement bien connu à la cause de la Reine eut fait supposer, dans des vues plus ou moins honorables, que mon départ pour Paris, au moment ou les événements venaient de prendre un biais anormal, avait un objet ou une cause politique; qu'on en eut cherché l'explication dans les doctrines que j'ai constamment soutenues en 1833, comme Rédacteur en chef de la *Revista*, et à une époque plus récente ou quoique devenu étranger à la rédaction de ce journal, je crus devoir rentrer dans la polémique politique pour y défendre de hauts intérêts sociaux que je jugeais menacés, il n'y aurait eu jusque-la qu'une de ces conjectures si familières à l'esprit de parti. Mais ceux-là connaissent bien mal l'Espagne, qui, pour mêler à cette fable le nom de la reine, présument qu'elle court le moindre danger ni comme mère

205

ni comme régente. Si dans des circonstances encore plus critiques les Espagnols furent fidèles, furent nobles et généreux envers un monarque qui cependant avait déjà déçu les plus légitimes espérances, pourraient-ils cesser d'être précisément vis-à-vis de l'auguste princesse à laquelle ils doivent le rétablissement des libertés que le dévouement des plus puissans citoyens avait en vain cherché à reconquérir? Non, assurément. Il est de certaines questions sur lesquelles tous les hommes bien nés sont d'accord dans ce pays essentiellement chevaleresque; et la reine, pour communiquer avec les princes de sa famille, n'a besoin ni de mon faible secours, ni de celui d'aucun agent mystérieux; elle peut s'en rapporter à la loyauté des serviteurs officiels qui l'entourent, loyauté que leurs adversaires politiques eux-mêmes ne sauraient mettre en doute.

Quant à mon voyage, dont on m'a fait le dangereux honneur d'entretenir le public, il s'explique bien naturellement. Le projet en était connu depuis plusieurs mois par tous mes amis de Madrid. Je ne suis porteur d'aucune dépêche; je n'ai reçu de personne la moindre mission. Je reviens en France, parce que la France est ma patrie, parce que je désirais ardemment de la revoir après quinze ans d'absence; et enfin parce que je m'occupe plus que jamais d'y fixer mon avenir, depuis que les déplorables scissions qui divisent les défenseurs de la bonne cause m'ont paru compromettre plus gravement que jamais la paix du beau et malheureux pays ou j'ai reçu un noble hospitalité que je n'oublierai jamais.

Paris, 15 septembre   Grimaldi

Notes

Introduction

1 Grimaldi appears in two *Episodios nacionales*, "Los apostólicos" and "De Oñate a la Granja."
2 Antonio Espina, *Romea o el comediante* (Madrid: Espasa-Calpe, 1935).
3 Antonio Buero Vallejo, *La detonación*, in *Estreno*, IV (Primavera, 1978).
4 Ramón de Mesonero Romanos, *Memorias de un setentón*, in *Obras de don Ramón de Mesonero Romanos*. VIII (Madrid: Renacimiento, 1926), p. 66.
5 José Zorrilla, "Hojas traspapeladas de los *Recuerdos del tiempo viejo*," (Valladolid: Santarén, 1943), p. 1998.
6 José Alberich, Review of S. García Castañeda, *Miguel de los Santos Alvarez* (Madrid: SGEL, 1979) in *Bulletin of Hispanic Studies*, 58 (1981), p. 146.
7 Frank M. Duffey, "Juan de Grimaldi and the Madrid Stage (1823–1837)," *Hispanic Review*, 10 (1942), pp. 147–56.
8 *Jean-Marie de Grimaldi et l'Espagne* (Mémoire pour le Diplôme d'Etudes Supérieures, Faculté des Lettres de Paris, 1962).

1 The Spanish stage, 1800–23

1 AHN: Consejos 11.411, n. 35. "The town of Madrid enjoyed the ancient privilege of being able to conscript the most distinguished actors from the provinces and bring them from wherever they were to Madrid and it exercised without any second thoughts this odious right." Emilio Cotarelo y Mori, *María del Rosario Fernández, La Tirana, primera dama de los teatros de la corte* (Madrid: Rivadeneyra, 1897), p. 12.
2 The actors complained that Felipe IV "established the privilege of forcing all outstanding provincial actors and actresses to come to the capital, depriving them of exercising their profession if they chose not to come; a decision and a practice observed until now [1824]. This obligation was so troublesome, and so offensive, that it deprived the actors of better earnings which could be made in the different theatres of provincial capitals, and of the choice of living where it best suited their health or their differing personal circumstances, choices influenced by the relative expense of foodstuff, clothing, and the higher costs which they had to bear for costumes in the capital, and in its theatres, where even their daily earnings were lower." AHN: Consejos 11.411, n. 35.
3 See "Jubilaciones de los actores de Madrid," *Eco del Comercio*, February 15, 1835.
4 As Emmanuel Larraz has noted, "On the eve of the War of Independence, the material situation of the actors was precarious, and they were not strangers to misery and hunger." See "Le statut des comédiens dans la société espagnole du début du XIXe siècle," *Culture et société en Espagne et en Amérique Latine au XIXe siècle*

(Lille: Centre d'Etudes Ibériques et Ibero-Américaines, 1980), pp. 27-40 (quote here from p. 27).

5 Cited by Jorge Campos, *Teatro y sociedad en España, 1780–1820*) (Madrid, Moneda y Crédito, 1969), p. 188. Leandro Fernández de Moratín wrote, "With him the glory of acting in our theatres began and ended." This respect for Máiquez has remained strong. He was "the one great light in the darkness of this theatrical night," according to P.P. Rogers ("The drama of pre-Romantic Spain," *Romanic Review*, 21 (1930), p. 324).

6 Matilde Muñoz, *Historia del teatro dramático en España* (3 vols. Madrid, Editorial Tesoro, 1948), pp. 238-9. Campos reports that the subsidies ranged from between 20,000 and 126,500 *reales* per month. Campos, pp. 170–1.

7 Larraz, p. 34.

8 Larraz writes of two instances in which actors refused to obey the call to the capital, one hiding behind medical excuses and another leaving the profession entirely in order to avoid disrupting his life in the provinces. Larraz, p. 34.

9 Narciso Díaz de Escovar and F.P. Lasso de la Vega, *Historia del teatro español*, (2 vols. Barcelona: Montaner y Simón, 1924), vol. I, p. 340. Contemporary observers remembered Máiquez as being "the most legitimate glory of our stage, the only rival of the divine French actor Talma, the only one who managed to elevate the art of acting to its highest grade of perfection, interpreting the thoughts of playwrights and expressing emotion with that sublime truth that makes us forget scenic fictions . . ." Wenceslao Ayguals de Izco, *Panteón universal* (4 vols. Madrid: Ayguals, 1853-4), p. 503.

10 Alberto Colao, *Máiquez, discípulo de Talma* (Cartagena: Ayuntamiento de Cartagena, 1980), p. 13. For additional information on Máiquez, see Emilio Cotarelo y Mori, *Isidoro Máiquez y el teatro de su tiempo* (Madrid: José Perales y Martínez, 1902), José de la Revilla, *Vida artística de Isidoro Máiquez* (Madrid: Medina y Navarro, 1845), José Vega, *Máiquez* (Madrid: Revista de Occidente, 1947), Antonio Espina, *Seis vidas españolas* (Madrid: Taurus, 1967), and José Rodríguez Cánovas, *Isidoro Máiquez* (Cartagena: Athenas Ediciones, 1968).

11 On audiences and performances in Madrid in the eighteenth century, see René Andioc's indispensable study, *Teatro y sociedad en el Madrid del siglo XVIII* (Madrid: Castalia, 1976).

12 Rodríguez, p. 40.

13 Cited by Rodríguez, pp. 23-4.

14 Colao, p. 54.

15 See Espina, *Seis vidas*, p. 6.

16 See Manuel Bretón de los Herreros, "Declamación. Progresos y estado actual de este arte en los teatros de España," *La Enciclopedia Moderna*, 12 (1852), pp. 698–700.

17 It is possible that the young Rodríguez had been acting since 1814. In her petition for retirement benefits, written in February, 1836, she claimed twenty-two years of "continuous work" AV: Secretaría, 2–476–1.

18 A. [Juan de Grimaldi], "Concepción Rodríguez," *El Artista*, II (1835), p. 193.

19 A., "Concepción Rodríguez," p. 193.

20 Arjona wielded enormous power in Madrid and, as a supporter of Fernando VII's politics, became a constant irritant to the actors and directors. His policies were marked by censorship, control, and repression. See Alfonso Barojos Garrido, *D. José Manuel de Arjona* (Sevilla: Imprenta Municipal, 1976).

21 For further details concerning these plays, see Emilio Cotarelo y Mori, *Isidoro Máiquez*, pp. 447-50, 831-7; and A.K. Shields, "The Madrid stage, 1820–1833" (unpublished Ph.D. dissertation; University of North Carolina, 1933).

22 Earl J. Hamilton, *War and Prices in Spain, 1651–1800* (Cambridge, MA: Harvard University Press, 1969), p. 153.

23 Gonzalo Anes, ed. *El Banco de España: una historia económica* (Madrid: Banco de España, 1970), p. 251.

24 Hamilton, Appendix A.

25 Angel Fernández de los Ríos, *Guía de Madrid (1876)* (Madrid: Monterrey Ediciones, 1982), pp. 644–5.

26 A., "Concepción Rodríguez," p. 194.

27 Bernardo Gil and Antonio González, *Manifiesto que dan los autores de los teatros de la Cruz y Príncipe* (Madrid: Repullés, 1820), p. 11.

28 Gil, *Manifiesto*, p. 12.

29 See Appendix 1 for Gil's listing of the special charges from 1820.

30 Marie-Thérèse Carrière, "Acerca de las pensiones de actores en la Cruz y el Príncipe a mediados del siglo xix," *Hommage à Jean-Louis Flecniakoska*, 1 (Montpellier: Université Paul Valéry, 1980), p. 119.

31 Carrière, p. 118.

32 See Gregorio Martín, "Periodismo y teatro en el siglo xix," paper read at the annual Kentucky Foreign Language Conference, April 28, 1984. I am grateful to Professor Martín for providing me with a copy of his paper.

33 AV: Secretaría 2-169-3; Martín, "Periodismo y teatro."

34 Jesús Pabón, *Narváez y su época* (Madrid: Espasa-Calpe, 1983), p. 190.

35 Zorrilla, p. 1998. The documentation on Grimaldi's early life in France is provided by Bernard Desfrétières in his superb thesis on *Jean-Marie de Grimaldi et l'Espagne*, pp. 9–18. Desfrétières includes several appendices with transcript copies of documents relating to Grimaldi's years in France, which will be referred to in due course.

36 Desfrétières, p. 17. Desfrétières cites from Grimaldi's military dossier.

37 Patricio de la Escosura, "Recuerdos literarios," *Ilustración Española y Americana* (March, 1876), p. 226.

38 Martín, "Periodismo y teatro," p. 4.

39 I refer, of course, to the role of don Simplicio in Grimaldi's *La pata de cabra*. See chapter 3.

40 See David T. Gies, "Juan de Grimaldi y el año teatral madrileño, 1823–24," *Actas del VIII Congreso Internacional de Hispanistas* (Madrid: Istmo, 1986) pp. 607–13.

41 Dionisio Chaulié notes that actors who did not belong to the capital's acting companies were not permitted to perform within one "legua" – approximately three and one half miles – of the main theatres. *Cosas de Madrid*, II (Madrid: Correspondencia de España, 1886), p. 53. A copy of the contract signed on September 30 by Manuel Rodríguez, director of the Cava Baja Theatre, and sent to Grimaldi stipulates that "I agree to the following conditions concerning Mr. Grimaldi: (1) that before beginning the performances I will present to him a list of all the plays that will be performed in my theatre so he can exclude from said list any which might jeopardize the performances to be given in the principal theatres in Madrid, (2) that I will pay him each day 30 *reales* for each performance to be given in this theatre, (3) that at the end of one month from the day the theatre opens I will sign a new agreement with him, without which he is free to put into effect his rights as granted by the city government" AV: Corregimiento 1-197-5.

42 See Martín, "Periodismo y teatro" for some of the financial details of this arrangement.

43 A detailed description of this entire process is to be found in the documents cited; AV: Secretaría 2-472-25. A similar version can be found in the AHP: Protocolo 22945.

44 It was here, in the café of the Príncipe Theatre, where one of the most famous literary gatherings of the nineteenth century, the "Parnasillo," would begin to form in 1827. See Mesonero Romanos, *Memorias*, pp. 66–7; Gregorio Martín, "'El 'Parnasillo': origen y circunstancias," *La chispa*, '*81*. *Selected Proceedings* (New Orleans: Tulane, 1981), pp. 209–18. We will return to the Parnasillo later.

45 For further discussion of the details of this contract, see Desfrétières, pp. 26–30 and Gies, "Juan de Grimaldi y el año teatral."

46 *DM*, August 24, 1824. The *Diario de Madrid* became the *Diario de Avisos* from 1825 through 1836, when its name reverted to the *Diario de Madrid* once again. I shall use *DM* throughout.

2 Grimaldi at the beginning of the "ominous decade"

1 Breton de los Herreros, "Declamación," p. 710.

2 Chaulié, ii, p. 53.

3 The inventory of the Príncipe was conducted on the morning of September 15, 1823, by seven individuals, including those people in charge of the various sections: lighting, wardrobe, sets, etc. The Cruz was inventoried the next day.

4 When the items were returned in March, 1824, a dispute erupted over several missing or broken things, in particular the absence of forty of the eighty candlesticks originally listed in the inventory. It was finally decided that there had been only forty, in spite of the fact that the inventory had been signed for eighty, "and in everything else the goods were found to be in acceptable condition" AV: Secretaría 2-472-45.

5 Chaulié, ii, p. 54.

6 See J.J. Allen's study of the history of the Príncipe during the Golden Age, *The Reconstruction of a Spanish Golden Age Playhouse: El Corral del Príncipe, 1583–1744* (Florida: University of Florida Press, 1983). Also, Augusto Martínez Olmedilla, *Los teatros de Madrid* (Madrid: 1947) and Federico Carlos Sainz de Robles, *Los antiguos teatros de Madrid* (Madrid: Instituto de Estudios Madrileños, 1952).

7 Fernando Fernández de Córdoba, *Mis memorias íntimas*, i (1886; Madrid: Atlas, 1966), p. 307.

8 Adolphe Blanqui, *Voyage à Madrid* (Paris: Doudey-Dupré, 1826), pp. 100–3.

9 Antonio Ferrer y Herrera, *Paseo por Madrid 1835* (Madrid: Colección Almenara, 1952), p. 37.

10 Adolphe de Custine, *L'Espagne sous Ferdinand VII* (2 vols., Paris: Ladvocat, 1838), vol. ii, p. 284.

11 Chaulié, ii, p. 54.

12 See the partial list of "the plays which have been censored for the Príncipe and Cruz theatres from 22 September 1823 to 6 February 1824" AV: Corregimiento 1-246-36.

13 In an article entitled "La razón," which he published under his journalistic pseudonym "A" in *RE*, December 26, 1835.

14 *DM*, September 21, 1823. The interest in Rossini's work would become a veritable frenzy over the next decade, and his popularity would reach such heights that his visit to Madrid in 1831 was treated almost as a state occasion. We shall return to the subject of opera and the Madrid stage.

15 See A.K. Shield's thorough listing of repertory offerings in his "The Madrid stage."

16 *DM*, September 21, 1823; Shields gives no information about the actors during this first season.

17 *DM*, September 26, 1823.

18 *DM*, September 26, 1823. Concepción Rodríguez starred in this play, and it enjoyed a four-day run.

19 *DM*, October 14, 1823.

20 Julio Cejador y Frauca, *Historia de la lengua y literatura castellana* (Madrid: RABM, 1917), IV, p. 404, mistakenly attributes it to Manuel Anselmo Nafría.

21 The announcements in the *DM* underscore the continued French presence in the capital; for several days, the notices were published in both Spanish and French.

22 For performance schedules, see Shields and Luis Carmona y Millán, *Crónica de la ópera italiana en Madrid* (Madrid: Manuel Minuesa de los Ríos, 1878).

23 Shields mistakenly lists December 16 as the performance date. Shields, p. 623.

24 On these actors' brotherhoods, see José Subirá, *El Gremio de Representantes Españoles y la Cofradía de Nuestra Señora* (Madrid: C.S.I.C., Instituto de Estudios Madrileños, 1960).

25 *DM*, March 1, 1824.

26 Shields erroneously gives November 23, 1824, as the first performance date of the *sainete* version of *El médico a palos*; the first performance was on November 11, 1823. See *DM*.

27 See Shields for information concerning these translations.

28 Chaulié, II, p. 57.

29 See AV: Contaduría 4-56-1 for bills which detail the sums spent on these and other repairs.

30 *DM*, November 26, 1823.

31 *DM*, November 27, 1823.

32 Carrière, p. 134. That same year he is listed as an "unemployed lottery agent," still living in the old theatre district in Madrid; AV; Contaduría 4-171-1.

33 Larra wrote in February 1836 that a Society of Actors, composed of García Luna, Latorre, Guzmán, Romea, and Matilde Díez was ready to take charge of the Príncipe. "Teatros," *El Español*, February 29, 1836.

34 Not all of his performances were successes. N.B. Adams reports that he "had to accomplish his stage death amid hisses" in his 1830 interpretation of *El bandido incógnito*, although the hisses were more for the play than for the performance. N.B. Adams, "Notes on dramatic criticism in Madrid: 1828–1833," *Studies in Romance Languages and Literatures* (Chapel Hill: UNC Press, 1945), p. 235.

35 John C. Dowling, "El anti-don Juan de Ventura de la Vega," *Actas del VI Congreso Internacional de Hispanistas* (Toronto: Department of Spanish and Portuguese, University of Toronto, 1980), p. 215.

36 Antonio de los Reyes, *Julián Romea. El actor y su contorno (1813–1868)* (Murcia: Academia Alfonso X el Sabio, 1977), p. 26.

37 AV: Secretaría 3-478-9. I write "incredible" since it is difficult to believe that such sums were available to actors, even good ones like Latorre. But the document clearly states that on June 16, this payment "To Mr. Latorre, for having performed the tragedy *Oscar*, four days" was made.

38 See Ayguals, *Panteón universal*, pp. 355–7.

39 Zorrilla, p. 1756. This paragraph is plagiarized, without attribution, by Carlos Guerra and Francisco Guerra y Alarcón in their *Músicos, poetas y actores* (Madrid: Impr. Maroto, 1884). Several curious images remain of this great actor. See Elena Paez Ríos, *Iconografía hispana. Catálogo de los personajes españoles de la Biblioteca Nacional*, (4 vols., Madrid Biblioteca Nacional, Sección de Estampas, 1966), vol 2, p. 36.

40 Gustave Hubbard, *Histoire de la littérature contemporaine en Espagne* (Paris: Charpentier, 1867), p. 100.

41 He was not the first named to the post. The distinguished elder actor, Joaquín Caprara, held the position for the first few months.

42 These included the Duque de Rivas, Antonio Alcalá Galiano, Grimaldi, Martínez de la Rosa, Mesonero Romanos, Bretón, Agustín Durán, Donoso Cortés, Quintana, Espronceda, etc. See Mesonero Romanos, *Memorias*, p. 165, and Rafael María de Labra, *El Ateneo de Madrid, 1835-1905* (Madrid, 1906), p. 58.

43 See Larraz, p. 40.

44 Carrière, p. 138.

45 A similar flurry of bills, accusations, and denials regarding rental space appeared in March, 1824, and by May, yet another storagekeeper, Francisco Magan, was demanding from Grimaldi 3,495 *reales* for unpaid rental bills; AV: Secretaría 2-139-47.

46 "The illness of Mr. Lencerini has temporarily shut down the performances of opera, especially of *Elisa and Claudio*, which should have been performed today; therefore, the theatre management wishes to offer its subscribers the best verse plays and Spanish operettas possible under the circumstances, as far as the illnesses or indispositions of the acting company will allow . . ." *DM*, January 11, 1824.

47 Bretón reported that Grimaldi was "stage director for many years under different managements." Bretón de los Herreros, "Declamación," p. 710.

48 Carnicer had been under contract since October 29 of the previous year, but Grimaldi was unable to live up to the contractual promises made to him and a dispute was submitted to arbitration in April, 1824 – a procedure "carried out in good faith and avoiding lawsuits, quarrels and expenses." AHP: Protocolo 22946, fos. 67-8.

49 See Gies, "Juan de Grimaldi y el año teatral." Gregorio Martín interprets this clause as indicative of Grimaldi's pro-Fernandine politics. He writes: "That the absolute power of Fernando VII was considered, as Grimaldi considered it, to be the best solution for dramatic societies, was something that the actors who had suffered it and who had lived and died in exile could not forgive him. To call that power enlightened, when it had jailed and exiled Máiquez, the idol of the national actors, is something that only could occur to the famous Father Carrillo. Without judging the artistic skills of Grimaldi, considerable according to authors of the period and as can be seen from his opinion of the sad state of Spanish theatre, his political ideas in these years are perfectly defined. He handed the theatre over to Fernandine absolutism . . ." Martín, "Periodismo y teatro," p. 9. But this can also be seen as another example, more of which will be evident later, of Grimaldi's opportunism, his ability to speak to the authorities in order to get his way. Had he not praised Fernando he would never have been given the theatres. Even the actors themselves were not exempt from such hollow statements of praise.

50 He might have added that in Paris Máiquez met and studied with Talma, who taught him the seriousness of his art. See Colao, *Máiquez, discípulo de Talma*.

51 An additional letter, posted the same day – March 16 – reviewed the circumstances of his takeover of the theatres in 1823; AHN: Consejos, 11.411, n. 35.

52 See also their lengthy petition of February 19, 1824, in which they describe the history of their rights to pension payments.

53 See the contracts and inventories in AV: Contaduría 4-56-1.

54 See the detailed financial statements for that year; AV: Secretaría 3-478-9.

55 Latorre does not appear in the annual listing of the actors in the companies published in the *DM* (April 17, 1824) nor does he appear in Shields, but documents show that he was indeed a salaried member of the company; AV: Secretaría 3-478-9.

56 The elder Rodríguez and his wife adopted a child that May. She was their niece's daughter, an eight-year-old girl named María Dolores Gutiérrez del Pozo, and they promised to raise her and to pay the expenses her parents could not afford for her care: AHP: Protocolo 22946, fos. 115–16.

57 Molins, *Bretón de los Herreros. Recuerdos de su vida y de sus obras* (Madrid: Tello, 1883), pp. 25–6.

58 Desfrétières discovered and copied the marriage certificate from Book 38, Fo. 276; Desfrétières, p. 185.

59 She appeared that season in a diverse collection of translated comedies, one-act plays and "original" productions: *El opresor de la familia* (a French comedy by Duval); *Los viajes de Pedro el Grande o el Carpintero de la Libonia* (a French comic opera based on a Duval play); *Del rey abajo, ninguno; Abre el ojo o sea aviso a los solteros* (a revision of a play by Francisco de Rojas); *La tertulia realista* (a new one-act play by Carnerero – this play was written for Fernando VII's Saint's Day and performed first on May 30. It enjoyed a modest success – it managed three performances that season [Shields records only two] – and at least at first, tickets were hard to get: "The actors at the Príncipe, in spite of having announced for next Sunday a repetition of the play performed last night in honor of the King, because of the extraordinary attendance at the spectacle and the large number of people who could not get tickets, will give tonight a special performance of the same function and under the same conditions as last night in order to please the capital's audience." *DM*, May 31, 1824); Molière's *El avaro*; *Don Quijote y Sancho Panza en el Castillo del Duque* (an original play by José Robreño, first performed that year); *Viajes del emperador Segismundo o el Escultor y el ciego* (a translation, also first performed that year); *La huerfanita o lo que son los parientes* (a three-act comedy by Carnerero); and *El pobre pretendiente* (a "play rewritten for the Spanish stage" by Carnerero).

60 A., "Concepción Rodríguez," p. 194. Grimaldi signed the article "A," for "Juan Aquiles," the nickname his friends had given him.

61 *Ibid.* p. 194.

62 *Ibid.* p. 195.

63 For a fuller analysis of this issue, see D.T. Gies, "Larra, Grimaldi and the actors of Madrid," in *Studies in Eighteenth-Century Spanish Literature and Romanticism* (Newark: Juan de la Cuesta, 1985), pp. 113–22.

64 Grimaldi credited Josefa Virg, a character actress from the Cruz company, Dionisio Solís, the translator and director, and Máiquez himself with having had considerable influence on Concepción in her first years in Madrid.

65 A., "Concepción Rodríguez", p. 193.

66 They named her Clotilde and had her baptized the next morning at San Sebastián. The baby's maternal grandmother, Rosa Velasco, stood as godmother. San Sebastián, Libro 68B, 89vo.

67 See, for example, similar injunctions issued by José Manuel de Arjona, Juez Protector de los Teatros, in 1819; AHN: Consejos 11.408, n. 41. The eighteenth century was likewise riddled with laws and decrees which sought to control the actors and their audiences. See Francisco Aguilar Piñal, *Sevilla y el teatro en el siglo XVIII* (Oviedo: Universidad de Oviedo, 1974).

68 See Gies, "Larra, Grimaldi and the actors of Madrid."

69 See Cotarelo, *María del Rosario Fernández*, pp. 5–6.

70 Bretón de los Herreros, "Escuela de Declamación Española," *El Correo Literario y Mercantil*, September 5, 1831.

71 *Cartas Españolas*, III, November 1, 1831.

72 Bretón de los Herreros, "Declamación," p. 713.

73 *Cartas Españolas*, II, July 24, 1831.

74 See "Diferentes sistemas de los actores para la representación de los dramas" (September 9, 1831) and "Sobre la acción teatral, o los gestos y movimientos que el actor asocia a la palabra" (October 24, 1831).

75 Bretón de los Herreros, "Declamación," p. 710.

76 *Correo*, April 15, 1833. Reprinted in *Obra dispersa*, ed. J.M. Díez Taboada and J.M. Rosas (Logroño: Instituto de Estudios Riojanos, 1965), pp. 405.

77 See also Bretón's comments in the *Correos* of March 29, 1833 and May 8, 1833.

78 Escosura, "Recuerdos literarios," p. 226.

79 "When Gorostiza withdrew from Spain in 1823, the *Moratinistas* remained without a leader. Had Martínez de la Rosa been in the country during the years that followed he would doubtless have been their chief. In October of 1824 the recognition and applause accorded a play bearing the title *A la vejez viruelas* passed the leadership of this group to a new and unknown author, Bretón de los Herreros." Rogers, p. 321. See also Patrizia Garelli, *Bretón de los Herreros e la sua 'formula comica'* (Imola, Italy: Galeati, 1983).

80 While associated with Grimaldi and his company during the Fernandine era, Bretón wrote and staged thirteen original comedies, one-act comedies, or allegorical *loas*: in addition to *A la vejez viruelas*, he saw performed his *Los dos sobrinos* (1825), *A Madrid me vuelvo*, *La autoridad paterna*, and *El rival de sí mismo* (1828), *El templo de Himeneo* (written to commemorate the marriage of Fernando VII and María Cristina in 1829), *La falsa ilustración* and *Marcela o ¿cuál de los tres?* – which "definitely opened the doors of fame to him" in 1831 (Ricardo Navas Ruiz, *El romanticismo español*, 3rd edn. [Madrid: Catedra 1982], p. 358. Fernando VII attended a performance on March 2, 1832. See the *DM* of that date.) – and *El carnaval*, *El músico y el poeta*, *El templo de la gloria*, *Un tercero en discordia*, and *El triunfo de la inocencia* (written, along with *El templo*, to commemorate the official recognition of Isabel as the legitimate heir to the Bourbon throne in 1833). His translations of French comedies and tragedies included pieces by Beaumarchais, Scribe, Champfort, Molière, Racine, Néricault, Monvel, Dancourt, and other lesser lights, and were concentrated in two years – 1828 and 1831 (he translated one play in 1824, three in 1825, four in 1826, one in 1827, eleven in 1828, one in 1829, two in 1830, ten in 1831, three in 1832, and four in 1833). For his "arrangements" of Spanish plays he plundered dramas by Calderón, Lope, Tirso and Ruiz de Alarcón. (See N.B. Adams, "Notes on Spanish plays at the beginning of the Romantic period," *Romanic Review*, 17 [1926], pp. 128–42.)

81 Payments varied: José María Carnerero received 800 for his short piece, *La tertulia realista*, and an additional 640 for "the works that he has turned over to the company" in October, while Ventura de la Vega was paid just 320 for his one-act comedy, *Virtud y reconocimiento*, that same month.

82 See José Yxart, *El arte escénico en España* (2 vols. Barcelona: La Vanguardia, 1894), vol. I, p. 18.

83 See Piero Menarini, "El problema de las traducciones en el teatro romántico español," *Actas del VII Congreso Internacional de Hispanistas* (Rome: Bulzoni, 1982), pp. 751–59.

84 Larra, "De las traducciones," *El Español*, March 11, 1836.

85 Larra, "*La redacción de un periódico*. Comedia original en cinco actos y en verso, por don Manuel Bretón de los Herreros," *El Español*, July 8, 1836.

86 In 1837 alone he had more than two dozen plays staged in Madrid. N.B. Adams, "French influence on the Madrid theater in 1837," *Estudios dedicados a D. Ramón Menéndez Pidal* (Madrid: CSIC, 1950), p. 139.

87 See Molins, *Bretón*, 1893, p. 11.

88 See Cotarelo, *Máiquez*, p. 440. The company thought that *Dido* would be a success, and prepared for it carefully: "The company, wishing to give the

production of this tragedy special proof of the care with which it attempts to please the public and to remain worthy of the special favors that the audience has always granted to the Príncipe theatre, has not spared any effort to make Mr. l'Franc's celebrated work worthy of the high esteem it enjoys in all of Europe . . . Without going into detail concerning the resources employed to add to the extravagance of the spectacle, as much by the whole company as by the actors performing in it, it can be stated that even the scenery, painted for this performance by professor don Antonio María Tadei is superior in magnificence and good taste to any which have been presented in this theatre." *DM*, October 21, 1826. Tadei had worked for Grimaldi as scenery painter since 1824.

89 Molins, *Bretón*, 1893, p. 10.
90 Georges Le Gentil, *Le Poète Manuel Bretón de los Herreros et la société espagnole de 1830 a 1860* (Paris: Hachette, 1909), p. 26.
91 Molins, *Bretón*, p. 30.
92 Molins, *ibid.*, pp. 30–1.
93 Frank Duffey, "Juan de Grimaldi and the Madrid stage (1823–1837)," *Hispanic Review*, 10 (1942), p. 151.
94 See J.K. Leslie, *Ventura de la Vega and the Spanish Theatre, 1820–1865* (Princeton, 1940) and J. Montero Alonso, *Ventura de la Vega: su vida y su tiempo* (Madrid: Editora Nacional, 1951).
95 Ángel Salcedo Ruiz, *La literatura española*, III (Madrid: Calleja, 1916), p. 476; cited by Duffey, "Madrid stage," p. 152.
96 See Hans Juretschke, *Vida, obra y pensamiento de Alberto Lista* (Madrid: CSIC, 1951).
97 Translations predominated: of the fourteen plays he is credited with writing or translating during the Fernandine era, only two (*El día de San Calixto*, 1825; *Don Quijote de la Mancha en Sierra Morena*, 1832) are original pieces. His broadest successes came after 1828 with his translations from Duval (*Shakespeare enamorado* and *El Tasso*, 1828), Scribe (*El gastrónomo sin dinero*, 1829; *El testamento*, 1831; *Hacerse amar con peluca*, 1832), and St. Aulaire (*La expiación*, 1831.) Andioc has written of *La expiación*: "The eighteen sessions dedicated to *La expiación*, also a play 'of great spectacle,' translated by Ventura de la Vega, reach an average of 6,500 *reales* during the 1831–2 theatrical year; in the next year, however, the number of performances is much lower than the preceding figures, with the subsequent reduction of the money collected . . ." René Andioc, "Sobre el estreno de *Don Alvaro*," *Homenaje a Juan López-Morillas* (Madrid: Castalia, 1982), p. 69.
98 Larra, "De las traducciones," *El Español*, March 11, 1836.
99 See Robert Marrast, *José de Espronceda et son temps* (Paris: Klincksieck, 1974.)
100 Zorrilla recounts an amusing anecdote about Ventura's rebellious tendencies and his refusal to conform to an arbitrary law which prohibited anyone except military officers from wearing a moustache. Zorrilla, p. 2000.
101 Marrast, p. 122.
102 See Eugenio Hartzenbusch e Hiriarte, *Periódicos de Madrid* (Madrid: Sucesores de Rivadeneyra, 1876), pp. 39–41, and Georges Le Gentil, *Les revues littéraires de l'Espagne pendant la première moitié du XIXe siècle* (Paris: Hachette, 1909).
103 Le Gentil, *Bretón*, p. 26.
104 Molins, *Bretón*, 1893, p. 18. See also Adams, "Notes on dramatic criticism," pp. 231–8. P.P. Rogers, commentating on Carnerero and Féliz Encisco Castrillón as playwrights, states that "Both were playwrights of little worth. The support they gave to the struggle for the supremacy of good taste may be counted as their service to the theatre." p. 32.
105 See Juan Luis Alborg, *Historia de la literatura española. El romanticismo* (Madrid: Gredos, 1980), vol. IV, pp. 627–34, and S.A. Stoudemire, "Gil y Zárate's

translation of French plays," *Modern Language Notes*, 48 (1933), pp. 321–5.

106 Chaulié, p. 58. On Carrillo and censorship, see Hubbard, *Histoire de la littérature*, p. 100.

107 See N.B. Adams, "Sidelights on the Spanish theaters of the Eighteen-Thirties," *Hispania*, 9 (1926), p. 2.

108 Mesonero Romanos, *Memorias*, p. 65.

109 Menarini, p. 752.

110 Gregorio Martín has shown that the *tertulia* began a few years before the date remembered by Mesonero Romanos. "'El Parnasillo'," pp. 209–18. See also his *Hacia una revisión crítica de la biografía de Larra* (Porto Alegre: PUC–EMMA, 1975), pp. 67–8.

111 Chaulié, pp. 63–6.

112 *Mis memorias íntimas*, vol. I, p. 188.

113 Molins, *Obras poéticas*, II (Madrid, 1857). The modern historian of the theatre, Matilde Muñoz, intensified the disagreeable descriptions by labeling it a "sordid locale full of cockroaches and rats," Muñoz, p. 212.

114 *Memorias* VIII, p. 61.

115 Duffey, "Madrid stage," p. 153.

116 *Mis memorias íntimas*, I, p. 188.

117 Romanticism hardly began at "El Parnasillo," as Edgar Allison Peers has made clear, but the nature of the discussions at the Príncipe Café and its function as a meeting place for those artists involved in the attempt to reanimate Spanish literature cannot be overestimated. See E.A. Peers, *Historia del movimiento romántico español* (2 vols., Madrid: Gredos, 1967), vol. II, pp. 484–5.

118 Molins wrote of the stimulating effect the *tertulia* had on Bretón: "There in his literary mode, when his behavior had been formed in barracks and encampments, and his style had been modeled on those of D. Diego de Torres and Gerardo Lobo, meeting Vega, Pezuela, Pardo, Escosura, Frías, Gallego, Alonso, Ortiz, Romea, *Grimaldi above all*, in short "El Parnasillo," cleared up, as he himself says, his intelligence." Molins, *Bretón*, 1883, p. 415. Emphasis added.

119 *Memorias*, pp. 66–7.

120 Larra, "¿Quién es el público?" *El Pobrecito Hablador*, August 17, 1832.

121 Pedro Gómez Aparicio, *Historia del periodismo español* (4 vols., Madrid: Editora Nacional, 1967), p. 192.

122 There were many others: see Mesonero Romanos' complete listing in *Memorias*, pp. 64–8.

123 *Memorias*, p. 74.

124 Duffey, "Madrid stage," p. 155.

125 See Desfrétières, p. 51. Grimaldi's manuscript is kept in the Biblioteca Municipal, Madrid (1-209-53).

126 See Shields, p. 559, and Desfrétières, p. 52. The two plays have been confused by critics, most recently by René Andioc, in his superb article, "Sobre el estreno de *Don Alvaro*," p. 69. Commenting on the popularity of *La huérfana* in 1831, he writes: "The same happens with *La huérfana de Bruselas (o El abate l'Epée y el asesino)*, translated from the French and already staged at the beginning of the century . . ."

127 Bretón, *Obra dispersa*, p. 266.

128 Desfrétières, p. 52.

129 It was performed numerous times in Seville, for example. See F. Aguilar Piñal, *Cartelera prerromántica sevillana, años 1800–1836* (Madrid: C.S.I.C., 1968), p. 28. Aguilar Piñal does not confuse it with Bouilly's play, the performances of which he lists on p. 9.

130 See Shields; *DM*; J. Simón Díaz, *Cartelera teatral madrileña: 1830–1839* (Madrid: CSIC, 1960), p. 80; and F. Herrero Salgado, *Cartelera teatral madrileña: 1840–1849* (Madrid: CSIC, 1963), p. 89.

131 See A. Rumeau, "Le théâtre à Madrid à la veille du Romantisme, 1831–1834," *Hommage à Ernest Martinenche. Etudes hispaniques et américaines* (Paris: D'Artrey, 1939), pp. 330–46.

132 Desfrétières, p. 53.

133 For a discussion of the importance of these key images in Spanish Romantic drama, see David T. Gies, "Imágenes y la imaginación románticas," *Romanticismo I: Atti del II Congresso sul Romanticismo* (Genoa: La Quercia Edizioni, 1982), pp. 49–59.

134 *La huérfana de Bruselas*, 2nd. edn. (Madrid: Pascual Conesa, 1862), p. 10.

135 *Diario de Valencia*, July, 1831, p. 94. The reviewer went on to praise the "naturalness" of her style, concluding that "The world is full of examples of such naturalness, but only genius can observe them fully; their exact and faithful imitation, as expressed by Mrs. Rodríguez, is the art's most sublime achievement."

136 Antonio García Llansó, *Historia de la mujer contemporánea* (Barcelona: A. J. Bastiños, 1899), p. 256.

137 Guerra and Guerra y Alarcón, *Músicos, poetas y actores*, pp. 273–4. A. Fernández de los Ríos wrote that she was twelve when she acted in this role. *Album biográfico. Museo universal de retratos y noticias de las celebridades actuales de todos los países* (Madrid, 1848), p. 72.

138 See Desfrétières, pp. 54–6. A manuscript of the translation, in the Biblioteca Municipal in Madrid (1-43-11), shows that the play was approved by the censors on March 25. Another manuscript is kept in the Biblioteca Nacional (15.818).

139 See Shields; *DM*; Simón Díaz, *Cartelera*; Herrero Salgado, *Cartelera*.

140 Aguilar Piñal, *Cartelera*, p. 30.

141 The Biblioteca Nacional's *Catálogo de piezas de teatro manuscritas* (Madrid, 1934) lists an edition published in Valencia in 1830, but this has never been located.

142 Duffey, "Madrid stage," p. 151.

143 Grimaldi himself wrote that Mendizábal pressured writers to support the "cause": "Mr. Mendizábal knows very well that his word at that time was frank, fiery; he knows very well, if we are to cite one example among many, that such was the meaning of the instructions he gave to the poets who were in charge of the compositions scheduled to be read at the first patriotic function created in the capital's theatres to benefit the national war effort; finally, he knows very well that the same authority was used to suppress a strophe written to flatter him personally, an incident we remember with pleasure for the honor it brings to someone we are today forced to fight against." "De la administración del señor Mendizábal (Artículo tercero)," *Revista Española* (July 19, 1836).

144 Molins, 1883, p. 104.

145 *Eco del Comercio*, February 15, 1836.

146 *DM*, December 5, 1835. See also *RE*, December 5, 1835.

147 Simón Díaz, *Cartelera*, p. 87.

148 *RE*, December 7, 1835.

149 *RE*, December 8, 1835.

150 *El Artista*, I, p. 287.

151 See in particular, "De la administración del señor Mendizábal (Artículo tercero)," July 19, 1836, as cited above.

3 On the eve of Romanticism

1 See Desfrétières, pp. 59–65. Grimaldi also had before him a Spanish translation of the play, called *La Pata de carnero*, which he claimed was not the source for his play. "There existed in the archives of the Cruz Theatre, since the year 1816, a magical comedy translated from French called *La pata de carnero*, passed by censors and ready for performance. Some people have suggested, in more or less good faith, that *La pata de cabra* is a translation or literal version of that French play. This is not true. While it is true that the author of *La pata de cabra* has had this original version before him, imitated from it many things and even translated others, and preserved the core of the character of don Simplicio, it still cannot be considered a *translation* . . ." "Advertencia," *Todo lo vence amor, o La pata de cabra*, 2nd edn. (Madrid: Repullés, 1836), p.v. In the *Índice de las comedias y sainetes que existen en el archivo de el teatro de la Cruz al cargo de Vicente Masi*, Legajo 2, n. 21, of the Biblioteca Municipal in Madrid, an odd handwritten note appears in the margin next to this work: "*La pata de carnero*: it was given to Mr. Grimaldi and he mislaid it." I am grateful to Professors Antonietta Calderone and Gabriella del Monaco for bringing this to my attention. The word "estorvó" which appears in the article by Paola Santoro, "La crítica giornalistica (1750–1850)," in E. Caldera, ed., *Teatro di magia* (Rome: Bulzoni, 1983), p. 213, is an obvious misprint.

2 D.L. Shaw, *A Literary History of Spain: The Nineteenth Century* (London: Benn, 1972), p. 5.

3 The newspaper *El Laberinto* reported on April 16, 1844 (following the first performances of *Don Juan Tenorio*) that it was received "coldly and had very few performances." Cited by Sainz de Robles, p. 19. "It seems as though the popularity of *Don Juan Tenorio* was not immediate . . ." A mere thirteen performances took place between its debut in 1844 and 1846, and only seventeen more until 1849. See Dowling, "El anti-Don Juan de Ventura de la Vega," p. 218.

4 There seems to be some confusion regarding this date. Several erroneous dates have been advanced, including 1824 (D. Poyán Díaz, *Enrique Gaspar, medio siglo de teatro español* [2 vols., Madrid: Gredos, 1957]), p. 134; 1825 (Le Gentil, *Bretón*, p. 26; Peers, *Historia*, I, p. 331); 1828 (*Enciclopedia Universal Ilustrada*, vol. 42, p. 682); February 19, 1829 (Joaquín Muñoz Morillejo, *Escenografía española* [Madrid: Blass, 1923], p. 103); April 19, 1829 (Desfrétières, p. 59); and even 1831 (Navas Ruiz, *El romanticismo español* [Madrid: Cátedra, 1982] p. 121). The title page of the second edition (1836) claimed that the play was "performed in Madrid for the first time on April 19, 1829" but the *DM* confirms that the play opened on February 18. Shields provides the correct date (Shields, p. 882).

5 *DM*, February 18, 1829.

6 *DM*, May 7, 1829.

7 "Soon a black cloud descended upon the theatrical managements, who had to suspend performances of *La pata de cabra*, and close the box offices, in order to join the public prayers for Queen María Josefa Amalia's health." Molins, *Bretón*, 1883, pp. 65–6.

8 *El Correo Literario*, July 31, 1829.

9 *DM*, November 3, 1829.

10 *DM*, November 11, 1829.

11 See Shields; *DM*; Simón Díaz, *Cartelera*, p. 88; Herrero Salgado, *Cartelera*, p. 100; *Veinticuatro diarios (Madrid, 1830–1900)* (4 vols., Madrid: CSIC, 1972), II, p. 391.

12 As late as 1898, newspapers were still praising its "interesting plot." *La Época*, January 10, 1898.

13 Blanqui, p. 74.
14 de Custine, vol. II, pp. 326–7. The infamous Casanova had similar tales to tell when he arrived in Madrid fifty years earlier. See *Histoire de ma vie* (Paris: Plon, 1961), x, p. 313.
15 Ferrer y Herrera, p. 19.
16 Zorrilla, p. 1999.
17 *Correo Literario*, October 19, 1829. Emphasis added.
18 Mesonero Romanos, *Manual de Madrid*. BAE 201 (Madrid: Atlas, 1967). Fernández de Córdoba gives similar figures for the 1825 period, when the central box cost 60 *reales*. *Mis memorias íntimas*, p. 44.
19 For further information concerning pricing during these years, see Manuel Espadas Burgos, "Abasto y hábitos alimenticios en el Madrid de Fernando VII," *Cuadernos de Historia*, 1973, pp. 237–90; and Pascual Madoz, *Diccionario geográfico, estadístico histórico* (Madrid, 1847), x.
20 Mesonero Romanos, *Manual de Madrid*, BAE vol. 201, p. 106.
21 Ricardo Sepúlveda provides some comparable figures from December 1831. *El corral de la Pacheca* (Madrid, 1888), p. 128.
22 Throughout December of that year, *La pata* averaged over 8,000 *reales* per performance. Professor René Andioc has pointed out to me that figures for these same performances of *La pata* from the Corregimiento section of the Municipal Archives are generally 1,010 *reales* higher than those listed here. Neither of us is sure why this is the case. I am grateful to Professor Andioc for this information.
23 *Correo Literario*, October 5, 1829.
24 Duffey, "Madrid stage," p. 155.
25 Duffey has speculated that it might have had as high as a half million spectators and as many as one thousand performances. It was still in repertory as late as the first quarter of this century. Carmen de Burgos, *Fígaro* (Madrid: Imprenta de 'Alrededor del Mundo', 1919), p. 78.
26 Sepúlveda reproduces the figures in *El corral de la Pacheca*, p. 130. Andioc mistakes the document for Corregimiento. Andioc, "Sobre el estreno de *Don Alvaro*," p. 70. The annual proceeds were 537,536 *reales* (1829–30 season), 84,099 (1830–1), 81,743 (1831–2), 227,517 (1832–3), and 39,023 (March to July 1833). For comparison's sake, a subscription to the *Correo Literario* cost 10 *reales* per month.
27 See Julio Caro Baroja, *Teatro popular y magia* (Madrid: Revista de Occidente, 1974).
28 Caro Baroja, p. 38.
29 "The appearance in 1715 of the first five plays by Juan Salvo y Vela titled *El mágico de Salerno, Pedro Vayalarde*, marks the rise of the *comedia de magia* genre; and, his plays as a whole establish those characteristic features by which the genre is defined." Donald C. Buck, "Juan Salvo y Vela and the rise of the *comedia de magia*: The magician as anti-hero," *Hispania*, 69 (1986), p. 251. Buck takes issue with Caro's judgment that the magic plays appealed to the audiences' craving for spectacle rather than to its artistic sense: "I would suggest instead that the spectacular element is not the *raison d'être* for the *comedia de magia*, but rather the means to a different, more intrinsically dramatic end: the development of the magician character type and his function in the exposition of the major theme of these plays: illusion and reality." Buck, pp. 251–2. See also J.L. Gotor, "El máxico de Salerno," in *Teatro di magia*, ed. Ermanno Caldera (Rome: Bulzoni, 1983), pp. 107–46. Caldera studies the visual impact of the stage effects of magic plays in "Entre cuadro y tramoya," *Dieciocho*, 9 (1986), pp. 51–6.
30 Mesonero Romanos, *Dramaturgos posteriores a Lope de Vega*, BAE 48 & 49 (2 vols., Madrid: Rivadeneyra, 1859) II, p. xx.
31 See José de Cañizares, *El anillo de Giges*, ed. Joaquín Alvarez Barrientos (Madrid:

CSIC, 1983), p. 30. Also, Ermanno Caldera, "Sulla 'spettacolarità' delle commedie di magia," in *Teatro de magia*, pp. 11–32.

32 A look at those magical scenes from Act 1 will enable us to view more clearly the problems he needed to surmount. (Citations from Juan de Grimaldi, *Todo lo vence amor o la pata de cabra*, ed. David T. Gies (Rome: Bulzoni, 1986). See Appendix 3 for examples from Acts 2 and 3.

Scene		Trick or Transformation
1.	1	The pistols with which don Juan is trying to kill himself "suddenly escape from his hands and fly through the air."
2.	1	Cupid appears out of the tree trunk on which don Juan is seated.
3.	2	Cupid draws a circle on the ground and another in the air with one of his arrows, and the circles – the moon and a waterfall – turn blood red.
4.	2	Lightning is followed by "horrible" thunder, a cave opens up, flames shoot out and several genies appear.
5.	2	The genies place a goat inside a cauldron, a lightning bolt incinerates it and one goat's foot is all that remains.
6.	2	Don Juan attempts to catch Cupid by his wings, but the God of Love flies off ("You try to hold love down?").
7.	6	The earth opens up and out walk four musicians carrying instruments.
8.	7	The musicians change into duennas.
9.	11	The mirror in Leonor's boudoir changes into "a throne of flowers."
10.	12	The four duennas/musicians change into nymphs.
11.	12	Leonor's vanity table reappears and the nymphs disappear.
12.	13	Don Juan, who has been hiding behind the mirror, mysteriously disappears as don Simplicio is about to reveal his presence.
13.	15	Don Juan and Leonor are locked behind bars in the towers of don Lope's house. Cupid flies by in a carriage, and as he passes each of the two prisoners "the towers collapse, and he is caught in the carriage."

33 The theatres had such a trap door, as indicated in the stage directions of the play, Act 3, Scene 8.
34 *Correo Literario*, October 5, 1829.
35 Matilde Muñoz reports that Blanchard painted seven new sets for *La pata*, Muñoz, p. 103.
36 Peers demonstrates little patience with these changes in *La pata*, particularly the end scene in Cupid's palace where Cupid is seated on a throne of roses between Juan and Leonor, although the final scene of *Don Juan Tenorio*, where don Juan ascends to Heaven in a bed of roses surrounded by fluttering cupids, is hardly much different from Grimaldi's trumped-up ending. See Peers, p. 331.
37 See Appendix 4.
38 *El Entreacto*, 1840, p. 45.
39 *Correo Literario*, October 23, 1829.
40 BM: 1-199-7. This manuscript also contains minor stage directions written into the margin as well as a long interpolated scene following Act 2, Scene 15. The added scene is a trivial interlude with the peasants and has little interest.
41 Chaulié, II, p. 55. See also Alonso Cortés, *Zorrilla. Su vida y sus obras*, 2nd edn. (Valladolid: Santaren, 1943) p. 45. She saw one of the very first performances, since she died in mid-May, 1829.
42 *Documentos del reinado de Fernando VII. III. Arias Tejero, diarios (1828–1831)* (3 vols., Pamplona: Universidad de Navarra, 1967), vol. II, p. 267.
43 *El Entreacto*, August 4, 1839.
44 "El hombre menguado o el carlista en la proclamación," *La Revista Española*, October 27, 1833. Similar references are found in his articles 'Representación de

Ana Bolena" (*Revista Española*, May 19, 1834), "Carta de Fígaro" (*Revista Española*, July 31, 1834), "El ministerial" (*Revista Española*, September 16, 1834), "La cuestión transparente" (*El Observador*, October 19, 1834), and "El hombre–globo" (*Revista Mensajero*, March 9, 1835).

45 *La Nación*, April 13, 1853. See also *La Epoca*, April 12, 1853.

46 "Don Simplicio returns from his fantastic journey, whose incidents he retells to his enthralled audience. 'I have seen the moon' the actor used to say, drawing out the 'oo' in 'moon' for comic effect, and adding several ad-libbed jokes to modernize what he had seen on his fabulous trip. But once, at the same time of the Revolution of 1868, when among the candidates for the Spanish throne was mentioned the Duke of Montpensier, it occurred to Fernández to say, 'I have seen . . . Montpensier munching stewed vegetables' ('comiendo pisto'). The theatre erupted in raucous laughter, and the joke cost the comic a huge fine." José Deleito y Piñuela, *Estampas del Madrid teatral fin de siglo* (Madrid: Editorial Saturnino Calleja, 1946), pp. 73–6.

47 *La Correspondencia de España*, January 24, 1890.

48 Mesonero Romanos, "Las tres tertulias," *Panorama matritense*, March, 1833.

49 *Correo Literario*, November 16, 1829.

50 Ferrer y Herrera, p. 41. Ferrer did not like Guzmán either, finding him "boring."

51 Alonso Cortés, p. 45.

52 Shaw, p. 5.

53 Mesonero Romanos, *Memorias*, p. 74.

54 N.B. Adams, "Notes on dramatic criticism," p. 235.

55 *Correo Literario*, September 2, 1831.

56 Zorrilla, p. 2004.

57 Ermanno Caldera, "La última etapa de la comedia de magia," *Actas del VII Congreso Internacional de Hispanistas* (Rome: Bulzoni, 1982), pp. 247–53. *El Heraldo* reported that don Simplicio, the protagonist of *La pata*, reappeared in a "second part" entitled *Los talismanes*, November 15, 1848. The playwright Tamayo y Baus wrote a *zarzuela de magia* ("pretty bad") based on Grimaldi's play, which received its first performance in Madrid on May 7, 1853. (See R. Esquer Torres, *El teatro de Tamayo y Baus* [Madrid: CSIC, 1965], p. 26.) Cristóbal Oudrid, a well-known composer, converted *La pata* into a *zarzuela*, which played in Madrid in 1858 (See *La Epoca* and *La Iberia*, June 17, 1858; also, Papeles de Barbieri, BM: ms. 14078.)

58 Enrique de Olavarría y Ferrari reported that "The new item at year's end was the magical comedy *La pata de cabra*, which was received with delirious applause on December 30, and went on to play in 1842 with numerous repetitions." *Reseña histórica del teatro en México*, ii (México, 1902), p. 45; cited by Duffey, "Juan de Grimaldi and the pre-Romantic drama in Spain," p. 35. It was playing in Mexico as late as 1887. Olavarría similarly reported the existence of a *zarzuela* entitled *Don Simplicio Bobadilla en México, op. cit.*, ii., p. 222.

59 *Correo Literario*, October 19, 1829.

60 *El Español*, July 12, 1836. See Susan Kirkpatrick, "Larra y *El Español*: Los artículos no firmados," *Cuadernos Hispanoamericanos*, 399 (1983), p. 61.

61 See Carnerero's *Cartas Españolas*, ii (July 11, 1831), p. 18. Andioc writes, "The most important debut of the theatrical year, 1831–2, is unquestionably the melodrama *Jocó o el orangután* [. . .]; the work was staged twenty days, with 7,600 *reales* on average, but it did not have more than eight performances during the next season, with 5,500 *reales* per day, and declining from there . . ." "Sobre el estreno de *Don Alvaro*," p. 69.

62 *Correo Literario*, July 31, 1829.

63 Ermanno Caldera, "La última etapa de la comedia de magia," p. 247. Caldera has done brilliant work on Spain's *comedia de magia* and has headed a research team which has produced important studies of this underappreciated genre. See his *La commedia romantica in Spagna* (Pisa: Giardini, 1978), his edited collection of essays on *Teatro di magia* (Rome: Bulzoni, 1983) and the new series of edited plays ("Tramoya: Teatro inédito de magia y 'gran espectáculo'") being published by Bulzoni under his direction.

64 See Ermanno Caldera, "La magia nel teatro romantico," in *Teatro di magia*, pp. 185–205.

65 Ermanno Caldera, "*La pata de cabra y Le pied de mouton*," *Studia historica et philologica in honorem M. Batllori* (Rome: Instituto Español de Cultura, 1984), pp. 567–75. I am grateful to Professor Caldera for providing me with a pre-publication typescript of this study.

66 "Advertencia," *La pata de cabra*, 2nd. edn. (Madrid: Repullés, 1836).

67 Caldera, "*La pata de cabra y Le pied de mouton*," p. 571.

68 Zorrilla, p. 2004. Zorrilla recounts a delicious anecdote concerning a priest from Segovia, who under the pretext of checking up on his nephew, comes to Madrid to see Grimaldi's play. When the Superintendent of Police (Zorrilla's father) is finished with his interrogation, he decides that not only is the priest's reason good enough, but he is ordered to remain in Madrid "to go back to see it again." pp. 2005–7.

69 Larra, "Yo quiero ser cómico," *RE*, March 1, 1833.

70 "What I want to say is that my people can never have faith in the future and that my many gifts cannot buy that happiness which can only be assured by the heart of a wife, the affection of children, a clear conscience, the triumph of merit, the cultivation of arts and sciences, and above all by virtue and honor."

71 Caldera, "*La pata de cabra y Le pied de mouton*," p. 567. Caldera concludes: "With all these modifications, and others that are omitted here, Grimaldi did not manage to write an original comedy; but at any rate it is undeniable that he knew how to breathe into the work of the French author a new life that found a perfect home on Iberian soil." Antonio de los Reyes also labels it a "simple plagiarism." *Julián Romea, el actor y su contorno (1813–1868)* (Murcia: Academia Alfonso X el Sabio, 1977), p. 38.

72 Duffey, "Juan de Grimaldi and the pre-Romantic drama in Spain," p. 74.

73 Duffey, *ibid.*, p. 82.

74 "Advertencia." Bretón, too, noted that "When *La pata de cabra* is announced, even the most ignorant spectator knows very well that he is not going to see a play of classical literature, that he is not going to see a traditional play; he is going to enjoy himself and laugh powerfully for three hours; he is going to a theatrical function that flatters his emotions, ignoring for that one night all theories and classifications." *Correo Literario*, September 2, 1831.

75 Zorrilla, p. 2004.

76 *Correo Literario*, September 2, 1831.

77 Yxart, *El arte escénico en España*, p. 19.

78 See also the Acting Magistrate Antonio José Galindo's letter of March 13. AV: Corregimiento 1-197-5.

79 Montero Alonso, *Ventura de la Vega*, p. 50. On Manuel Gaviria, father and son, see AHP: Protocolo 23799; AHP: Protocolo 22949; and Martín, "Periodismo y teatro."

80 Muñoz, p. 240. Gaviria was also involved with entertainments (horse shows,

acrobats) at the Bull Ring during these years. See J.E. Varey, *Los títeres y otras diversiones populares de Madrid: 1758–1840* (London: Támesis, 1972).

81 Sepúlveda, p. 489.

82 Cited in the article, "Reales concesiones hechas a los teatros de Madrid por varios Señores Reyes, para el pago de las jubilaciones, viudedades y horfandades," *Semanario Teatral*, April 28, 1834, p. 20.

83 Martín, "Periodismo y teatro."

84 See Molins, *Bretón*, 1893, p. 13.

85 See Appendix 5.

86 See Mesonero Romanos's article, "La filarmonía," published first in March, 1833, and collected in his *Panorama matritense*. BAE 199 (Madrid: Atlas, 1967), pp. 175–8. See also Le Gentil, *Bretón*, p. 26.

87 Bretón wrote that Grimaldi directed one of the companies: "At that time the Príncipe Theatre had the good fortune to be taken over by our unforgettable friend, Juan de Grimaldi, who had directed one of the above-mentioned Italian companies . . ." "Declamación," p. 710. For the expenses of mounting a company in 1824, see AV: Secretaría 3-478-9.

88 Carmona y Millán, pp. 62–85. See also Antonio Peña y Goñi, *España desde la ópera a la zarzuela* (Madrid: Alianza, 1967), p. 41, and William M. Bussey, *French and Italian Influence on the Zarzuela, 1700–1750* (Ann Arbor: UMI Research Press, 1982), especially the chapters entitled "The Italian invasion" and "The rise of Neoclassicism: the debate over the new musical style".

89 Montero Alonso, *Ventura de la Vega*, p. 50.

90 Victor Tamayo, in an anecdotal article on "La Rodríguez, Grimaldi y Guzmán," wrote: "The comedy had the virtue of making people abandon the Cruz Theatre, where fervent adoration was paid to *bel canto*, and imagine how a perishable and absurd play had more power to force people away from their favorite spectacle than all the more or less cruel and poetic satires written against the "philharmonic furor" at that time . . ." *Blanco y Negro*, May 27, 1928. I am grateful to Professor Victor Ouimette for bringing this article to my attention.

91 Duffey, "Juan de Grimaldi and the pre-Romantic drama in Spain," p. 28.

92 Mesonero Romanos, *Memorias*, p. 191.

93 In the opening scene, Juan, while enumerating the various professions he has tried and failed, says, "I write music . . . but boy! without being Italian . . . well, you know . . ."

94 "But my anger, Anfriso, does not permit me to accept that we praise Italian singers while insulting Spanish theatre. Heap praise upon a foreign voice, but let's not forget that in Madrid there are plays and actors. It shouldn't be all bravos and exaggerated praise when the Syrians pay homage to their queen while we yawn as we listen to Inarco [Moratín]. Let us not deliriously applaud some duet while acting as if Calderón or the famous Moreto, instead of providing pleasant calm, made us suffer."

95 *RE*, December 22, 1833. Cited by José Escobar, *Los orígenes de la obra de Larra* (Madrid: Editorial Prensa Española, 1973), pp. 153–4.

96 "One question which has never been properly discussed is the relationship between the Italian opera and the Romantic drama. Surely the music of composers such as Rossini, Donizetti, and Bellini, and the sentimental and melodramatic plots of their operas helped to mould Romantic taste." N.B. Adams, "French influence on the Madrid theater in 1837," p. 136.

97 Eventually, instrumental music became the dominant musical interest of the Spanish upper and middle classes, but that interest took until mid-century to

develop fully. See Claude Poullain, "Apuntes sobre la vida musical en España en la época romántica," *Iris*, 3 (1982), pp. 189–215. Opera never completely lost its hegemony over the lives of Spain's middle and upper classes, however, as has been beautifully documented by Galdós (*Miau*) and Clarín (*La Regenta*).

98 Hubbard, p. 100.
99 "Teatros," *El Español*, March 8, 1836.
100 January 22, 1833. Cited by José Escobar, "Un episodio biográfico de Larra, crítico teatral, en la temporada de 1834," *Nueva Revista de Filología Hispánica*, 25 (1976), p. 52. As we shall see, Grimaldi's contract proposals did indeed include clauses which promised the existence of an opera company. He had even paid to bring a famous singer, Giulietta Grisi, to Madrid, *before* his contract with the City Council was signed. This proved to be a mistake.
101 Desfrétières, p. 66.
102 Desfrétières, p. 67.
103 Bretón wrote to his mother: "This year hasn't been a loss; and if in order to earn a crust of bread I needed to travel to Norway next year, I would not hesitate to do so." Cited by Duffey, "Madrid stage," p. 150.
104 Pilar Lozano Guirao, "El archivo epistolar de don Ventura de la Vega," *Revista de Literatura*, 13 (1958), p. 123. See also Escosura, "Recuerdos literarios," pp. 226–7.
105 Additional repertory information is available in Aguilar Piñal, *Cartelera* and Molins, *Bretón*, 1883, pp. 76–7.
106 Ayguals, *Panteón universal*, p. 356.
107 Molins incorrectly reports that Matilde went with the company to Seville. Molins, *Bretón*, 1893, p. 13.
108 García Llansó, *Historia de la mujer contemporánea*, p. 256.
109 Larra, "Reposiciones teatrales," *RE*, April 9, 1834.
110 *El Universal*, April 9, 1834.
111 *Semanario Teatral*, May 28, 1834. A story has been recounted – by Sepúlveda, Sainz de Robles and Reyes – that Grimaldi, upon seeing the young actress in *Don Alvaro*, warned his wife that Matilde Díez would replace her as the first actress of the Spanish stage ("but tonight someone has been born on stage who is going to eclipse you." "Who?," asked the startled Rodríguez. "The girl who played the part of Preciosilla." "The gypsy girl? Díez?" "That very one.") It hardly seems reasonable to assume that Grimaldi waited so long to make such an announcement, since he (and indeed his wife, too) had known Matilde for nearly five years at that point. Cited by Antonio de los Reyes, p. 57.
112 Pedro Romero Mendoza mocked Matilde's physical appearance, along with that of other actresses of the Romantic stage, finding them "strong, wide, crass, massive or spongy, but without that slimness derived from the restrictions put on a healthy appetite or from excessive exercise. The aesthetics of the body," he continued, "was not cultivated, as it is today, among women . . . They ate whatever they wanted, and physical exercise was not the rule." His description of a period engraving of Matilde produced the following ruminations: "Black and shining hair, so stuck onto her head that it seems like a wig and collected in the back in a bun. Long nose and lightly arched eyebrows. A very full face, vigorous neck, that emerges out of the swelling and robustness of the breast. Girdled waist, with the violence of imprisoned flesh, that seems to be begging for a breach between the whalebones of the corset in order to escape. The arms thick, fleshy, bulgy, adorned with small hands, each one looking like a coiled snake. In her entire figure there is a visible incivility of flesh." He then snidely called Concepción Rodríguez "a real beauty" ("hermosota"). "El teatro romántico," *Alcántara*, 8 (1952), p. 6.

113 The following week it appointed Agustín Durán, the famous collector of the *Romancero*, as Director of Archives of Plays, and Carnerero as Director of Archives of Dramatic Pieces. Durán, however, nearly refused the appointment since it was linked to a loyalty oath which he found insulting.

114 On Rossini in Madrid, see Mesonero Romanos, *Memorias*, pp. 192–4, and José Subirá, *Historia de la música española e hispanoamericana* (Barcelona: Salvat, 1953).

115 *Cartas Españolas*, I, p. 47 (April 11, 1831).

116 The Commission voted bonuses of 5,000 *reales* each for Latorre and Guzmán and 8,000 for García Luna. Some records of monthly payments can be found in AV: Contaduría 3-575-1.

117 For example, 1,000 *reales* might be paid by a stage manager for the rights to put on a play. It is not known how Grimaldi's salary compared to his income as author and translator.

118 de Custine, vol. II, p. 325. (Mesonero quoted a full theatre as producing 9,699 *reales*. *Manual de Madrid*, p. 106.) Numerous performances earned little more than two or three thousand *reales*. See AV: Contaduría 3-181-2.

119 Ismael Sánchez Estevan, *Mariano José de Larra, 'Figaro'. Ensayo biográfico* (Madrid: Hernando, 1934), p. 55.

120 Mesonero Romanos, *Manual de Madrid*, p. 106.

121 Between 1820 and 1833 only nine productions played more than 50 times. Five were operas (*Il barbiere di Seviglia* led the list). See Shields, *op. cit.* and Duffey, "Juan de Grimaldi and the pre-Romantic drama in Spain," p. 28.

122 Most, but not all, of the relevant correspondence is reproduced by Desfrétières, pp. 187–225.

123 During these negotiations, of course, Grimaldi continued to work at the Príncipe. It is possible that he translated *La loca o el testamento de una inglesa*, a three-act comedy first performed at the Príncipe on February 27, 1832. The French original by G. de Wailly, *La folle ou le testament d'une Anglaise*, dates from 1827. See *Cartas Españolas*, IV (March 1, 1832).

124 Bretón de los Herreros, "Novedades teatrales," *Correo Literario* (April 13, 1832). *Obra dispersa*, p. 229.

125 See Grimaldi's and the doctor's statements of February, 1836, which refer to these matters. AV: Secretaría 2-476-1.

126 Bretón de los Herreros, "Novedades teatrales," *Correo Literario* (April 13, 1832). *Obra dispersa*, p. 229.

127 Gregorio Martín, "Larra, crítico teatral," paper read at the VIII Congreso Internacional de Hispanistas (Venice, 1980). I am grateful to Professor Martín for providing me with a copy of this paper. Martín recounts that one of the new actors was Nicolás Puchol, who returned to Madrid in June without fulfilling his contract to Grimaldi. Grimaldi sued him and Larra defended Grimaldi in several articles published in Madrid that summer. See also Martín, *Hacia una revisión crítica de la biografía de Larra*, pp. 94–104.

128 Molins, *Bretón*, 1883, p. 343.

129 Bretón de los Herreros, "Teatro de provincias," *Correo Literario* (July 23, 1832). *Obra dispersa*, p. 276. See also "Teatro de Cádiz," *Correo Literario* (July 30, 1832). *Obra dispersa*, p. 280.

130 Bretón de los Herreros, "Teatro–Noticias," *Correo Literario* (September 24, 1832). *Obra dispersa*, p. 311.

131 The Council, chastened by its previous experiences of last-minute decisions, resolved as early as August, 1832, to initiate the process of ownership for the 1833–4 season. In a meeting of August 29 it decided to offer the theatres up for public auction. The plan was to have all petitions in by October 2 and the decisions made by the 15th of that month. AV: Secretaría 2-474-7. The

announcement in the *Diario de Avisos* reads: "Since it has been decreed by His Majesty that the theatres of the capital should be run by a private concern, the Town Council announces to the public that anyone interested in this venture, which should begin on Easter Sunday, 1833, should acquire a copy of the conditions and present in writing his proposals to the Secretary, D. Faustino Domínguez, before October 2." *Diario de Avisos*, September 6, 1832.

132 Sepúlveda, p. 129.

133 AV: Secretaría 2-474-7. Emphasis added. Additional documents relevant to the case are located in AV: Corregimiento 1-78-54. Most, but not all, of these documents are reproduced by Desfrétières, pp. 227-88.

134 He pointed specifically to the issue of the free seats and the 400,000 *reales* which needed to be paid to "all sorts of people" – retirees, the disabled, and the various charitable establishments.

135 He recognized the advances made with the actors by praising the Queen's protection of the acting school at the Real Conservatorio. "The creation of a dramatic school directed by two of our best actors, under the immediate protection of a Queen who has done so much good for our country, engenders great hopes." ·

136 Cited by Escobar, "Un episodio biográfico de Larra," p. 52.

137 The list of their holdings is kept in the AV: Secretaría 2-474-7.

138 The legal point they were debating was an old ruling which stipulated that farmers ("labradores") were not permitted to enter into financial contracts. Technically, Burgueños was a farmer since his land produced goods, but the lawyers failed to distinguish between a peasant farm hand and the rich owner of many acres of productive land. Grimaldi addressed this point in his response to the lawyer's decision.

139 Alonso was a poet and teacher, as well, who was a good friend of not only Grimaldi, but also of Larra, Vega, Gil, Bretón, Espronceda, and Escosura. See Marrast, pp. 127 and 443.

140 Molins, *Bretón*, 1893, p. 13.

141 See Zorrilla, p. 1754, and Martínez Olmedilla, p. 13.

142 García Llansó, pp. 268-71.

143 "El teatro romántico," *Alcántara*, p. 9.

144 Alfonso Par, *Representaciones shakespearianas en España* (2 vols., Madrid: Victoriano Suárez, 1936), I, p. 157.

145 Guerra, p. 273; Shields, p. 878; Espina, *Romea o el Comediante*, p. 36. Espina's novel is riddled with factual errors, but it does capture the excitement of the period. See in particular his novelization of Romea's victory party at the Príncipe Café following the debut of *El testamento*, pp. 40-51. A more reliable study of Romea is by Reyes.

146 Mesonero Romanos, *Memorias*, p. 192. Molins claimed that Romea's first big success came on October 4, 1835, in Delavinge's *Los hijos de Eduardo*, in which he also acted opposite Concepción Rodríguez and Latorre. *Bretón*, p. 139.

147 *RE*, April 23, 1833.

148 "With no reason the part of the troubadour has been given to Mr. Latorre, who was not right for it, as he is not right for any tender and amorous role. His stature, and his kind of talent are better suited to hard and energetic characters; that is why it would have been better to have given him the role of Count Nuño. Just the opposite happens with Mr. Romea, who should have played the troubadour." *El Español*, March 4, 1836.

149 AV: Secretaría 6-311-3.

150 See Dowling, "El anti-don Juan de Ventura de la Vega," pp. 215-18.

151 Romea wrote: "At that time the modern comedy was in such a state of prostration that, with very rare exceptions, it was enough to announce one on the marquee for the theatre to be deserted. I dedicated my energies to bringing it out of that extreme, and nobly aided by the distinguished actresses doña Matilde Díez, doña Teodora Lamadrid, doña Josefa Palma, doña Jerónima Llorente, doña Plácida Tablares and others, and by the actors don Carlos Latorre, don José García Luna, don Antonio Guzmán, don Luis Fabiani, don Mariano Fernández, my brother don Florencio and some others, we managed to raise up the comedy, enabling it to recover its ancient rights and managing later, under its own steam, to begin to reign, as it had done before, in the theatre." Cited by Espina, p. 35.
152 "Lettres Espagnoles I," *Mémorial Diplomatique* (Paris), September 19, 1867.
153 *Memorias*, p. 74.
154 Escosura, "Recuerdos literarios," p. 226.
155 See the financial reports published in the *Semanario Teatral*, April 21, 1834.

4 The Romantic stage

1 All of the actors individually signed a petition to María Cristina on October 15, 1833, asking her to prevent them from being "afflicted by the most deplorable misery" AHN: Consejos 11.387, n. 17. See also *Semanario Teatral*, April 24, 1834. The following anecdote, recounted by Jean Descola in an otherwise worthless book has some truth to it: "That is how María Cristina became the soul of the liberal movement and the idol of the progressives and, at the same time, the *bête noire* of the absolutists. Everyone expected that when the King died there would be a bloody settling of scores. Fernando lived out his last days wavering between physical suffering and resignation. No one was deceived about his popularity. When he was told that many people were praying for his health, he responded: 'I'm sure they are. Especially the actors, who are afraid that their theatres will be closed down.'" *La vida cotidiana en la España romántica, 1833–1868* (Barcelona, Argos Vergara, 1984), p. 24.
2 The theatres did not close, but their losses were immense – as much as 6,000 *reales* per day, according to *La Revista Española* (August 1, 1834) – because people were afraid to venture out in public.
3 Rumeau, "Le Théâtre à Madrid," p. 339.
4 *El Universal*, April 2, 1834. For observations regarding the general status and condition of the theatre at this time, see N.B. Adams, "Sidelights," pp. 1–12.
5 See Escobar, "Un episodio biográfico de Larra," pp. 53–4.
6 There are several excellent studies of Larra's life and ideas. See Sánchez Estevan; Pierre Ullman, *Mariano de Larra and Spanish Political Rhetoric* (Madison: University of Wisconsin Press, 1971); Escobar, *Los orígenes de la obra de Larra*; Martín, *Hacia una revisión crítica de la biografía de Larra*; Susan Kirkpatrick, *Larra: El laberinto inextricable de un romántico liberal* (Madrid: Gredos, 1977); and José Luis Varela, *Larra y España* (Madrid: Espasa-Calpe, 1983).
7 Ricardo Navas Ruiz, *Imágenes liberales (Rivas, Larra, Galdós)* (Salamanca: Ediciones Almar, 1979), p. 44. Larra's five-act comedy, *No más mostrador*, an adaption of Scribe's one-act *Les adieux au comptoir*, was his first produced work. It appeared at the Cruz on April 29, 1831. "Larra wrote it at the impresario [sic] Juan Grimaldi's urging." J.L. Alborg, p. 270.
8 "Mi nombre y mis propósitos," *RE*, January 15, 1833.
9 Mesonero Romanos, *Memorias*, p. 92.
10 See *El Universal*, May 7, 1834.

11 N.B. Adams, *The Romantic Dramas of García Gutiérrez* (New York: Instituto de las Españas en los EE UU, 1922), p. 10.

12 Sánchez Estevan, p. 49.

13 Cited by G. Martín, "Larra, crítico teatral," p. 13. Not all of the financial arrangements had been worked out, however, and some of the same problems which had plagued Grimaldi (difficulty in raising guarantees, for one) also plagued the new owner. In the May 12, 1834 issue of the *Semanario Teatral* we read: "Much has been said concerning the presentation of guarantees by the management, as outlined in the contract which was signed for taking over the theatres. These guarantees could not be given at that time and a period of two months was granted for them to be verified. During that time a business firm has given its guarantee. When the time arrived to present the guarantees demanded in the contract, there were presented, according to what has been told to us, guarantees of nearly one million *reales* – mortgages on properties not far from Madrid. But since they did not cover the entire cost of the guarantees demanded by the authorities, it is said that the City Council has refused to accept them, and has raised up to the Queen its concerns that the city's funds are uncovered. . . ."

14 *El Universal*, April 1, 1834.

15 Excluding May 2, a traditional holiday. See also, *Semanario Teatral*, April 28, 1834.

16 "*La conjuración de Venecia*," *RE*, April 25, 1834.

17 *Semanario Teatral*, May 12, 1834.

18 See J.L. Patake Kosove, *The "Comedia Lacrimosa" and Spanish Romantic Drama (1773–1865)* (London: Tamesis Books, 1978). Also, Russell P. Sebold, "Una lágrima, pero una lágrima sola: sobre el llanto romántico," *Insula*, 380–1 (1978), pp. 8–9.

19 Muñoz, p. 103. Blanchard did equally stunning sets for the popular French melodrama, *La expiación*, translated by Ventura de la Vega, and for Ducange's *El verdugo de Amsterdam*. In fact, the sets for *La expiación* were so complicated that musical interludes were planned between the acts, "which must be longer than usual in order to give the stage hands time to change the sets." *RE*, May 9, 1834.

20 See Jean Sarrailh, *Un homme d'état espagnol: Martínez de la Rosa 1787–1862* (Bordeaux-Paris: Feret et Fils, 1930).

21 Shields, p. 678. Rumeau records only sixteen. "Le théâtre à Madrid," p. 338.

22 *Cartas Españolas*, February 2, 1832. Cited by Adams, "Notes on Spanish plays," p. 136.

23 Ayguals, *Panteón universal*, p. 356. Molins wrote, "In Seville *Edipo*, by our Martínez de la Rosa, until that period prohibited *in odium autoris*, was staged with unusual elegance and naturalness." *Recuerdos*, p. 71.

24 Rumeau, "Le théâtre à Madrid," pp. 340–1.

25 Peers, I, p. 330.

26 Cited by Rumeau, "Le théâtre à Madrid," p. 342.

27 Letter to *El Castellano*, September 26–30 (?), 1836. Reproduced by Carmen de Burgos, *Fígaro*, p. 191, and Desfrétières, pp. 298–9. I have been unable to locate this publication. Earlier, Larra had praised "the skill with which [his play] was put on stage." "Teatro y algo más," *El Español*, April 18, 1836.

28 Adams, "Sidelights," p. 3.

29 Larra, *Obras completas*, vol. 4 (BAE 130) (Madrid: Atlas, 1960), p. 278. See also Martín, *Hacia una revisión crítica de la biografía de Larra*, pp. 112–13.

30 See F.C. Tarr, "More light on Larra," *Hispanic Review*, 4 (1936), p. 97.

31 A. Rumeau, "Mariano José de Larra et le Baron Taylor," *Revue de Littérature Comparée*, 16 (1936), p. 481.

32 See Ferrer del Río, *Galería de la literatura española* (Madrid: Mellado, 1846), pp. 132–5; Molins, *Recuerdos*, pp. 100–8; Burgos, *Fígaro*, pp. 185–206; Sánchez Estevan; Rumeau, "Mariano José de Larra et le Baron Taylor," p. 481.

33 Grimaldi was producing masked balls at the Oriente, as we shall see.

34 Mesonero Romanos, *Memorias*, p. 165. The 165 individuals in attendance included most of Grimaldi's group: Molins, Mesonero, Vega, Carnerero, Latorre, Romea, Gil, Espronceda, Bretón, etc. *Eco del Comercio*, December 13, 1835. See also Labra, *op. cit.*, Victoriano García Martí, *El Ateneo de Madrid (1835–1935)* (Madrid: Dossat, 1948) and Antonio Ruiz Salvador, *El Ateneo científico, literario y artístico de Madrid* (London: Támesis, 1971).

35 *Actas* of the Ateneo, Saturday, October 31, 1835. Grimaldi attended a total of just ten meetings between October 31, 1835, and June 8, 1836.

36 F.C. Tarr finds Bretón's signature on Grimaldi's petition insufficient evidence that the Bretón–Larra hostilities had subsided by early January. "The fact that Bretón is one of the sponsors... is by no means conclusive evidence that they were still friends at that time. The application may have been signed by Bretón in order to further hypocritically a pretense of innocence. After all, the incident in itself is of minor importance, although not without value for the study of Larra's character and his relations with his friends. With Bretón, as with Carnerero and Delgado, his friendship had its decided 'altibajos.' " "More light on Larra," p. 97.

37 The letter is kept at the Ateneo. See Jenaro Artiles, "Larra y el Ateneo," *Revista de la Biblioteca, Archivo y Museo (Ayuntamiento de Madrid)*, 8 (1931), pp. 137–51.

38 It was customary for actors to travel off to the provincial theatres during the summer recess in Madrid in order to augment their salaries. Rodríguez, Guzmán, Latorre, etc., did so frequently, and their travels were often documented in the newspapers in the capital. See, for example, *Cartas Españolas*, II, p. 23 (July 24, 1831), which reports that Concepción was in Barcelona and Valencia that summer. Reviews of her performances can be found in the *Diario de Valencia*, July 7, 1831 and July 15, 1831.

39 See Sánchez Estevan, pp. 55–6, 86–7.

40 *Cartas Españolas*, I, p. 215 (June 25, 1831).

41 Díaz de Escovar, II, p. 145.

42 *Cartas Españolas*, II, p. 70 (August 6, 1831). Carnerero was quoting the review in the *Diario de Valencia* of July 15. That reviewer went on to write: "If it is true that this defect is not noted as much in Miss Rodríguez as in other actors of the same school, still those who recognize her merit regret seeing her contaminated, even a little bit, by a vice which has invaded Spanish acting in modern times."

43 Sánchez Estevan, p. 90.

44 "El Colegio de Tonnington," *RE*, May 27, 1834.

45 *Semanario Teatral*, June 2, 1834. See Escobar, 'Un episodio biográfico de Larra," p. 67.

46 "Teatros de Madrid," *El Entreacto*, 60 (October 24, 1839).

47 Ferrer y Herrera, p. 39.

48 "Salida del señor Nicanor Puchol en *Pelayo*, tragedia de don Manuel José Quintana," *RE*, June 19, 1833.

49 Natalio Rivas Santiago, *Curiosidades históricas contemporáneas* (Barcelona, 1942), p. 76. Reprinted in *Anecdotario histórico contemporáneo* (Madrid, 1946).

50 Marrast, p. 347.

51 Rivas Santiago, *Curiosidades*, p. 76.

52 *Recuerdos*, p. 138. Likewise, "Miss Rodríguez gave new proof of her theatrical mastery in several scenes." Review of Dumas' *Teresa*, *RE*, February 3, 1836.

53 See Andioc, "Sobre el estreno de *Don Alvaro*."

54 Díaz de Escovar, ii, p. 146.

55 "Teatros y algo más," *El Español*, April 18, 1836.

56 AHN: Consejos 11.416, n. 3. An additional decree, issued in April, 1849, stipulated that all individuals not directly involved in dispatching tickets were barred from entering the ticket booths. AHN: Consejos 50.932, n. 16.

57 Larra complained that the roles were distributed poorly and that Concepción, instead of playing the easy role of Leonor, should have performed that of Azucena: "For the same reason the role of the gypsy was poorly assigned. This was the most original, the newest creation in the drama, the most difficult character as well, and consequently the one with the most luster; if Miss Rodríguez is the first lady of these theatres, she should have played the role, even though she would appear ugly and old (as if Miss Rodríguez could ever be ugly or old). The character of Leonor is one of those whose success is in the role itself; it must be said: an actress like Miss Rodríguez should reject such easy triumphs." "El Trovador," *El Español*, March 4, 1836.

58 *El Español*, March 23, 1836.

59 See document reproduced by Sepúlveda, pp. 610–12.

60 Grimaldi seems to have had two brothers living in Madrid as well. Leopoldina's godfather was one Alfredo de Grimaldi (Iglesia de San Sebastián, Libro 71B, folio 272) and Cecilia's godfather was Estanislao de Grimaldi, "bachelor" (San Sebastián, Libro 72B, folio 32). The Grimaldis also had a son, but reference to him only appears in documents from their later years in Paris. It is not known when he was born.

61 "Miss Concepción Rodríguez, a retired actress from the theatres of this capital, most respectfully informs Your Majesty that since her husband, D. Juan Grimaldi, has gone back to his own country, France, she wishes to join him there. The petitioner is well aware of the regulations which stipulate that no public servant can collect a pension outside of Spain without permission; however, others who have found themselves in the same situation have been forced to request a Royal License, and that is what has happened these days to Miss Lorenza Correa and Miss Loreto García, who with permission are receiving their pensions abroad. The petitioner was also granted by Your Majesty, as a reward for the services rendered in these theatres, a position as ticket-seller in the theatres. Her absence from the capital will make it impossible for her to continue in this position, but other actors in Madrid and even several who live outside of the capital have been able to fill those positions by substitutes. With this in mind, the petitioner humbly requests permission to receive her retirement payments abroad as well as permission to continue as ticket-seller through a substitute, just as Joaquín Caprara is doing now from his residence in Andalusia. February 12, 1837." AHN: Consejos 11.387, n. 120. See also, Carrière.

62 Except for Antera Baus, Bernardo Gil's widow, Concepción Rodríguez was the highest-paid retiree. Wages for her "work" as a ticket-seller might have totaled one-third more. AV: Secretaría 9-449-26. These payments were considerably lower than the salary she received as an actress. In 1831, for example, she was earning 89 *reales* per performance, or 895 for a ten-day period. AV: Contaduría 3-575-1 and AV: Contaduría 3-181-2.

63 Ayguals, *Panteón universal*, p. 356.

64 Lozano Guirao, p. 195.

65 See, for example, Bretón's "artículo de costumbres," "Las máscaras," in *El Correo Literario y Mercantil*, March 7, 1832; the story "Yago Yasck," in *El Artista*,

vol. III; or the anonymous "Un baile de máscaras," in *El Eco del Comercio,* January 8, 1837.

66 Díaz de Escovar, I, p. 390. Interesting information on the masked balls in Valladolid can be found in Rosa Díez Garretas, *El teatro en Valladolid en la primera mitad del siglo XIX* (Valladolid: Institución Cultural Simancas, 1982), pp. 109–16.

67 Madrid: Repullés, 1834.

68 "*La conjuración de Venecia,*" *RE,* April 25, 1834. Interesting comments on the carnival atmosphere in later romantic dramas, in particular, Zorrilla's *Don Juan Tenorio,* can be found in Robert ter Horst, "Ritual time regained in Zorrilla's *Don Juan Tenorio,*" *Romanic Review,* 70 (1979), 80–93; and Gustavo Pérez Firmat, "Carnival in *Don Juan Tenorio,*" *Hispanic Review,* 51 (1983), 269–81. The most serious analysis of carnival is that of M. Bakhtine, *Rabelais and His World,* tr. Hélène Iswolki (Cambridge, MA: Harvard University Press, 1965).

69 *Diccionario de las gentes del mundo, para uso de la corte y de la aldea, escrito en francés por un joven eremita. Tr. al castellano y aumentado con muchas voces por tres amigos.* (Madrid: Ibarra, 1820). I am grateful to Pedro Alvarez de Miranda for bringing this item to my attention.

70 Sepúlveda recounts the following horrifying tale about a masked ball held at the Príncipe Theatre on February 3, 1821: "In those days the floorboards were not examined carefully, as they are today, nor did the people worry too much about being burned by the candle wicks or the oil lamps that were beginning to be used. It has been said for a while that the Pacheca [Theatre] wasn't in good repair and that the flooring was patched together without being adequately tested: that to dance on it was like dancing over a volcano . . .; but nothing stopped the people. The women covered up their faces with a wax mask and headed onto the floor to dance. The men followed them as always, disguised, too . . . When the crowd was largest and the dancing most lively, the floorboards gave off a loud 'crack!' and hundreds of masked dancers fell tumbling down to the very foundations of the ancient Corral . . . There were broken arms and heads, there were ripped costumes and wounded prides, and finally a few deaths; there was everything. But wait! When the conductor declared the disaster over the orchestra began to play a minuet, the people returned to their dancing as though nothing had happened." Sepúlveda, pp. 327–8.

71 Zorrilla, p. 2000.

72 Mesonero Romanos, *Memorias,* p. 194; Larra, "Bailes de máscaras," *El Observador,* December 17, 1834.

73 The regulations forbade wearing masks in the streets, hovering in front of the site of the dance, wearing costumes imitating religious individuals or public officials, wearing firearms or swords, insulting other guests, etc. See AV: Secretaría 2-481-34.

74 See, for example, the notices in *La Abeja* (January 20, 1836, January 24, 1836, February 25, 1836, etc.) concerning tickets for the balls held at Santa Catalina.

75 Desfrétières notes that this fact contradicts the general belief that the first masked balls given at the Teatro de Oriente date from the 1850–1 season. Desfrétières, pp. 105–6. See also José Subirá, *Historia y anecdotario del Teatro Real* (Madrid: Plus-Ultra, 1949). The theatre was formally inaugurated in 1850.

76 This was not a serious point during these negotiations, since the police demanded only three such seats. AV: Corregimiento, 1-68-59; Desfrétières reproduces many of the pertinent documents from this file and from AHN: Consejos 11.387, n. 109, pp. 289–97.

77 The balls were given on January 22, January 30, February 7, February 11, February 14, February 15 and February 16. An additional ball, announced for February 21, was cancelled (see *DM*, February 21, 1836). See D.T. Gies, "Juan de Grimaldi y la máscara romántica," *Romanticismo 2: Atti del III Congresso sul Romanticismo* (Genoa: Edizioni Realizzazioni Grafiche, 1984), pp. 133–40.

78 *RE*, January 26, 1836.

79 See the diagram and description of the Teatro de Oriente published in *Cartas Españolas*, II, p.47.

80 Kirkpatrick, "Larra y *El Español*," p. 54.

81 *ibid.*, p. 55.

82 *La Abeja*, January 29, 1836.

83 *Histoire de ma vie*, x (Paris: Plon, 1961), p. 327.

84 *La Abeja*, January 28, 1836.

85 *La Revista Española* attributed the frequent low attendance at some of the other balls to the proliferation of them in Madrid: "Attendance is excessively low in the capital since there is no street or corner where there isn't a corresponding ball, at any price, for any type of people." January 30, 1836.

86 *El Español* (January 25, 1836). See Kirkpatrick, "Larra y *El Español*," p. 56.

87 Acevedo provided a hilarious description of the crush of the mob to get into the theatre. "It was a little after midnight when we arrived at the Plaza de Oriente, and winding around as best we could among the huge mass of vehicles and carriages from all periods and styles that were parked three rows deep around the building, we managed to arrive at the door, completely obstructed by an unruly collection of masked and unmasked revelers, scalpers, servants and footmen, night watchmen and onlookers. Those who were there in cruel expectation were desperate, and as the possibility of being able to make it through the exceedingly narrow door through which the crowd was expected to pass began to seem more and more remote, they cursed the hour when they thought of going to the ball and the impresario who had created this carnival atmosphere. Finally, and none too soon, the notice arrived that one of the side doors would be opened. Those of us besieging the front door abandoned our position and headed straight for the door they indicated to us, managing (after doling out a hundred blows) to gain access through the needle's eye that was opened up; some sideways, some head on, and many back first, helping one another to make it up the narrow and long stairway that led up to the salons, as though we were pushing our way up a greased pole, where the first one is pushed onwards by the force of those behind him . . . ; floating on the immense compact mass that we formed, and in which everyone could consider himself a small molecule . . . ; it was a Saracen invasion: the Valley of Jehosaphat: the trumpet of the final judgment seemed to have sounded calling out for all mortals, who meekly gathered on that very spot to heed the call."

88 *El Artista*, I, p. 71.

89 See *El Eco del Comercio*, January 3, 1837 and January 6, 1837.

90 Kirkpatrick, 'Larra y *El Español*," p. 53.

91 See the increased incidence of masked balls as listed in José Simón Díaz (ed.), *Madrid en sus diarios; 1830–1844* (Madrid: CSIC, 1961), pp. 18–25.

92 See Ferrer del Río, pp. 253–70; Cayetano Rosell, "Don Antonio García Gutiérrez," *Autores dramáticos contemporáneos*, (Madrid: Fortanet, 1881–82), I, pp. 81–96; Adams, *The Romantic Dramas of García Gutiérrez*; Alborg, pp. 515–32.

93 Enrique Piñeyro, *El romanticismo en España* (Paris: Garnier, 1900), p. 96.

94 Rosell reported that Grimaldi was not particularly impressed with the play and moved to have it staged at the Cruz Theatre, whose actors opposed it. Rosell,

p. 85. According to Antonio Montoro, the actors laughed and commented sarcastically when the play was read to them. *El romanticismo literario europeo* (Madrid: Biblioteca Nueva, 1959), p. 230.

95 Adams, *The Romantic Dramas*, pp. 13–14.

96 See Ferrer del Río's eye-witness account in *Galería*.

97 See Appendix 6. I have reproduced the article from Desfrétières, pp. 296–7.

98 *El Castellano*, September 26, 1836. I cite from the transcription of Desfrétières, p. 297.

99 Desfrétières, p. 121.

100 Burgos, p. 191.

101 Escobar has noted that Larra's defense of Grimaldi was related to his own political situation. He had been elected on the Istúriz Moderate ticket as a representative from Avila, but the actions at La Granja annulled the election "and, now, with the progressives in power, he was forced to defend his liberalism and recognize his friendship with Grimaldi." "Un episodio biográfico de Larra," p. 70.

5 Juan de Grimaldi: journalist, historian, diplomat

1 Eugenio Hartzenbusch e Hiriarte, *Periódicos de Madrid* (Madrid: Sucesores de Rivadeneyra, 1876), p. 41; Mesonero Romanos, *Memorias*, p. 180.

2 See María Cruz Seoane, *Historia del periodismo en España. 2. El siglo XIX* (Madrid: Alianza, 1983), p. 135.

3 See Pedro Gómez Aparicio, *Historia del periodismo español* (Madrid: Editora Nacional, 1967), p. 180.

4 The article in *El Castellano* (September 26, 1836; reproduced by Desfrétières, pp. 297–8) claimed that "Mr Grimaldi has also served as editor and writer for newsp̃ ̃ers. When the *Revista* began to become important, in the beginning of 1833, with the intervention and impulse of his friend D. José Mariano [sic] de Larra, Grimaldi went aboard as editor in chief of that paper . . ." Larra, however, corrected this statement in a later issue: "I think that I must make clear to you that at that time I was a mere theatre editor for *La Revista*, with no influence over the composition of the editorial board. My intervention and my impulse got nobody a job. It is, therefore, false what you say in your article; I mean that the man who wrote it does not know what he is talking about, or he is lying, if he does know."

5 Mesonero Romanos, *Memorias*, p. 74.

6 Desfrétières, who identifies the articles but gives no discussion of them, erroneously lists twenty-four articles. As we shall see, three of them are not Grimaldi's.

7 Letter dated November 12, 1867. RAH: Narvaez, 56. All of the correspondence cited here between Grimaldi and Narváez is kept in the Archivo de Narváez in the Real Academia de la Historia. I shall cite them by date and box number. I am grateful to Professor Carlos Seco Serrano for his assistance in helping me to secure copies of these important letters.

8 Reproduced by Desfrétières, p. 113.

9 Desfrétières errs, I believe, in attributing to Grimaldi the article entitled "Brief Observations on an Article from the *Diario de los Debates*," which begins on the front page of this issue of the *Revista* and which appears to be signed with the pseudonymous "A." However, a closer look at the article reveals that in the middle, with no space break, we read the words "Mr Editor of the *Revista Española*," the usual beginning of a letter to the editor. The subject matter of the first half differs markedly from the second half (a French commentary on the

brewing "crisis" in Spain versus comments on public education and economic well being). "A" clearly wrote only the "second" part.

10 Burgos, who had learned public administration as an *afrancesado* liberal during the reign of Joseph Bonaparte, was to become one of the outstanding leaders of the Moderates, a staunch supporter of the Queen Regent, and a key figure in the "modernization" of the Spanish bureaucracy.

11 Desfrétières has found evidence of Grimaldi's participation on this Commission in 1851, 1856, 1865, 1867 and 1869. Desfrétières, p. 310.

12 Desfrétières lists an article entitled "Sobre los últimos sucesos de Barcelona" as Grimaldi's (Desfrétières, p. 116), but I think this is an incorrect attribution. The author of the article, published January 17, 1836, claims to have been an eye witness in Barcelona to the events of January 3–5, when Catalan troops exacted a bloodthirsty revenge against some Carlist troops who had mistreated their Catalan prisoners. But Grimaldi was in Madrid at the time, working on getting Larra into the Ateneo, as his letter of January 2 and the *Actas* of the Ateneo of January 4 prove. Desfrétières lists another article, published on May 7, as Grimaldi's, but this is in reality a response to Grimaldi's May 4 article.

13 See Raymond Carr, *Spain 1808–1939* (Oxford: Clarendon Press, 1966), pp. 158–62.

14 This article is the first time he mentioned Guizot, who would excite from him in 1867 some of the most impassioned articles about Spain he ever wrote.

15 "Tentatives de Régicide. Inviolabilité du Roi. Liberté de la Presse" (Paris: Le Normant, 1837).

16 *RE*, May 29, 1836, note 11.

17 See D.T. Gies, "Larra and Mendizábal: A Writer's Response to Government," *Cithara*, 12 (1973), pp. 74–90.

18 The details of the period preceding Mendizábal's resignation fall outside the realm of this study. See Peter Janke, *Mendizábal y la instauración de la Monarquía constitucional en España, 1790–1855* (Madrid: Siglo XXI, 1974), pp. 214–15.

19 *El Español*, August 2, 1836; reproduced by Kirkpatrick, "Larra y *El Español*," p. 72.

20 Janke, p. 214.

21 *El Español* had also issued detailed rebuttals of Aniceto de Alvaro's arguments, but Grimaldi, believing correctly that "there still remains much to be said," offered new data "which *El Español* has probably not seen."

22 Larra voiced similar complaints against Mendizábal in "El ministerio Mendizábal," *El Español*, May 6, 1836.

23 Gómez Aparicio, *Historia del periodismo español* (Madrid: Editora Nacional, 1967), pp. 181–2.

24 See Carr, *Spain, 1808–1939*, pp. 169 ss.

25 The following diplomatic communiqué from 1839 provides one such example of Grimaldi's continued intervention in Spanish affairs of state: "My dear Sir: I have just received notice of the royal order dated the ninth of the present month which you have sent in reply to my communication 229, and according to your wishes I have informed D. Juan Grimaldi of the queen's resolution to the effect that from the first of July next he is relieved of the assignment given to him by this embassy. Paris, June 27, 1839. Marqués de Miraflores" AHN: Estado, Legajo 5295, no. 293.

26 (Paris: Bohaire, 1841), 151 pp. All citations from this edition.

27 Luis Fernández de Córdoba, *Memoria justificada* (Paris, 1837); Eugenio de Aviraneta e Ibargoyen, *Vindicación de D. Eugenio de Aviraneta de los calumniosos cargos que se le hicieron por la prensa . . . y observaciones sobre la guerra civil de España* (Madrid: Sánchez, 1838).

28 The reference, of course, is to Lope's play, *El mejor alcalde, el rey.*

29 See pp. 166–81 below.

30 See documents relating to his planned promotion to Officer in the French Legion of Honor, July, 1870. Archives de France: AF: F^{ld} III, 14^{10}.

31 MAE: Legajo 125, n. 6071. The file is reproduced by Desfrétières, pp. 300–9.

32 One documented case involved his intervention with the Director of the French Academy of Music to release two well-known performers to travel to Madrid to perform at the Oriente. Grimaldi himself lent them money for the trip (60,000 francs), which he thought was guaranteed by nature of the contract the performers had with the government's theatre, the Oriente. When he found out that the contract had been underwritten by a private impresario who had subsequently gone bankrupt (*plus ça change*), he made immediate claim for reimbursement of his expenses. See letter dated March 12, 1851. MAE: Legajo 125, n.6071; reproduced by Desfrétières, pp. 305–6. Also AHN: Consejos 11.376.

33 Pabón, *Narváez*, p. 253.

34 November 20, 1849; Pabón, *ibid.*, p. 266. The correspondence is kept in the Narváez documents (letters exchanged with Riánsares) at the Real Academia de la Historia, Madrid.

35 Recounted by Pabón, *Narváez*, pp. 270–1.

36 "Elysée Palace, December 10, 1849 / I have received from Mr. Grimaldi the sum of 100,000 francs on account for the loan which he is making to me. / Louis Napoleon Bonaparte." Reproduced by Pabón, *ibid.*, p. 273.

37 Pabón, *ibid.*, p. 275.

38 See his angry and defensive explanation of his actions. RAH: Narváez, 10. Letter dated March 10, 1851.

39 "The Queen has read the attached letter by D. Juan Grimaldi, recently consul of Spain in Paris, in response to the Royal Order of the 8th of last month accepting his resignation; she has ordered me to send it to you to be returned to the writer, letting him know that the less than decorous tone it is written in prohibits it from being filed in this office." Letter dated May 20, 1851. MAE: Personal, Legajo, 125, n.6071.

40 Two coded telegraph dispatches (May 21 and 22, 1854) read:
1. Si no ha comunicado V.S. 4698-2846-4614-4541-944-240-221-suspenda hacerlo, guarde sigilo y devuelva el traslado por el correo. ("If you have not told anyone of Grimaldi's appointment, do not; keep quiet and send the transcript back by return mail.")
2. El nombramiento de G- ri- mal- di no ha s- i- 4698. 2846. 4614. 4541. 9414. 200. 221. 2837. 3351. 5145. 2048.
do comuni- cado- a na- die de oficio pero lo conocen muchas 4715. 4166. 5567. 6448. 4544. 59. 4614. 766.
personas. ("Grimaldi's nomination has not been told to anyone officially but many people know of it.") MAE: Personal Legajo 125, n.6071.

41 See his letter to Narváez, dated July 4, 1867; RAH: Narváez, 56.

42 San Luis (Luis José Sartorius) went on to inquire about "what Grimaldi thinks about what is happening and what is going to happen" and "if there has been any change in his relations with Riánsares. If he has seen and is on good terms with Narváez." San Luis also asked Vega to check into a sale of paintings which Grimaldi was arranging for him. Letter dated June 21, 1853. Lozano, "El archivo epistolar," p. 195. Grimaldi stayed in touch with his old protégé Vega in other ways as well. The Conde de Cheste reported that Grimaldi gave him set decorations, drawings, and costumes for the projected opening of his play, *La muerte de César*, in 1865. Conde de Cheste, "Elogio fúnebre del excelentísmo señor

D. Ventura de la Vega," *Memorias de la Academia Española*, II (Madrid, 1870), pp. 464-5.

43 Letter dated February 6, 1865. Lozano, "El archivo epistolar," p. 173. Grimaldi suffered from gout, the traditional disease of excess.

44 Desfrétières has researched Grimaldi's activities in the Council. See pp. 129-33, 310.

45 Archives de France: AF: F^{ld} III, 14^{10}. One of those improvements was the statue he had erected to a famous local hero, General Jean-Joseph Cler, the youngest general in the Napoleonic army. Grimaldi gave a speech at the unveiling ceremony in front of all the dignitaries of the region in which he highlighted Cler's allegiance to the Napoleonic cause and issued strong praise for Napoleon III. Cler seemed to be another example (like Grimaldi himself) of a man of little formal education who had become influential and successful. The funeral address was published in 1859.

46 Desfrétières cites a confidential report from the Prefect of Salins who supported Grimaldi's selection, naming him "as much because of his financial status as his long-standing devotion to the Prince President, the most important and the most resp ected man in my province." Desfrétières, p. 131. As late as 1867, Narváez was congratulating him on a recent "honor" received from Salins and praising Napoleon III for "placing at his side a man of your talents." Undated letter (mid-September), 1867; RAH: Narváez, 56.

47 Grimaldi, *Discours prononcé . . . à l'ouverture de la session de 1853* (Paris, n.d.).

48 Letter written by a long-time acquaintance (and current President of the Council), Edouard Dalloz, on July 7, 1870. Archives de France, *op. cit.*

49 Grimaldi was still involved with the *Journal de Bordeaux* as late as 1867. He sent it articles for publication which propagated the Narváez government's positions. See letter dated September 11, 1867; RAH: Narváez, 56.

50 Desfrétières, p. 310.

51 Gabriel Tortella Casares, *Los orígenes del capitalismo en España* (Madrid: Editora Tecnos, 1973), pp. 163-70.

52 Rondo E. Cameron, *France and the Economic Development of Europe, 1800-1914* (Princeton: Princeton University Press, 1961), p. 248 ss, and Francisco Wais, *Historia de los ferrocarriles españoles* 2nd. edn. (Madrid: Editora Nacional, 1974).

53 Article entitled "Finances de l'Espagne," *Mémorial diplomatique*, November 7, 1867.

54 "The Law of Stock Societies of 1848 gave Parliament the exclusive right to grant concessions to railway companies. After a few calm years, Parliament became, after 1851, a hunting ground for provisional concessions, which were obtained through influence and bribery of the representatives and senators, and which later were sold at increasing prices, passing from hand to hand without anyone ever making the smallest effort to begin construction of the line in question. Railway scandals during these years stimulated the opposition party to support the coup of 1854, the famous Vicalvarada coup." Tortella Casares, p. 168.

55 Archives de France: AF: F^{ld} III, 14^{10}.

56 He must have meant "jip" or "gyp," from "gypsy," connoting a rogue.

57 Letters dated November 7, 1867 and December 5, 1867, respectively. The *Mémorial diplomatique* was a newspaper published in Paris, in which, as we shall see, Grimaldi had a direct interest.

58 The articles appeared in the *Mémorial diplomatique* on October 24, November 7, November 14, November 21, and December 5, 1867.

59 *El Español*, October 20, 1867. Narváez sent a copy of *El Español's* report to Grimaldi the day after its publication.

60 See Diego Mateo del Peral, "Los orígenes de la política ferroviaria en España (1844–1877)" in Miguel Artola, ed., *Los ferrocarriles en España, 1844–1943* (Madrid: Servicio de Estudios del Banco de España, 1978), pp. 29–163.

61 Neither Grimaldi's name nor the Gerona-Venta de Sales line appears in the excellent study of "Las compañías ferroviarias en España (1855–1935)" by Pedro Tedde de Lorca. See *Los ferrocarriles en España, 1844–1943*, ed. Miguel Artola (2 vols., Madrid: Servicio de Estudios del Banco de España, 1978) pp. 13–354.

62 See Francisco Wais, *Historia de los ferrocarriles españoles*, 2nd edn. (Madrid: Editora Nacional, 1974), p. 719.

63 José Luis Comellas, *Los moderados en el poder: 1844–1854* (Madrid: CSIC, 1970), p. 238.

64 François Pierre Guillaume Guizot, *Mémoires pour servir à l'histoire de mon temps* (8 vols., Paris; Michel-Lévy, 1867), vol. 8, pp. 147–8.

65 Guizot, p. 150.

66 Guizot, p. 248.

67 Guizot, p. 248.

68 Introduction to the "Lettres espagnoles," *Mémorial diplomatique*, September 19, 1867.

69 See Grimaldi's letter to Narváez, dated December 15, 1867, for details of the paper's ownership.

70 David had already made an oral contract to purchase a half interest in the *Mémorial* for 75,000 francs, but he was unable to raise the sum by his August 31 deadline and asked Debrauz for an extension. But Debrauz was already negotiating with Grimaldi so he ignored David's request, which prompted David to initiate a lawsuit against him. Debrauz felt that if he could seal his contract with Grimaldi right away, David would not have a legitimate case. Grimaldi sent a transcript of Debrauz' proposal to Narváez in his letter of September 19.

71 Grimaldi added: "Just arrived in Madrid, his correspondent thought he knew and could judge Spanish men and things which the most astute foreign observer however only begins to understand after having lived in the Spanish world for some time . . . Thus, for example, he arrives in Madrid on March 3, and on the 11th he writes to Mr. Guizot: 'jealousy, ambition and vengeance are the principal characteristics of the men who figure here on the political scene'."

72 Narváez corrected this error in a letter to Grimaldi on September 30: "You have been mistaken in the first letter where you say that González Bravo was the organizer of the Civil Guard; this organization owes its existence to me; the Decree is signed by me as Minister of War; the idea was mine, I organized it; I named the Duke of Alhumada as Director; and once it was organized and established, I handed it over one day to the Queen in the Plaza de Oriente, and to the Minister of the Home Office, Mr. Pidal." But Grimaldi, while he had initially believed that Narváez had created the Civil Guard, had read recently that González Bravo was the real initiator of the project. He asked Narváez about this in one of his letters and directed him to send a coded telegram immediately in order to confirm whether the "company" (the Civil Guard) was really begun by "Pelayo" (Narváez) or by "García" (González Bravo). The telegram arrived: "The *company* was created by *Pelayo* . . . Details will be sent by mail. Martínez [Narváez]." The two old men rather enjoyed playing at spies, exchanging their little secrets through coded telegrams.

73 These included the revision of the Constitution of 1837, the promulgation of an electoral law, a revision of the laws governing freedom of the press, organization of the Council of State, the creation of provincial councils, the liquidation of the floating debt, presentation of the first "normal" budget, reorganization of the army, establishment of the Civil Guard, etc.

74 Grimaldi was not the only person to complain of Guizot's anecdotal history. Other Spaniards (especially Alejandro Mon) raised their voices in protest as well.

75 One such area was Grimaldi's proposed discussion of the involvement of a man named Mercier de Lostende with Ambassador Bresson in Madrid, but Narváez dissuaded Grimaldi from mentioning Mercier since he was currently an ally of the Spanish head of state: "At the same time I received your letter of the 17th . . . and although what you propose to do in your future publications seems perfectly acceptable, it would be convenient if you would say nothing against Mercier because he's on my side on this matter and he says that all that Bresson and his allies are saying about me are lies; and besides that, the truth of the matter is that Bresson was afraid of me; and since it is good to have friends, and since he is proving to be so favorable to our position on this matter, we should not antagonize him." It was too late for Grimaldi to omit any allusion to Mercier, but as he explained to Narváez, "Don't worry: he's too stupid to have understood the allusion, and from here on in I shall be careful to pardon him as a poor soul, or keep him behind the scenes." October 24, 1867; RAH: Narváez, 56.

76 "I'm sorry that you said that I didn't want to side with Mon and Pidal because I respect the memory of Pidal and want to maintain good relations with Mon and I am sorry, I repeat, that this has been said. It seems to me that it would be better to mount a defense without hurting other people because the polemic is really only hostile to Guizot and Bresson." Undated letter (early November, 1867); RAH: Narváez, 56.

77 See Carr, *Spain 1808–1939*, pp. 256–304.

78 In his letter to Narváez of November 12, he explained his views this way: ". . . I shan't miss the opportunity to add weight to my real goal, that is, to say that O'Donnell was a royalist, partisan of the absolute monarchy when you were a liberal; that O'Donnell was a substitute for you when you headed the constitutional coalition of the years 52 and 53 . . ."

79 Grimaldi informed Narváez: ". . . Debrauz stays as owner and as such his agreement to publish our articles during the year remains in effect." (January 2, 1868; RAH: Narváez, 56.)

80 See correspondence on his behalf in his dossier at the Archives de France: F^{ld} III: 14^{10}.

81 Desfrétières reproduces Grimaldi's death certificate, p. 311.

6 Conclusion

1 See Dowling, "El anti-don Juan de Ventura de la Vega," pp. 215–18.

2 Théodore Anne, *Madrid ou Observations sur les moeurs et usages des espagnols au commencement du XIXème siècle* (Paris: Pillet Aîné, 1825), p. 162. Anne went on: "Mr Grimaldi, in charge of the two theatres when they were permitted to reopen, has tried to bring them out of the deep chaos which they are in. I know what his plans were, and I can say that one cannot achieve success in a more noble, surer or less selfish way. His work in just eight months, of little advantage to himself, has managed to pull the theatre out of a rut. He has put the theatres back on course: and that is quite an accomplishment."

3 The "magical comedies" had always contained complicated stage apparatus, but few were as successful as Grimaldi's. As Andioc described the popularity of a production of *Marta la Romarantina* (1796): " 'Flight', 'balance beam', 'rack', 'trap door': these are terms which we find regularly in the reports of the staging of such plays. They all designate the machinery used to help the characters defy the laws of gravity: the protagonists rise up in the air or disappear beneath the earth;

carriages, ships, and even palaces and mountains appear on stage." *Teatro y sociedad*, p. 51.

4 Artiles, "Larra y el Ateneo," p. 140.

5 See Mesonero Romanos, Zorrilla, García Llansó, Sepúlveda, Duffey, etc. As Escosura wrote, "his speciality, as we say today, was the theatre, and we owe him, without a doubt, the great service of having galvanized, to put it one way, our theatre, reduced since the death of Máiquez to a terrible state, and preparing it as was proper and necessary so that a few years later *La conjuración de Venecia*, *El trovador* and *Los amantes de Teruel* could be staged." "Recuerdos literarios," p. 226.

6 "Declamación," p. 710.

7 He kept in frequent contact with businessmen in London, and read the London *Times*. Letter dated September 11, 1867; RAH: Narváez, 56.

8 Desfrétières, p. 128.

Bibliography

I. Primary sources: works by Grimaldi

A. Plays

1. *El abate l'Epée y el asesino o La huérfana de Bruselas* (1825)
   a. Ms. BM: 1-209-53 (1835).
   b. Valencia: José Gimeno, n.d.
   c. Madrid: Prados e hijos, 1846.
   d. Madrid: Pascual Conesa, 1862 (in series, *Biblioteca dramática*, vol. 29).
2. *En un momento de error o Lord Davenant* (1826)
   a. Ms. BM: 1-43-11 (1826).
   b. Ms. BN: 15.818.
   c. Valencia, 1830.
3. *Todo lo vence amor o la pata de cabra* (1829)
   a. Ms. BM: 1-199-7 (1829).
   b. Ms. BM: 1-178-10.
   c. Ms. BN: 14.181[6].
   d. Madrid: Repullés, 1836.
   e. Madrid: Repullés, 1841.
   f. Madrid: Sucesores de Cuesta, 1899.
   g. Rome: Bulzoni, 1986. Ed. David T. Gies.
4. *Lo que es y lo que será* (with Bretón and Vega, 1835)
   a. (no extant copies)

B. Articles

1. *La Revista Española*
   a. "Breves observaciones sobre un artículo del Diario de los debates," January 8, 1835.
   b. "Sobre la decadencia de las lanas españolas," February 1, 1833.
   c. "Sobre instrucción pública," March 19 and 29, 1833.
   d. "Instrucción pública. Escuelas de primeras letras," May 22, 24, and 30, 1834.
   e. "Secretos del año 1835 que el tiempo ha de revelar," October 29, 1833.

f. "Deseganos de los carlistas," November 5, 1835.

g. "Gaceta de don Carlos," November 9, 1835.

h. "A la unión," November 13, 1835.

i. "La razón," December 26, 1835.

j. "Remitido," May 4, 1836.

k. "De la dimisión del Ministerio Mendizábal," May 26, 1836.

l. "Remitido," May 29, 1836 (notes only).

m. "De la elección de los sucesores del Ministerio Mendizábal," June 5, 1836.

n. "Inviolabilidad del Rey," July 4, 1836.

o. "De la administración del señor Mendizábal," July 12, 13, 19, and 21, 1836.

p. "El triunfo de la Constitución no acelera el triunfo de don Carlos," August 21, 1836.

2. *El Artista*
   a. "Concepción Rodríguez," II, 1835, pp. 193–6.

3. *La Presse* (Paris)
   a. "Etudes biographiques sur Espartero," June 29, July 2, 5, 8, 14, and 18, 1841. (Reprinted as *Espartero: Etudes biographiques* [Paris: Bohaire, 1841]).

4. *Mémorial diplomatique* (Paris)
   a. "Lettres espagnoles," September 19, 26; October 3, 10, 17, 24; November 7, 1867.
   b. "O'Donnell," November 14, 1867.
   c. "Finances de l'Espagne," October 24; November 7, 14, 21; December 5, 1867.

C. *Published speeches*

1. *Rapport fait au nom de la Commission de l'Instruction Publique. Conseil Général du Jura. Session de 1851.* (Lons-Le-Saunier: F. Gauthier, 1851).

2. *Discours prononcé par M. de Grimaldi, Président du Conseil Général du Jura, à l'ouverture de la session de 1853.* (Paris, n.d.).

3. *Funérailles du Géneral Cler.* (Paris: N. Chaix, 1859).

II. Secondary sources

Adams, Nicholson B. "French influence on the Madrid theater in 1837." *Estudios dedicados a D. Ramón Menéndez Pidal.* Madrid: CSIC, 1950, 135–51.

"Notes on dramatic criticism in Madrid, 1828–1833." *Studies in Romance Languages and Literatures.* Chapel Hill: University of North Carolina Press, 1945, 231–8.

"Notes on Spanish plays at the beginning of the Romantic period." *Romanic Review*, 17 (1926), 128–42.

The Romantic Dramas of García Gutiérrez. New York: Instituto de las Españas en los Estados Unidos, 1922.

"Sidelights on the Spanish Theaters of the Eighteen-thirties." *Hispania*, 9 (1926), 1-12.

Aguilar Piñal, Francisco. *Cartelera prerromántica sevillana, años 1800–1836.* Madrid: CSIC, 1968.

Alberich, José. Review of S. García Castañeda, *Miguel de los Santos Alvarez. Bulletin of Hispanic Studies*, 58 (1981), 146–7.

Alborg, Juan Luis. *Historia de la literatura española. El romanticismo.* Madrid: Gredos, 1980.

Alcalá Galiano, Antonio. *Literatura española siglo XIX.* Tr. by Vicente Llorens. Madrid: Alianza, 1969.

Historia de España, desde los tiempos primitivos hasta la mayoría de la reina Isabel II. 7 vols. Madrid: Sociedad Literaria y Topográfica, 1844–6.

Memorias. 2 vols. Madrid: E. Rubiños, 1886.

Recuerdos de un anciano. Madrid: Victor Saiz, 1878.

Alonso Cortés, Narciso. *Zorrilla. Su vida y sus obras.* 2nd. edn. Valladolid: Santarén, 1943.

"El teatro español en el siglo XIX." *Historia general de las literaturas hispánicas,* IV. Barcelona: Barna, 1949–58, 261–337.

Andioc, René. "Sobre el estreno de *Don Alvaro*." *Homenaje a Juan López-Morillas.* Madrid: Castalia, 1982. 63–86.

Teatro y sociedad en el Madrid del siglo XVIII. Madrid: Castalia, 1976.

Anes, Gonzalo, ed. *El Banco de España: una historia económica.* Madrid: Banco de España, 1970.

ed. *La economía española al fin del Antiguo Régimen.* 4 vols. Madrid: Alianza, 1982.

Anne, Théodore. *Madrid ou Observations sur les moeurs et usages des espagnols au commencement du XIXème siècle.* Paris: Pillet Aîné, 1825.

Arrieta, Emilio. "La música española al comenzar el siglo XIX." *La España del siglo XIX. Colección de conferencias históricas celebradas en el Ateneo durante los cursos 1885–1886 y 1886–1887,* II. Madrid: Impr. La Libertad, 1886–7, 157–85.

Artiles, Jenaro. "Larra y el Ateneo." *Revista de la Biblioteca, Archivo y Museo (Ayuntamiento de Madrid)*, 8 (1931), 137–51.

Artola, Miguel. *La burguesía revolucionaria (1808–1869).* Madrid: Alianza, 1973.

ed. *Los ferrocarriles en España, 1844–1943.* 2 vols. Madrid: Servicio de Estudios del Banco de España, 1978.

Arzadún y Zabaleta, Juan. *Fernando VII y su tiempo.* Madrid: Summa, 1942.

Ayguals de Izco, Wenceslao. *Panteón universal.* 4 vols. Madrid: Ayguals, 1853–4.

Azpitarte Almagro, J.M. "La ilusión escénica en el siglo XVIII," *Cuadernos Hispanoamericanos*, 303 (1975), 657–73.

Bahamonde Magro, A. and J. Toro Mérida. *Burguesía, especulación y cuestión social en el Madrid del siglo XIX.* Madrid: Siglo XXI, 1978.

Blanqui, Adolphe. *Voyage a Madrid.* Paris: Doudey-Dupré, 1826.

Barojos Garrido, Alfonso. *D. José Manuel de Arjona, Asistente de Sevilla, 1825–1833.* Sevilla: Imprenta Municipal, 1976.

Bretón de los Herreros, Manuel. *Contra el furor filarmónico o más bien contra los que desprecian el teatro español.* Madrid: Burgos, 1828.

"Declamación. Progresos y estado actual de este arte en los teatros de España." *La Enciclopedia Moderna*, 12 (1852), 659–716.

"Diferentes sistemas de los actores para la representación de los dramas." *Correo Literario y Mercantil*, September 5, 1831.

Obra dispersa. ed. by J.M. Díez Taboada and J.M. Rosas. Logroño: Instituto de Estudios Riojanos, 1965.

Recuerdos de un baile de máscaras. Cuento en verso. Madrid: Repullés, 1834.

"Sobre la acción teatral, o los gestos y movimientos que el actor asocia a la palabra." *Correo Literario y Mercantil*, October 24, 1831.

Bretón y Orozco, C., ed. "Apuntes sobre la vida y escritos de don Manuel Bretón de los Herreros." *Manuel Bretón de los Herreros. Obras*, 1. Madrid: M. Ginesra, 1883, 3–17.

Buck, Donald C. "Juan Salvo y Vela and the rise of the *comedia de magia*: the magician as anti-hero." *Hispania*, 69 (1986), 251–61.

Burgos, Carmen de. *Fígaro.* Madrid: Impr. de 'Alrededor del Mundo', 1919.

Bussey, William M. *French and Italian Influence on the Zarzuela, 1700–1750.* Ann Arbor: UMI Research Press, 1982.

Caldera, Ermanno. "Entre cuadro y tramoya." *Dieciocho*, 9 (1986), 51–6.

La commedia romantica in Spagna. Pisa: Giardini, 1978.

"La magia nel teatro romantico." *Teatro di magia*, ed. by Ermanno Caldera. Roma: Bulzoni, 1983, 185–205.

"*La pata de cabra* y *Le pied du mouton.*" *Studia historica et philologica in honorem M. Batllori.* Rome: Instituto Español de Cultura, 1984, 567–75.

"Sulla 'Spettacolarità' delle commedie di magia." *Teatro di magia*, 11–32.

"La última etapa de la comedia de magia." *Actas del VII Congreso Internacional de Hispanistas* (Rome: Bulzoni, 1982), 247–53.

Cameron, Rondo E. *France and the Economic Development of Europe*, 1800–1914. Princeton: Princeton University Press, 1961.

Campos, Jorge. *Teatro y sociedad en España (1780–1820).* Madrid: Moneda y Crédito, 1969.

Cañizares, José de. *El anillo de Giges*, ed. by Joaquín Alvarez Barrientos. Madrid: CSIC, 1983.

Carmona y Millán, Luis. *Crónica de la ópera italiana en Madrid desde 1738 hasta nuestros días.* Madrid: Manuel Minuesa de los Ríos, 1878.

Caro Baroja, Julio. *Teatro popular y magia.* Madrid: Revista de Occidente, 1974.

Carrière, Marie-Thérèse. "Acerca de las pensiones de actores en la Cruz y el Príncipe a mediados del siglo XIX." *Hommage a Jean-Louis Flecniakoska*, 1. Montpellier: Paul Valéry, 1980. 119–41.

Casanova, Jacques. *Histoire de ma vie.* Paris: Plon, 1961.

Castro, Concepción de. *Andrés Borrego: Romanticismo, periodismo y política.* Madrid: Tecnos, 1975.

Chaulié, Dionisio. *Cosas de Madrid*, II. Madrid: Correspondencia de España, 1886.

Cheste, Conde de. "Elogio fúnebre del Excelentísimo señor D. Ventura de la Vega." *Memorias de la Academia Española*, II. Madrid, 1870, 434–67.

Christiansen, E. *The Origins of Military Power in Spain: 1800–1854*. Oxford: Oxford University Press, 1967.

Colao, Alberto. *Máiquez, discípulo de Talma*. Cartagena: Ayuntamiento de Cartagena, 1980.

Coe, Ada M. *Catálogo bibliográfico y crítico de las comedias anunciadas en los periódicos de Madrid de 1661 a 1819*. Baltimore: Johns Hopkins, 1935.

Comellas, José Luis. *Los moderados en el poder: 1844–1854*. Madrid: CSIC, 1970.

Cotarelo y Mori, Emilio. *Isidoro Máiquez y el teatro de su tiempo*. Madrid: José Perales y Martínez, 1902.

——— *María del Rosario Fernández, La Tirana, primera dama de los teatros de la corte*. Madrid: Rivadeneyra, 1897.

——— *Orígenes y establecimiento de la ópera en España hasta 1800*. Madrid, 1917.

Custine, Adolphe de. *L'Espagne sous Ferdinand VII*. 2 vols. Paris: Ladvocat, 1838.

Deleito y Piñuela, José. *Estampas del Madrid teatral fin de siglo*. Madrid: Editorial Saturnino Calleja, 1946.

Dent, Edward J. *The Rise of Romantic Opera*. Cambridge: Cambridge University Press, 1976.

Descola, Jean. *La vida cotidiana en la España romántica, 1833–1868*. Barcelona: Argos Vergara, 1984.

Desfrétières, Bernard. *Jean-Marie de Grimaldi et l'Espagne*. Mémoire pour le Diplôme d'Etudes Supérieures, Institut d'Etudes Hispaniques, Faculté des Lettres de Paris, 1962.

Díaz de Escovar, Narciso, and Lasso de la Vega, F.P. *Historia del teatro español*. 2 vols. Barcelona: Montaner y Simón, 1924.

Díaz-Plaja, Fernando. *El siglo XIX (La historia de España en sus documentos)*. Madrid: Instituto de Estudios Políticos, 1954.

Didier, Charles. *Une année en Espagne*. 2 vols. Paris: Dumont, 1837.

Díez Garretas, Rosa. *El teatro en Valladolid en la primera mitad del siglo XIX*. Valladolid: Institución Cultural Simancas, 1982.

Documentos del reinado de Fernando VII. III. Arias Tejero, diarios (1828–1831). 3 vols. Pamplona: Universidad de Navarra, 1967.

Dowling, John C. "El anti-don Juan de Ventura de la Vega." *Actas del VI Congreso Internacional de Hispanistas*. Toronto: Department of Spanish and Portuguese, University of Toronto Press, 1980, 215–18.

Duffey, Frank. "Juan de Grimaldi and the Madrid Stage (1823–1837)." *Hispanic Review*, 10 (1942), 147–56.

——— "Juan de Grimaldi and the pre-Romantic Drama in Spain." Master's Thesis, University of North Carolina, 1940.

Escobar, José. *Los orígenes de la obra de Larra*. Madrid: Editorial Prensa Española, 1973.

——— "Un episodio biográfico de Larra, crítico teatral, en la temporada de 1834." *Nueva Revista de Filología Hispánica*, 25 (1976), 45–72.

Escosura, Patricio de la. "Teatros de Madrid." *Entreacto* 62 (November 3, 1839).

"Recuerdos literarios." *Ilustración Española y Americana* (March, 1876), 225–7.

Espadas Burgos, Manuel. "Abasto y habitos alimenticios en el Madrid de Fernando VII." *Cuadernos de Historia* (1973), 237–90.

Espina, Antonio. "Isidoro Máiquez o el contorno mágico." In *Seis vidas españolas*. Madrid: Taurus, 1967.

Romea o el Comediante. Madrid: Espasa-Calpe, 1935.

Esquer Torres, Ramón. *El teatro de Tamayo y Baus*. Madrid: CSIC, 1965.

Fernández de Córdoba, Fernando. *Mis memorias íntimas*. Madrid: Atlas, 1966.

Fernández de los Ríos, A. *Album biográfico. Museo universal de retratos y noticias de las celebridades actuales de todos los países*. Madrid, 1848.

Guía de Madrid (1876). Madrid: Monterrey Ediciones, 1982.

Ferrer del Río, A. *Galería de la literatura española*. Madrid: Mellado, 1846.

Ferrer y Herrera, Antonio C. *Paseo por Madrid 1835*, ed. J.M. Pita Andrade. Madrid: Colección Almenara, 1952.

Flynn, Gerard. *Manuel Bretón de los Herreros*. Boston: Twayne, 1978.

Fontana, Josep. *Cambio económico y actividades políticas en la España del siglo XIX*. Barcelona, 1973.

La crisis del Antiguo régimen, 1808–1833. 2nd. edn., Barcelona: Editorial Crítica, 1983.

García Llansó, Antonio. *Historia de la mujer contemporánea*. Barcelona: A.J. Bastiños, 1899.

García Martí, Victoriano. *El Ateneo de Madrid (1835–1935)*. Madrid: Dossat, 1948.

Garelli, Patrizia. *Bretón de los Herreros e la sua 'formula comica'*. Imola, Italy: Galeati, 1983.

Gies, David T. " 'Inocente estupidez': *La pata de cabra* (1829), Grimaldi, and the regeneration of the Spanish stage," *Hispanic Review*, 54 (1986), 375–96.

"Juan de Grimaldi y el año teatral madrileño, 1823–24." *Actas del VIII Congreso Internacional de Hispanistas*. Madrid: Istmo, 1986, 607–13.

"Juan de Grimaldi y la máscara romántica." *Romanticismo 2: Atti del III Congresso sul Romanticismo*. Genova: Edizioni Realizzazioni Grafiche, 1984, 133–40.

"Larra and Mendizábal: A Writer's Response to Government." *Cithara*, 12 (1973), 74–90.

"Larra, Grimaldi and the actors of Madrid." *Studies in Eighteenth-Century Spanish Literature and Romanticism*. Newark: Juan de la Cuesta Press, 1985. 113–22.

Gil, Bernardo and González, Antonio. *Manifiesto que dan los autores en la representación de los individuos de los teatros de la Cruz y Príncipe al respetable público de esta heróica villa*. Madrid: Repullés, 1820.

Gómez Aparicio, Pedro. *Historia del periodismo español*. Madrid: Editora Nacional, 1967.

Gotor, L.L. "El máxico de Salerno." *Teatro di magia*, ed. Ermanno Caldera. Rome: Bulzoni, 1983, 107–46.

Guerra, Carlos and Guerra y Alarcón, Francisco. *Músicos, poetas y actores*. Madrid: Impr. Maroto, 1884.

Guizot, François Pierre Guillaume. *Mémoires pour servir a l'histoire de mon temps*. 8 vols. Paris: Michel-Lévy, 1858–67.

Hamilton, Earl J. *War and Prices in Spain, 1651–1800*. Cambridge, MA.: Harvard University Press, 1969.

Hartzenbusch, Juan Eugenio. *Los amantes de Teruel*, ed. Jean-Louis Picoche. Madrid: Alhambra, 1980.

Hartzenbusch e Hiriarte, Eugenio. *Periódicos de Madrid*. Madrid: Sucesores de Rivadeneyra, 1876.

Unos cuántos seudónimos de escritores españoles con sus correspondientes nombres verdaderos. Madrid: Sucesores de Rivadeneyra, 1904.

Herrero Salgado, Félix. *Cartelera teatral madrileña: 1840–1849*. Madrid: CSIC, 1963.

Hubbard, Gustave. *Histoire contemporaine de l'Espagne*. Paris, 1869–78.

Histoire de la littérature contemporaine en Espagne. Paris: Charpentier, 1867.

Janke, Peter. *Mendizábal y la instauración de la Monarquía Constitucional en España, 1790–1855*. Madrid: Siglo XXI, 1974.

Juretschke, Hans. *Vida, obra y pensamiento de Alberto Lista*. Madrid: CSIC, 1951.

Kirkpatrick, Susan. *Larra: El laberinto inextricable de un romántico liberal*. Madrid: Gredos, 1977.

"Larra y *El Español*: Los artículos no firmados." *Cuadernos Hispanoamericanos*, 399 (1983), 47–76.

Labra, Rafael María de. *El Ateneo de Madrid, 1835–1905*. Madrid, 1906.

Lafarga, Francisco. *Las traducciones españolas del teatro francés (1700–1835)*, I. *Bibliografía de Impresos*. Barcelona: Universidad de Barcelona, 1983.

Larraz, Emmanuel. "Le statut des comédiens dans la société espagnole du début du XIXe siécle." *Culture et société en Espagne et en Amerique latine au XIXe siécle*. Lille: Centre d'Etudes Iberiques et Ibero-Americaines, 1980. 27–40.

Le Gentil, Georges. *Le poète Manuel Bretón de los Herreros et la société espagnole de 1830 à 1860*. Paris: Hachette, 1909.

Les revues littéraires de l'Espagne pendant la première moitié du XIXe siècle. Paris: Hachette, 1909.

Leslie, John K. *Ventura de la Vega and the Spanish Theatre, 1820–1865*. Princeton: Princeton University Press, 1940.

Lozano Guirao, Pilar. "El archivo epistolar de don Ventura de la Vega." *Revista de Literatura*, 13 (1958), 121–72, and 14 (1959), 170–97.

Madoz, Pascual. *Diccionario geográfico, estadístico, histórico*. Madrid, 1847.

Marichal, Carlos. *Spain (1834–1844)*. London: Támesis, 1977.

Marrast, Robert. *José de Espronceda et son temps*. Paris: Klincksieck, 1974.

Martín, Gregorio. *Hacia una revisión crítica de la biografía de Larra*. Porto Alegre: PUC-EMMA, 1975.

"Larra: cronista del teatro español." Paper presented at VII Congreso Internacional de Hispanistas (Venice, 1980); unpublished.

" 'El Parnasillo': origen y circunstancias." *La chispa, 81. Selected Proceedings*. New Orleans: Tulane, 1981, 209–18.

"Periodismo y teatro en el siglo XIX." Unpublished paper.

Martínez Olmedilla, Augusto. *Los teatros de Madrid*, 1947.

Menarini, Piero. "El problema de las traducciones en el teatro romántico español." *Actas del VII Congreso Internacional de Hispanistas.* Rome: Bulzoni, 1982. 751–9.

Menarini, Piero, Garelli, Patrizia, et. al. *El teatro romántico español (1830–1875). Autores, obras, bibliografía.* Bologna: Atesa Editrice, 1982.

Mesonero Romanos, Ramón de. *Dramaturgos posteriores a Lope de Vega.* 2 vols. BAE 47 & 49. Madrid: Rivadeneyra, 1859.

Manual de Madrid. BAE 201. Madrid: Atlas, 1967.

Memorias de un setentón. Madrid: Renacimiento, 1926.

Molins, marqués de (Roca de Togores). *Bretón de los Herreros.* Madrid: La España Moderna, 1893.

Bretón de los Herreros. Recuerdos de su vida y de sus obras. Madrid: Tello, 1883.

Montero Alonso, José. *Ventura de la Vega: su vida y su tiempo.* Madrid: Editora Nacional, 1951.

Morena Garbayo, Natividad. *Catálogo de los documentos referentes a diversiones públicas conservados en el Archivo Histórico Nacional.* Madrid: Junta de Archivos, Bibliotecas y Museos, 1958.

Muñoz, Matilde. *Historia del teatro dramático en España.* 3 vols. Madrid: Editorial Tesoro, 1948.

Muñoz Morillejo, Joaquín. *Escenografía española.* Madrid: Blass, 1923.

Navas Ruiz, Ricardo. *Imágenes liberales (Rivas, Larra, Galdós).* Salamanca: Ediciones Almar, 1979.

El romanticismo español. Madrid: Cátedra, 1982.

Oliva Marra-López, Andrés. *Andrés Borrego y la política española del siglo XIX.* Madrid: Instituto de Política, 1959.

Ossorio y Bernard, Manuel. *Ensayo de un catálogo de periodistas españoles del siglo XIX.* Madrid: J. Palacios, 1903.

Pabón, Jesús. *Inventario del archivo de Narváez.* Real Academia de la Historia: Sala 9/ 7809–7875.

Narváez y su época. Madrid: Espasa-Calpe, 1983.

Pacheco, Joaquín Francisco. *Historia de la regencia de la reina Cristina.* Madrid: F. Suárez, 1841.

Paez Ríos, Elena. *Iconografía hispana. Catálogo de los personajes españoles de la Biblioteca Nacional.* 4 vols. Madrid: Biblioteca Nacional, Sección de Estampas, 1966.

Par, Alfonso. *Representaciones shakespearianas en España.* 2 vols. Madrid: Victoriano Suárez, 1936.

Peers, Edgar A. *Historia del movimiento romántico español.* 2 vols. Madrid: Gredos, 1967.

Peña y Goñi, Antonio. *España desde la ópera a la zarzuela.* Madrid: Alianza, 1967.

Pérez Firmat, Gustavo. "Carnival in *Don Juan Tenorio.*" *Hispanic Review*, 51 (1983), 269–81.

Piñeyro, Enrique. *El romanticismo en España.* Paris: Garnier, 1900.

Plessis, Alain. *De la fête impériale au mur des fédérés (1852–1871).* Paris: Editions du Seuil, 1974.

Poullain, C. "Apuntes sobre la vida musical en España en la época romántica." *Iris*, 3 (1982), 189–215.

Poyán Díaz, Daniel. *Enrique Gaspar, medio siglo de teatro español*. 2 vols. Madrid: Gredos, 1957.

Rees, M.A. "The Spanish Romantics and theatre as a visual art." *Staging in the Spanish Theatre*, ed. M.A. Rees. Leeds: Trinity and All Saints' College, 1984. 27–49.

Revilla, José de la. *Vida artística de Isidoro Máiquez, primer actor de los teatros de Madrid*. Madrid: Medina y Navarro, 1845.

Reyes, Antonio de los. *Julián Romea, el actor y su contorno (1813–1868)*. Murcia: Academia Alfonso X el Sabio, 1977.

Ridley, Jasper. *Napoleon III and Eugenie*. London: Constable, 1979.

Ringrose, David. *Transportation and Economic Stagnation in Spain, 1750–1850*. Durham: Duke University Press, 1970.

Rivas Santiago, Natalio. *Curiosidades históricas contemporáneas*. Barcelona, 1942.

Rodríguez Cánovas, José. *Isidoro Máiquez*. Cartagena: Athenas Ediciones, 1968.

Rogers, P.P. "The drama of pre-Romantic Spain." *Romanic Review*, 21 (1930), 315–24.

Romero de Solís, Pedro. *La población española en los siglos XVIII y XIX*. Madrid: Siglo XXI, 1973.

Romero Mendoza, Pedro. "El teatro romántico." *Alcántara*, 8 (1952), 3–16.

Rosell, Cayetano. "Don Antonio García Gutiérrez." *Autores dramáticos contemporáneos*. Madrid: Fortanet, 1881, 81–96.

Ruiz Salvador, Antonio. *El Ateneo científico, literario y artístico de Madrid*. London: Támesis, 1971.

Rumeau, Aristide. "Mariano José de Larra et le Baron Taylor." *Revue de Littérature Comparée*, 16 (1936), 477–93.

'Le théâtre à Madrid à la veille du Romantisme, 1831–1834." *Hommage à Ernest Martinenche*. Paris: D'Artrey, 1939, 330–46.

Sainz de Robles, Federico Carlos. *Los antiguos teatros de Madrid*. Madrid, Instituto de Estudios Madrileños, 1952.

Sánchez, Roberto. "Emilio Mario, Galdós y la reforma escénica del XIX." *Hispanic Review*, 52 (1984), 263–79.

Sánchez Estevan, Ismael. *Mariano José de Larra, 'Fígaro'. Ensayo biográfico*. Madrid: Hernando, 1934.

Sardá, Juan. *La política monetaria y las fluctuaciones de la economía en el siglo XIX*. Madrid: CSIC, 1948.

Sarrailh, Jean. *Un homme d'état espagnol: Martínez de la Rosa (1787—1862)*. Bordeaux: Etudes Hispaniques, 1930.

Seoane, María Cruz. *Historia del periodismo en España. 2. El siglo XIX*. Madrid: Alianza, 1983.

Sepúlveda, Ricardo. *El corral de la Pacheca*. Madrid, 1888.

Shaw, Donald L. *A Literary History of Spain. The Nineteenth Century*. London: Benn, 1972.

Shields, A.K. "The Madrid stage, 1820–1833." Unpublished Ph.D. thesis, University of North Carolina, 1933.

Simón Díaz, José. *Cartelera teatral madrileña: 1830–1839.* Madrid: CSIC, 1960.

(ed.), *Madrid en sus diarios: 1830–1844.* Madrid: CSIC, 1961.

Simón Palmer, María del Carmen. "Construcción y apertura de los teatros madrileños en el siglo XIX." *Segismundo,* 19–20 (1975), 85–137.

Subirá, José. *Historia de la música española e hispanoamericana.* Barcelona: Salvat, 1953.

Historia y anecdotario del Teatro Real. Madrid: Plus-Ultra, 1949.

Tamayo, Victor. "La Rodríguez, Grimaldi y Guzmán." *Blanco y Negro* (May 27, 1928).

Tarr, F.C. "More Light on Larra." *Hispanic Review,* 4 (1936), 89–110.

"Reconstruction of a Decisive Period in Larra's Life (May–November, 1836)." *Hispanic Review,* 5 (1937), 1–24.

ter Horst, Robert. "Ritual time regained in Zorrilla's *Don Juan Tenorio.*" *Romanic Review,* 70 (1979), 80–93.

Tortella Casares, Gabriel. *Los orígenes del capitalismo en España.* Madrid: Editora Tecnos, 1973.

Varela, José Luis. *Larra y España.* Madrid: Espasa-Calpe, 1983.

Vida y obra literaria de G. Romero Larrañaga. Madrid: CSIC, 1948.

Varela Hervias, Eulogio. *Don Ramón Mesonero Romanos y su círculo.* Madrid: Caja de Ahorros de Madrid, 1975.

Varey, John E. *Los títeres y otras diversiones populares de Madrid: 1758–1840.* London: Támesis, 1972.

"Popular Entertainments in Madrid, 1758–1859," *Renaissance and Modern Studies,* 22 (1978), 26–44.

Vega, José. *Máiquez. El actor y el hombre.* Madrid: Revista de Occidente, 1947.

Veinticuatro Diarios (Madrid, 1830–1900). Colección de Indices de Publicaciones Periódicas. 4 vols. Madrid: CSIC, 1968–75.

Vico y López, Antonio. "Isidoro Máiquez, Carlos Latorre, Julián Romea. La escena española desde principios del siglo. La declamación en la tragedia, en el drama histórico y en la comedia de costumbres." *La España del siglo XIX.* 3 vols. Madrid: Impr. 'La Liberal', 1886–7.

Wais, Francisco. *Historia de los ferrocarriles españoles.* 2nd. edn. Madrid: Editora Nacional, 1974.

Yxart, José. *El arte escénico en España.* 2 vols. Barcelona: La Vanguardia, 1894.

Zorrilla, José. *Recuerdos del tiempo viejo.* In *Obras completas,* II. Valladolid: Santarén 1943. 1729–2103.

Index

Printed in the United Kingdom
by Lightning Source UK Ltd.
100419UKS00001B/116